# INTERSECTIONS OF HARM

# INTERSECTIONS OF HARM

## Narratives of Latina Deviance and Defiance

LAURA HALPERIN

Rutgers University Press

NEW BRUNSWICK, NEW JERSEY, AND LONDON

LIBRARY OF CONGRESS CATALOGING-IN-PUBLICATION DATA

Halperin, Laura, 1974–
    Intersections of harm : narratives of Latina deviance and defiance / Laura Halperin.
        pages cm. — (American literatures initiative)
    Includes bibliographical references and index.
    ISBN 978-0-8135-7037-2 (hardback)
    ISBN 978-0-8135-7036-5 (pbk.)
    ISBN 978-0-8135-7038-9 (e-book (web pdf))
    1. American literature—Hispanic American authors—History and criticism.
2. American literature—Women authors—History and criticism. 3. Hispanic American
women in literature. I. Title.
PS153.H56H35 2015
810.9'928708968—dc23

                                                                        2014040946

A British Cataloging-in-Publication record for this book is available
from the British Library.

Copyright © 2015 by Laura Halperin

Visit our website: http://rutgerspress.rutgers.edu

Manufactured in the United States of America

THE
AMERICAN
LITERATURES
INITIATIVE

A book in the American Literatures Initiative (ALI), a collaborative
publishing project of NYU Press, Fordham University Press, Rutgers
University Press, Temple University Press, and the University of Virginia
Press. The Initiative is supported by The Andrew W. Mellon Foundation.
For more information, please visit www.americanliteratures.org.

*Para mi familia*

*Para mi familia*

# Contents

# ACKNOWLEDGMENTS

This book would not exist without the immeasurable support I have received from countless people over the years. There are far more people I would like to thank than I can possibly name here. Please know how grateful I am for all of your encouragement.

I would like to begin by acknowledging those who helped make this book a reality. Frances Aparicio, María Cotera, and John González: you have seen me through this project from its inception until its final stages, providing me with the type of mentorship most people can only dream of finding. Frieda Ekotto and Rosie Ceballo, you gave me invaluable advice and encouragement in this project's early stages. All five of you have also taught me the importance of humility. There are four colleagues at the University of North Carolina, Chapel Hill to whom I am forever grateful: María DeGuzmán, Ruth Salvaggio, Minrose Gwin, and Ariana Vigil. I cannot thank you enough for the incredibly insightful comments you provided on different chapters of this book. I feel privileged to work with such an amazing, generous, and thoughtful group of women.

Thank you to Jimmy Longoria for giving me permission to reproduce "Cara de la Llorona" on this book cover and for being the dedicated social activist I can only aspire to be. I would also like to acknowledge *Latino Studies*, as parts of chapter 4 (and parts of the description of chapter 4) previously appeared in "Still Hands: Celia's Transgression in Cristina García's *Dreaming in Cuban*," *Latino Studies* 6, no. 4 (2008): 418–35.

I cannot believe the good fortune I have had both to work with Katie Keeran as my editor and to publish this book with Rutgers University

Press. Katie, you have believed in this project from the moment we first talked about it; you have been patient and understanding throughout my writing process; and you carefully chose two extraordinarily thoughtful reviewers to read my manuscript. I could not have asked for better reviewers; I am so grateful for their generosity, attention to detail, and suggestions for revision. I only wish I could thank them in person to let them know that this manuscript is so much stronger thanks to their feedback.

I have benefited from the assistance of multiple people who helped set this project in motion, and I have been fortunate enough to receive fellowships that have given me time and resources to work on the manuscript. Although a number of people helped me in the early stages of this project, four friends merit particular mention: Pavitra Sundar, Constanza Svidler, Meredith Martin, and Bénédicte Boisseron. Thank you for the countless hours you spent talking with me about my work, reading my work, and sharing a writing space with me. Thank you to the Rackham Merit Fellowship Program, the Global Ethnic Literatures Seminar Fellowship, and the Institute for Research on Women and Gender at the University of Michigan, Ann Arbor and the Carolina Postdoctoral Fellowship for Faculty Diversity at the University of North Carolina, Chapel Hill.

There are people who may not have realized the powerful impact they have had and continue to have on me. These include students and colleagues at UNC and elsewhere. When I teach my classes, when I meet with students outside of the classroom, when I attend conferences where I find my larger Latina/o studies community, I realize why I am in this profession and why this work matters. When students thank me for teaching works in which they can see themselves reflected perhaps for the first time in their educational careers, when students want to continue the conversations begun in the classroom outside of the classroom, when colleagues across the country engage in passionate discussions about Latina/o literary and cultural studies while also addressing the systemic challenges of being duly recognized for the groundbreaking work they do because their work gets dismissed as "trendy" or too specialized instead of being rightfully recognized as critically important, I am motivated to continue doing the work I do, and I realize just how much more work there is to be done. Thank you to my extended Latina/o studies community: Randy Ontiveros and Marissa López (my conference buddies since our graduate school days and now my good friends), Larry La Fountain-Stokes, Ana Patricia Rodríguez, Suzanne Bost, Elena

Machado Sáez, Marta Caminero-Santangelo, Ricardo Ortiz, Tony López, José David Saldívar, Claudia Milian, and Jenny Snead Williams. I would especially like to thank Suzanne Oboler. You introduced me to Latina/o studies before I knew what I wanted to do with my life, and you have believed in me ever since.

I am surrounded by a wonderful group of people in North Carolina. These include friends, current and former colleagues, and staff in the English, Comparative Literature, Romance Languages and Literatures, and American Studies departments and the Latina/o Studies and Carolina Postdoctoral Fellowship programs. I would particularly like to acknowledge Beverly Taylor and Jennifer Ho for the immeasurable advice and support that you have extended to me over the years. JoAnna Poblete, Rebecca Walsh, Stephanie Elizondo Griest, Jordynn Jack, Heidi Kim, Matt Taylor, and Rebecka Rutledge Fisher: I cannot thank you enough for being there for me personally and professionally. Michelle Robinson, Jenny Tone-Pah-Hote, Angeline Shaka, Ben Frey, and Gaby Calvocoressi: I could not ask for a better, more diligent group of people with whom to have regular work sessions. Special thanks to those of you who brought me to UNC and who have formed an important part of my North Carolina community, namely Bill Andrews, James Thompson, Bland Simpson, Tony Waldrop, Sibby Anderson-Thompkins, Joy Kasson, Priscilla Wald, GerShun Avilez, Donna Bickford, Paul Cuadros, Josmell Pérez, John Ribó, Ashley Lucas, Matthew Grady, Elisha Taylor, Ricci Wolman, Ferol Vernon, Kim and Josh Boggs, Beth Richardson, Steven Kent, and my FARM friends.

My community also consists of remarkable friends who are spread across the country. I am grateful to all of you. Tyrone Brown, Alpa Patel, Annmarie Perez, Vanessa and Alex Rein, Kate Destler, and Johann Neem: you have been there for me for over twenty years. In no small part thanks to your friendship and support, this book has come to fruition. Jamie Rosenthal, Neel Ahuja, Mark Sheftall, Oswaldo Estrada, and Cristina Carrasco: I met all of you in North Carolina, and you have quickly become the best of friends. You have been there for me through good times and tough times; you have been my pillars of strength; you have provided me with sage advice; you have listened to me talk about work; you have helped me find work-life balance; you have made me smile and laugh; and you have made me feel at home.

Since much of this manuscript is about the importance of re-turning, it is only fitting that I end my acknowledgments by thanking my family; and since much of this manuscript is about the importance of attempting to articulate oneself in one's own voice, it is only fitting that I code-switch here. *Quisiera agradecer primero a los miembros de mi familia que ya no están aquí físicamente, aunque sigan aquí en mi corazón. Abuelo Luis, Abuela Chola, Abuela Claire, y Tía Dora: los extraño un montón. Ustedes me han enseñado la importancia de ser humilde, de tratar a la gente con cariño y respeto, de luchar para que este sea un mundo más justo, de creer en mí misma, y aprovechar el tiempo que tenemos con la gente que queremos. Tío* Eduardo, *Tía* Fanny, Marina, and Lucila: you have taught me about the importance of family, and I will gladly listen to your *humor Halperin* any day. Marta, *gracias por haberme ayudado a crecer y por haberme mostrado lo que significa tener una ética increible de trabajo.* Alejandra and Rob, you have taught me about dedication, loyalty, and understanding, and you inspire me in all you do while raising three incredible children. Emma, Sofia, and Thomas, I am so lucky to be your *tía*! The three of you are my world, and I love you with all of my heart. Finally, Mom and Dad (Mirta and Ricardo), I cannot begin to thank you enough for all that you have done and continue to do for me. I would not have been able to write this book without you. You instilled a powerful work ethic in me; you put your lives on hold when I needed a helping hand; you have always believed in me; and you have always been there for me. *Les agradezco del fondo de mi corazón.*

# INTERSECTIONS OF HARM

# Introduction: Contextualizing Harm

*"We're going to have to control your tongue," the dentist says. . . . My tongue keeps pushing out the . . . cotton, . . . drills, . . . needles. "I've never seen anything as strong or stubborn," he says. And I think, how do you tame a wild tongue, train it to be quiet, . . . bridle and saddle it . . . make it lie down?*

—GLORIA ANZALDÚA, *BORDERLANDS/LA FRONTERA: THE NEW MESTIZA*

At first glance, this epigraph might appear to be about a woman at a dentist's office whose physical tongue is getting in the way of the medical attention she is there to receive. But the passage is about much more than this: it is explicitly about a female patient—and implicitly about a Latina, *mestiza* patient—whose body part is being manipulated by a male, arguably Anglo, dentist.[1] It is about a gendered and racialized struggle for control, exemplified by the power the dentist wields as a medical practitioner with drills and needles in hand while standing over his patient, and illustrated through the power the patient questions and seeks to take back for herself in her stubbornness and refusal to be tamed. It is about a personified body part that pushes back and will not lie down, a body part that stands for something more than a physical entity. A tongue also represents language, and, as the Chicana writer Gloria Anzaldúa asserts, language is integrally connected to ethnic identity and ethnic pride: "Ethnic identity is twin skin to linguistic identity—I am my language."[2] The tongue bridges the corporeal, linguistic, and psychological, as it is tied to the construction of self and collective. By identifying the patient's tongue as something that needs to be tamed, the dentist dismisses his patient's desires and constructs his patient as deviant in her (tongue's) wildness and defiant in her (tongue's) stubbornness. Resorting to control instead of cooperation, he imposes coercive power over his patient. Questioning the dentist's insistence that her tongue needs to be bridled and saddled, the patient fights back against the control wielded over her (tongue) and attempts to reassert her own voice/tongue.

This epigraph illustrates the major polemics explored in *Intersections of Harm*. It highlights a complicated portrayal of the medical system and alludes to the medicalization of a *latinidad* that is gendered female. It speaks to questions of power, control, and coercion in relation to structural subjugation; it reveals the limitations and possibilities of resistance; and it emblematizes the intersections of physical, psychological, and geopolitical harm, as well as the junction of harm and hope. Although this excerpt (taken out of the context in which it appears) does not explicitly reference geopolitical harm, its positioning in a text that emphasizes the primacy of the borderlands grounds it in a geopolitical framework. The hope in this passage can be found in the patient's refusal to let her voice/tongue be tamed. Just as the patient thinks, "How do you tame a wild tongue, train it to be quiet, how do you bridle and saddle it? How do you make it lie down?," *Intersections of Harm* asks these same questions.[3] But I also ask: How can the patient's (mis)treatment be linked to broader, collective struggles with institutionalized oppression? Why does the patient's tongue need to be tamed, trained, bridled, and saddled? What is at stake in the ready suppression of Latina tongues as portrayed in contemporary Latina literature? And how do Latinas resist the efforts to clamp their tongues?[4]

While posing these questions, I examine the crossroads of psychological, physical, and geopolitical harm in two memoirs and four novels written by and about Latinas at the end of the twentieth century and the beginning of the twenty-first. Analyzing the Puerto Rican author Irene Vilar's memoirs *The Ladies' Gallery: A Memoir of Family Secrets* (1996) and *Impossible Motherhood: Testimony of an Abortion Addict* (2009), the Dominican American novelist Loida Maritza Pérez's *Geographies of Home* (1999), the Xicana writer Ana Castillo's novel *So Far from God* (1993), the Cuban American author Cristina García's novel *Dreaming in Cuban* (1992), and the Dominican American writer Julia Alvarez's novel *How the García Girls Lost Their Accents* (1991), I explore how the ascriptions of Latina deviance in Latina literature are entwined with the damage wreaked on Latinas' bodies and minds and on the places they inhabit.[5] This deviance sometimes manifests itself as mental illness and at other times presents itself as a general aberrance from or defiance of socially constructed norms. I therefore position the individual harm that befalls Latina subjects alongside collective forms of harm, including structural oppression, subjugation, and dispossession.

My analysis emphasizes the junction of various types of harm and signals the hope that can be found amid so much harm. Harm presents itself in myriad and sometimes paradoxical ways; it spreads in multiple directions from multiple sources; and it consists of psychological, physical, and geopolitical damage experienced by, and imposed on and within, individuals and communities. While similar to pain, it encompasses more than pain, moving beyond the individual psychological and/or physical suffering to which pain refers. In the case of this introduction's epigraph, harm presents itself through the dentist's physical manipulation of the patient's tongue and silencing of her voice that affects her psyche and that cannot be extricated from the subjugation of Chicanas who live in the borderlands. I adopt the term *harm* because I am interested in the relation among individual suffering, the catalysts that produce such hurt, and the collective wounding that ensues from such injury. The terminological shift from pain to harm is but one way to emphasize the integral connection between individual and collective, oppressor and oppressed, and among body, mind, *and place.*

Harm carries an abundance of connotations—medical, legal, philosophical—arguably all of which are linked to the notion of an ethical imperative that in some way is challenged. The harm stems from the breach of ethics. The idea of an ethical imperative is central to this book; I emphasize that the representations of harm in Latina literature elucidate grave social injustices that demand rectification. Part of such rectification consists of recognition, and part of this recognition entails acknowledging the intersectional ways in which harm can manifest itself.

The hope that glimmers even amid pervasive harm is connected to these ethical concepts of rectification and recognition. In *Borderlands*, the patient actively pushes back against the dentist's oral invasion; in this way, she demands recognition on her terms. Hope doesn't just consist of vocalization or a refusal to be silenced, though. In a number of cases in *The Ladies' Gallery, Impossible Motherhood, Geographies of Home, So Far from God, Dreaming in Cuban*, and *How the García Girls Lost Their Accents*, the Latina protagonists attempt to express themselves, but doing so does not guarantee that anyone will listen. All too often in these stories, the amount and degree of harm is so excruciating that hope may seem like an illusion or even delusion. These texts do not support a facile neoliberal, individualist ethos of advancement that suggests that if one just tries hard enough, one can get ahead. Hope does not exist in such false promises, nor is it the pretty thing neoliberalism paints it to be. Hope exists in the attempts at resistance, however futile these attempts may be or seem. It exists in the sharing of often painful individual and collective *historias* (histories *and* stories) and in the remembrance of harm in order to move past it and seek to rectify it. Remembering in these narratives doesn't just consist of recollecting the past; it entails recalling the past so as to remember it, giving it new shape in order to move forward toward a less harmful world. These texts elucidate how hiding harm does nothing to alleviate it or to prevent its future imposition. On the contrary, in positioning harm at the center of their tales and presenting narratives that disrupt time, Vilar, Pérez, Castillo, García, and Alvarez underscore that acknowledging harm and recognizing the forces that have led to its infliction are critical to avoid repeating the mistakes of the past. Although recognition and remembrance cannot guarantee change, they are instrumental for effecting it.

These writers' portrayals of harm and the hope that can arise from confronting it are intersectional and situated in the interstices. I thus foreground the term *intersections* to draw attention to my subject matter and theoretical approach alike, as the term connotes a sense of place (whether physical or psychological) and a mode of theorization that recognizes important connections among race, ethnicity, gender, sexuality, and class. The image of an intersection is one of a physical location where multiple roads converge and diverge. This image instantly evokes the primacy of place, and each of the texts I analyze foregrounds place. Place is not strictly a geographical location or marker, though, just as intersections do not simply delineate physical or mathematical points of convergence. Intersections are also sites where place and space merge; where the geographical, psychological, and corporeal simultaneously collide, fragment, and fuse; and where multiple identity markers entwine. The idea of intersections thus merges the literal with the figurative, content with concept, such that theory meets praxis. The parallel between subject matter and theoretical approach positions this as a U.S. Third World feminist project.

Informing my understanding of intersections and influencing the overarching theoretical thrust of this book is Anzaldúa's conceptualization of the borderlands. Building on Anzaldúa's description of the borderlands as a site where the geopolitical, psychological, sexual, spiritual, and corporeal meet, and drawing on her depiction of the borderlands as a place that creates *heridas, hendiduras, y rajaduras*—wounds, fissures, and ruptures—I elucidate how intersections serve a similar function. As with *Borderlands, Intersections of Harm* examines the split that can ensue from a bordered subjectivity and the preoccupation with the (w) hole that accompanies such a state.

My rationale for shifting the language from one of borders to one of intersections stems from a recognition that the texts I analyze do not succumb to the binary rhetoric that potentially can follow from the idea of borders, nor do they all focus on actual borders. Like Anzaldúa, I call for "a third perspective—something more than mere duality or a synthesis of duality."[6] The "third perspective" that operates within and beyond duality is precisely the type of perspective that is needed to understand the portrayals of multifaceted harm in Latina literature. The movement within and beyond dualistic modes of thought is not specific to Anzaldúa's work. Other Latina/o studies scholars, including Chela Sandoval, Mary Pat Brady, and Suzanne Bost, similarly have addressed the importance of such movement. Drawing from their theories of mobility and building on the postcolonial studies scholar Homi Bhabha's emphasis on interstitiality, liminality, cultural hybridity, and ambivalence, I locate my textual analyses in the interstices, or the "topographical space [that lies] 'between and among' oppositional ideologies."[7] I situate my readings in the interstices because this is where the writers themselves position their subjects and because interstices are fluid spaces associated with fissures and openings alike. The rupture that is affiliated with interstices connotes that something has been broken. This break might well suggest that something has been harmed, potentially irreparably, just as it might indicate a need for change, away from that which harms. The interstices accordingly are paradoxical sites of harm *and* hope.

## The Pervasiveness of Pathology

In their representations of multilayered harm, *The Ladies' Gallery, Impossible Motherhood, Geographies of Home, So Far from God, Dreaming in Cuban,* and *How the García Girls Lost Their Accents* comment on historical, sociopolitical, and geopolitical conditions faced by different groups of Latinas and illustrate the pervasiveness of pathology. This pathology most overtly presents itself in the narratives' preoccupation with the figure of the Latina "madwoman" but also in the texts' attention to the ways pathological structural forces impact the physical and psychological places the Latina protagonists inhabit. By situating pathology within and outside the self and implicating structural forces in its perpetuation, these works underscore the integral relation among mind, body, and place.

If Vilar, Pérez, Castillo, García, and Alvarez are illustrating the multipositionality of pathology, why locate the figure of the Latina "madwoman" in the center of their narratives? After all, doing so risks emphasizing an intrapsychic notion of pathology, risks reinscribing essentializing constructions of Latinas/os as prone to developing mental illness and dominant notions of hysteria as a women's disease, and risks undermining the ethnic pride at the foundation of the field of Latina/o studies. To address this question, it is important to place these contemporary writers' works in historical, literary, and theoretical context. Such contextualization allows me to examine how these literary portrayals of female madness challenge dominant dissociations of mind from body and place, extend beyond a pathologization of the individual, and destabilize essentializing gendered and racialized constructions of Latinas as "mad."

In placing these texts in the contexts out of which they emerged, emphasizing an intersectional reading of these books, and underscoring the relation between individual ascriptions of Latina "madness" and collective experiences of oppression in these narratives, my approach borrows from postcolonial psychoanalysis. Scholars of postcolonial psychoanalysis such as David Eng, David Kazanjian, Anne Cheng, and Ranjana Khanna insist on the pivotal roles that environments and social constructs (like race, ethnicity, class, gender, and sexuality) play in the development of individuals' psyches and demand that literary analysis attend to sociohistorical context. I too argue that any literary understanding of the ways psychological harm affects protagonists of color must move beyond an intrapsychic analysis and must acknowledge how psychological harm is connected to physical and geopolitical harm.

I accordingly provide some basic background information about Latina/o mental health care in the United States to help historicize the psychological strains of thought found in recent Latina literary production. Such background shows that this literature did not emanate from a sociopolitical vacuum. Rather, it followed from the same sets of conditions that led to an attention to Latina/o mental health care in this country just a few decades earlier.

Prior to the civil rights movement of the 1960s, the mental health needs of Latinas/os and other people of color were largely ignored in mainstream considerations of mental illness and well-being, primarily because the mental health care system in this country was designed to cater to the needs of white Anglos.[8] During the 1960s and 1970s, though, Latina/o mental health needs were finally being recognized. This newfound consideration arguably correlated with an attentiveness to the civil rights discourses of the time, the impact of President Lyndon

B. Johnson's Great Society programs, the demands articulated by the Chicano Movement and the Young Lords Party, the growth of Latinas/os in the United States spurred by the Immigration Act of 1965, and the burgeoning national awareness of the rising Latina/o population.[9] It also likely corresponded to the increased national interest in broader mental health issues following World War II.[10] However, the mental health needs of Latinas/os were not unproblematically brought to the forefront of psychological discussions, especially since these needs were—and continue to be—presented as excessive.[11] Indeed, when the mental health care needs of Latinas/os were put on the map, these needs not only were depicted as dire, but they were not being met.

Government-issued documents like the 1978 *Report to the President's Commission on Mental Health* and the 2001 *Mental Health: Culture, Race and Ethnicity* suggest as much, citing structural factors to explain why Latinas/os apparently underutilize mental health care services.[12] These publications link structural factors to what they label a "culture of poverty." The 1978 report presents Latinas/os as a population especially "at risk" for developing mental illness, for reasons including stress resulting from (im)migration, linguistic barriers, unemployment, poverty, limited education, extended families, and acculturation difficulties; the 2001 report similarly describes Latinas/os as undereducated, family-oriented, and "at risk" for developing mental illness due to poverty, criminality, acculturation difficulties, and language barriers. Despite both reports' emphases on the heterogeneity among Latinas/os and calls to provide more ethnically sensitive modes of care and develop fewer ethnocentric models of research in the United States, they ironically succumb to certain stereotypes of their own that could be used to counter their aims, as they risk portraying Latinas/os as a monolithic group that is poor and particularly vulnerable to mental instability by virtue of their *latinidad.* Rather than underscore the sociocultural conditions surrounding Latinas/os as socially produced, both reports biologize such conditions.

Despite the 1978 report's self-proclaimed intent to "respond to the . . . atmosphere of concern and ethno-racial activism" regarding "de facto inequality in the state's treatment of Latinos," the report has perpetuated essentialized constructions of Latinas/os as susceptible to developing mental illness.[13] In part, such constructions spring from the report's tendency to homogenize Latinas/os, as it underscores commonalities among Latinas/os and posits that "many mental health needs . . . are shared by all Hispanic-Americans." The report "conclude[s] that Hispanic Americans are a population 'at risk,' in the actuarial sense, concerning all aspects of mental illness," and it claims that Latinas are especially susceptible to mental disorders because of their gender as well as their race and ethnicity.[14] The report thus walks a fine line between positioning Latinas/os as prone to developing mental illness because of a perceived ontological essence or because of social variables that contribute to mental distress. Such paradoxical constructions arguably, and ironically, could be seen to feed into the inequality to which the report's creators—interestingly enough, a group of Latina/o mental health care professionals—were reacting in the first place. The 1978 report was commissioned by President Jimmy Carter in response to the fast-growing number of Latinas/os in the United States, outlining concerns similar to those espoused by the Hispanic Health Institute one year earlier. The problems with the 1978 report notwithstanding, the report nonetheless has affected the type of psychological care given to Latinas/os since its publication. During the mid-1980s, for instance, the Congress for Hispanic Mental Health and Latina/o-focused mental health care programs in New York City relied on the 1978 report in their organizational efforts and to legitimate their existence.[15] Johanna Lessinger, a cultural anthropologist, has noted the report's long-lasting impact in the development of Latina/o-based mental health care programs.[16] In 2001, such programs still referred to the 1978 report when expressing the need for "culturally sensitive" mental health care programs.[17]

In 2001, President George W. Bush commissioned *Achieving the Promise: Transforming Mental Health Care in America* as part of his New Freedom Initiative, and the 2001 report accompanied this document. Neither *Achieving the Promise* nor its more specific companion piece indicates that much has changed since the report written over two decades earlier. Like the 1978 report, the 2001 report homogenizes, essentializes, and pathologizes Latinas/os by virtue of their *latinidad*. Although the 2001 report (like the 1978 one) comments on the diversity of Latinas/os, it still lumps them together as a monolithic, generalized group, using phrasing like "Latinos are often referred to as" or "Overall, Hispanics have."[18] Likewise, whereas the 2001 report (like the 1978 one) recognizes the roles that social and historical factors play in the development of mental illness, and whereas it devotes separate sections to different national-origin Latina/o groups, it nonetheless risks identifying Latinas/os as a unitary group that is collectively "in great need of mental health services."[19] Considering the analogous language and conclusions in both reports and bearing in mind the acknowledged impact of the 1978 report more than two decades after its dissemination, the 1978 report arguably set a model by which Latina/o mental health was to be treated even until the beginning of the twenty-first century.

The difficulties of access to culturally sensitive care for Latinas/os help contextualize Vilar's, Pérez's, Castillo's, García's, and Alvarez's complicated portrayals of the mental health care system. The slippery slope down which the 1978 and 2001 reports slide as they risk essentializing *latinidad* to improve the care given to Latinas/os parallels the fine line these Latina writers sometimes cross as they occasionally waver between biologically and socially constructed depictions of Latinas' mental health. Not only were their texts published in a sociopolitical landscape undoubtedly influenced by the 1978 report, but they illustrate similar concerns as those articulated in both reports, even while they are not psychological or medical treatises about the "status" or quality of Latina/o mental health care in this country.

Although these texts grapple with issues of mental health, they underscore how mental health concerns are connected to bodily and geopolitical concerns, and they present these issues in literary genres for a general audience. By highlighting the ways mind, body, and place are interconnected, and by revealing the relation between the individual and the collective, while including storylines centered on Latina "madwomen," these writers present ambiguous and often contradictory portraits regarding Latina mental health. These depictions trouble Cartesian dualist and neoliberal individualist ideologies that position body and mind, or individual and collective, as separate entities; they also emphasize the multiple variables that contribute to psychic distress and underscore connections among various forms of harm. Even while Vilar, Pérez, Castillo, García, and Alvarez do not exclusively focus on psychological harm, the increased consideration of Latina/o mental health care needs in this country in the latter half of the twentieth century helps explain their preoccupation with the figure of the Latina "madwoman."

However, these writers' attention to an issue as painful, and arguably taboo, as mental illness and their emphasis on manifold harms could be considered to mark a shift from the tone of and focus on ethnic and racial identification, celebration, and resistance characteristic of Latino literature published just a few decades earlier.[20] Not only do Vilar, Pérez, Castillo, García, and Alvarez deviate in tone and focus from the Latino literary traditions that preceded them, but the subject matter of their works ostensibly risks positioning Latinas as vulnerable victims rather than strong and proud women. The Latina protagonists are potentially stripped of subjectivity and agency not only by arguably being cast as victims, but also by virtue of being the *recipients* of harm, even if they sometimes are the ones harming themselves and/or others. When they are the recipients of harm, they effectively are relegated to an object position (harm is exacted on them), whereas the forces perpetrating the harm are those put in a subject position (the forces mete out the harm). Given such negative and ostensibly damaging repercussions of focusing on the multifaceted harm that befalls Latinas, why would Vilar, Pérez, Castillo, García, and Alvarez place harm at the center of their tales? Are they presenting Latinas as victims? Or are they doing something different with their portrayals of harm, such that being the recipient of harm need not consist of a lack of agency?

I maintain that these writers' focus on harm does not cast their Latina protagonists as victims or strip their protagonists of all agency, nor does this focus altogether stray from the resistant Latino literature of the 1960s. Indeed, just as Elena Machado Sáez and Raphael Dalleo argue that post-1960s Latina/o literature needs to be read as consistent with and following from the resistant politics of 1960s Latino literature, I contend that these contemporary texts that grapple with intersections of harm are profoundly political. They vehemently critique hegemony from without *and* within, as they criticize both interethnic and intraethnic hegemonic discourses. This critique admittedly presents itself quite differently from that of Latino literature produced during the civil rights era, and this different manifestation might explain why post-1960s Latina/o literature has been accused of "selling out" to market forces.[21] Recent literature written by and about Latinas arguably feeds into anxieties that are specifically gendered and sexualized; perhaps *this* is an unspoken reason for the allegations from Latino/a scholars that such literature is apolitical.[22] Considering that a male-centered rhetoric dominated various Latino movements during the civil rights era and that some of these movements prioritized ethnic unification above all else, dismissing or downplaying concerns about gender and sexuality, it is not altogether surprising that contemporary Latina literature would modify the type of discourse of resistance from one of exclusively or predominantly ethnic pride to one of ethnicized, racialized, classed, gendered, and sexualized harm.[23]

Such a turn emphasizes the intersectional concerns affecting Latinas and, instead of silencing these concerns, draws attention to questions of voice and agency that are (not) available to Latinas. Circumscribed agency is not the same as victimhood, though; it is about survival in the face of adversity. Indeed, the terminology of victimhood is problematic at best, as it connotes an individual passivity that fails to recognize the oppressive forces that limit agency and also the myriad forms survival can take. As seen in the epigraph to this introduction, voice, or at least a refusal to be silenced, is key to this survival. Openly addressing the intersectional forms of harm that Latina protagonists experience does not minimize concerns about race, ethnicity, or class, for that matter. Instead, in underscoring how questions of gender and sexuality are integrally entwined with those of race, ethnicity, and class, the contemporary Latina texts in this study firmly locate themselves as successors to resistant 1960s Latino literary traditions by engaging in an equally oppositional politics, even if this oppositionality does not consist of binarisms as much as multiplicity.

Apart from extending the boundaries of what might constitute resistant Latino/*a* literary traditions, Vilar's, Pérez's, Castillo's, García's, and Alvarez's focus on Latina "madwomen" also locates their texts within Eurocentric and Anglocentric literary traditions that readily cast female characters as mad, while simultaneously reconfiguring what those traditions look like and refashioning their parameters. Not only do contemporary Latina writers present "madwomen" protagonists, but they also allude to female characters associated with madness in canonical Eurocentric and Anglocentric texts (for example, *Jane Eyre's* Bertha Mason and *Wide Sargasso Sea's* Antoinette Cosway [renamed Bertha Mason], *Hamlet's* Ophelia, *The Odyssey's* Sirens) as well as folkloric and historical Latina, Latin American, and indigenous female figures who have been cast aside because of their perceived deviance (for example, La Malinche/Marina/Malinalli/Malintzín, La Llorona, Pocahontas/Rebecca). In the process, these Latina writers claim a space within literary traditions that have tended to focus exclusively on white(ned) women by positioning gender as the common denominator uniting Latina literature with Eurocentric and Anglocentric literature. Just as these Latina writers broaden the parameters of what resistant Latino/a literary traditions might look like by adding concerns about gender and sexuality to traditions that have focused on race, ethnicity, and class, they add an exploration of race, ethnicity, and class to a Eurocentric and Anglocentric canon that has focused on the roles gender and sexuality play in the construction of literary "madwomen." In both cases, they insert an intersectional lens.

While analyzing Latina texts that place the "madwoman" at their center, *Intersections of Harm* is in dialogue with critical studies on "madwomen" in literature but situates these studies in relation to the broader polemics the works present. What is helpful about the extant scholarship is that it examines the roles patriarchal systems of oppression play in the creation and perpetuation of a specifically gendered psychological harm. Sandra Gilbert and Susan Gubar, Elaine Showalter, and Marta Caminero-Santangelo, for instance, have grappled with questions of voice, silence, power, and powerlessness in relation to the figure of the literary "madwoman," arguing either that a type of agency can be found within her—even if such agency seemingly has been stripped from her—or that there is nothing about her madness that is or ever can be empowering. I build on such polemics to examine representations of Latina protagonists who are cast as deviant by their surrounding societies, communities, families, and selves. What takes me in a different direction from the type of work done by these scholars who focus on the gendering of madness in literature is that I explore how the representations of deviance in Latina literature are not only connected to expressions of female defiance but are also linked to other forms of harm that include but extend beyond patriarchal and psychological violence.

The Latina writers in this study reveal the roles that race and ethnicity necessarily play in classifications of female madness and in the infliction of harm at large, as they illustrate how Latina "madwoman" subjects are like their white(ned) literary precursors, but with differences. Vilar, Pérez, Castillo, García, and Alvarez bring race, ethnicity, sexuality, and class into a discussion that has ignored these constructs for too long, has concealed them, or has tossed them to the periphery. These writers position the protagonists dismissed as deviant in the center of their narratives, while distinctively blending Eurocentric and Anglocentric references with Latina, Latin American, and indigenous historical and folkloric ones, thereby adding to the field of literary studies. Part of their contribution lies in sidestepping the colonizing gesture of solely relying on Eurocentric or Anglocentric allusions and alternatively grounding literary constructions in particular (post)colonial histories that have treated women who sought escape from the oppressive conditions in which they lived as traitors to their gender *and* race. Highlighting this blend of references, *Intersections of Harm* contributes to the extant scholarship about literary "madwomen" by underscoring that Latina "madwomen" protagonists need to be considered alongside the canonized Eurocentric and Anglocentric ones and emphasizing that understandings of female lunacy in literature cannot continue to privilege an analysis of gender at the expense of an examination of race, ethnicity, sexuality, and class. In underscoring that psychological harm needs to be understood in relation to physical and geopolitical harm, this book further adds to such scholarship by revealing how multiple forms of institutionalized oppression affect mind *as well as* body and place.

*Intersections of Harm* contests the very label "madwoman." I place the term in scare quotes to call it into question given the ready pathologization of Latinas, the individualization and medicalization associated with the label, and the romanticization and violence that have accompanied it. Perhaps, however, there is a way to construe the figure of the "madwoman" in Latina literature in terms that are not entirely essentializing, completely romantic (or agentic), or violent (or bleak). If and when this is possible, then hope can emerge "between and among" the harmful ascriptions of Latina madness. This hope, in large part, ironically springs from the same defiance that often causes Latinas to be labeled deviant or mad in the first place. Hope can exist in these paradoxical, interstitial spaces because the same defiance that readily gets re-cast as deviance has the potential to deviate from the very cycles that brand it as such.

By emphasizing the combination of harm and hope, deviance and defiance, my argument borrows and departs from the work of Caminero-Santangelo and Bost. Caminero-Santangelo asserts that madness ultimately traps the "madwoman" in silence and therefore is always utterly disempowering. Rather than focus on representations of psychological harm, Bost focuses on representations of pain and illness in Chicana literature. Positioning herself in contradistinction to the pain theorist Elaine Scarry, Bost arrives at much more hopeful conclusions than either Scarry or Caminero-Santangelo, for that matter. Unlike Scarry, who maintains that "pain is world-destroying," Bost contends "that pain opens up new perceptions of the relationship between one's body and the world around it and creates new ways of moving through the world."[24] I stand somewhere in the middle of these perspectives in terms of subject matter and argument: I examine the intersections of psychological, physical, and geopolitical harm, and I maintain that the multifaceted harm experienced by Latina protagonists is simultaneously disempowering and potentially transformative. My positioning "between and among" Caminero-Santangelo and Bost's perspectives resonates with the place where the Latina writers in my study locate themselves: they paradoxically demonstrate how psychological injury can be simultaneously disabling in the damage it wreaks and enabling in the resistance that often precipitates such injury and that frequently follows from it.

With its interstitial approach, positioning in the intersections, and call for a "third perspective," *Intersections of Harm* speaks to some of the same sets of concerns expressed by women of color during the 1970s and 1980s, and it builds on their intersectional feminist platforms that centered on a shared oppositional politics. Along with the emergence of U.S. Third World feminism that brought together concerns faced by women of color came the development of different strands of Latina feminisms and the proliferation of Latina writings. In the 1960s, 1970s, and 1980s, many Latinas were feeling left out of Latino-based movements that minimized their specific concerns about gender and sexuality. U.S. Third World feminism, and the groundbreaking interventions made by Anzaldúa and Cherríe Moraga, as well as the other contributors to the anthology *This Bridge Called My Back*, for example, allowed for a place where Chicanas and other Latinas and women of color felt as if their voices mattered. Writing played a significant role in giving due attention to the voices of women of color and helping them articulate a U.S. Third World feminist consciousness, with the 1980s marking the decade when this writing began to flourish. Such writing by Latinas, and the coalition building that came with the development of U.S. Third World feminism, emerged from "political necessity" and was designed to effect much-needed social change.[25]

Central to the platform of U.S. Third World feminism is an expressed commitment to a "theory in the flesh." This theory is about a prioritization of lived experience, of theory in praxis as applied to women of color in this country, and this theory entails a combination of "physical and psychic struggle."[26] The Latina texts analyzed in this book engage in a theory in the flesh in their own right. They blur the boundaries dividing theory from literature and illustrate how theory can be extrapolated from literature just as often as it can be applied to literature. Vilar's, Pérez's, Castillo's, García's, and Alvarez's intersectional foci and emphases on "physical and psychic [and geopolitical] struggle" reveal their commitment to presenting their own "theories in the flesh." *Intersections of Harm* underscores this juxtaposed struggle and theorization. The portrayals of mental illness in *The Ladies' Gallery, Impossible Motherhood, Geographies of Home, So Far From God, Dreaming in Cuban,* and *How the García Girls Lost Their Accents* are accompanied by representations of devastating corporeal harm. The bodily injury in these texts takes multiple forms, including miscarriage, abortion, assault, (attempted) suicide, disease, and damage to disparate body parts. Despite Scarry's sharp differentiation between the physical and the psychological, these texts elucidate that the two phenomena cannot be readily disentangled. Physical and psychological pain alike can emanate from and refer to different forms of structural subjugation. In the texts I examine, the two forms of pain are set alongside one another, suggesting that the two necessarily are intertwined, and they are also significantly positioned alongside geopolitical harm.

While analyzing representations of corporeal harm, I draw from the theories presented by Bost and Anzaldúa to explore how the literary depictions of bodily injury can illustrate a theory in the flesh that advances an activist—and gendered, sexualized, racialized, ethnicized, and classed—political agenda. Vilar's, Pérez's, Castillo's, García's, and Alvarez's texts present the type of theory in the flesh outlined by U.S. Third World feminists, and they portray bodily harm through explorations of the ways gender, sexuality, race, ethnicity, and class are scripted onto Latina protagonists' bodies and affect Latinas' psyches. The Latina subjects of these books often are marked according to their physical traits, or at least by socially constructed ideas that subsequently are harmfully imposed on their bodies. At times this harm comes from without, and at times it comes from within. An attention to grooming, for instance, allows Vilar, Pérez, Castillo, García, and Alvarez to comment on how socially produced gender norms affect the ways Latina protagonists view and sometimes disparage their bodies and selves. Likewise, these writers underscore that public perceptions of race influence self-perceptions of race. Just as Frantz Fanon notes in *Black Skin, White Masks* that blackness is always already marked on him and helps instigate what he terms a third-person consciousness, the Latina works I examine emphasize that racism imposed from without can foster an internalized racism felt on and in the body and mind at once and often is attached to protagonists' sense of place or displacement. Through such portrayals, Vilar, Pérez, Castillo, García, and Alvarez underscore that harm (re)produces itself in various sites and in multiple ways.

This harm is exacted on Latina subjects' bodies and minds, and it is foisted on the places they inhabit. These places may be geographical locations where subjects reside, psychological spaces where subjects dwell, or even the physical sites of subjects' own bodies. In this sense, the damage wreaked on geographical place is entwined with that inflicted on Latina protagonists themselves. In their characterizations of place, Vilar, Pérez, Castillo, García, and Alvarez position their settings in the fore of their narratives, underscoring their centrality in the tales these writers tell. The geopolitical devastation elucidated in their books presents itself in myriad ways, be it through histories of colonization, imperialism, dictatorship, or revolution, land appropriation and dispossession, or environmental genocide. In addition to these forms of geopolitical harm, there are times when the environments themselves are depicted as unwelcoming sites that render Latina protagonists vulnerable, such that the inhospitableness of geographical place makes the protagonists feel out of place psychologically. In my analysis of such representations, I draw from theories of space and place, ecocriticism, ecofeminism, and environmental justice put forth by Mary Pat Brady, Raúl Homero Villa, Henri Lefebvre, bell hooks, Kamala Platt, Doreen Massey, and Laura Pulido and connect these theories to ideas of unbelonging. Building on the work advanced by these scholars, I apply theories of place and space to literary analysis and position such geopolitical theories in conversation with literary studies, Latina/o studies, gender studies, psychology, pain theory, theories about the body, and U.S. Third World feminism.

## Situating Intersections of Harm

This book explores the manifold harms that Latina protagonists experience. Although each chapter could stand on its own, each also could be—and is *intended* to be—read in conversation with the others. Looking at the chapters as speaking to one another invites readers to find points of divergence and convergence among the texts and to determine patterns among them, as all of the texts underscore the relation between individual and collective and emphasize that the individual psychological and physical harm Latina subjects experience is entwined with collective histories of geopolitical violence. The chapters are also structured in parallel ways, divided into sections that primarily focus on individual protagonists within each narrative (although sometimes protagonists are paired together within a section). This structure invokes a particularly U.S. Third World feminist way of reading that emphasizes connections between individual and collective and that signals the importance of affirming Latina subjecthood. A character-by-character analysis challenges the ready homogenization and essentialization of Latinas/os and critically underscores specificities pertinent to each Latina subject's experiences. The structure reveals how these individual experiences must be understood in relation to a collective experience, given shared contexts of struggle. The structure thus emblematizes the ideas of identity-in-difference and identity-in-solidarity that underpin U.S. Third World feminist thought.

Chapter 1, "Rape's Shadow: Seized Freedoms in Irene Vilar's *The Ladies' Gallery* and *Impossible Motherhood*," analyzes the multigenerational, matrilineal legacies of mental illness, abandonment, and abuse in Vilar's two memoirs and positions these alongside Puerto Rico's history of colonization. I examine both books together since Vilar herself admits that, in the process of writing *Impossible Motherhood*, "My personal history alters constantly as more is 'remembered.'"[27] I also jointly analyze the two memoirs because they inform one another and together form one larger narrative of Vilar's life and that of her family and birthplace. Beginning *The Ladies' Gallery* with her grandmother Lolita Lebrón opening fire on Congress in a political declaration of Puerto Rican independence from the United States, Vilar connects her grandmother's subsequent imprisonment and institutionalization in a mental hospital with her mother Gladys's depression and suicide and her own psychiatric institutionalization, depression, and attempted suicide. Early in the narrative, Vilar emphasizes, "Where I come from, rape, metaphorical and literal rape, is considered the spark of our history, and solitude its human consequence."[28] *Impossible Motherhood* implicitly expounds on this same idea, as it grapples with what is largely unspoken in *The Ladies' Gallery*, namely that Vilar underwent fifteen abortions in fifteen years. Although Vilar concedes that she abused her right to "choose," she links her abortions—and her fraught relationship with her body and with motherhood—to her own sense of abandonment as a child, a familial narrative of abandonment and sexual abuse, and a national narrative of abuse of women's bodies, seen through the mass sterilization of Puerto Rican women and the oral contraceptive testing imposed on them.[29] I accordingly read Vilar's memoirs through the lens of rape as she defines it above, and I explore important moments of female resistance that accompany the seized freedoms highlighted in both texts. In the process, I depart from the type of argumentation advanced by Scarry, who distinguishes between physical and psychological pain, and I posit that the multifaceted types of harm portrayed in Vilar's memoirs cannot be readily compartmentalized.

Chapter 2, "Violated Bodies and Assaulting Landscapes in Loida Maritza Pérez's *Geographies of Home*," extends the analysis of rape provided in the previous chapter and examines the connections Pérez draws among bodily violation, mental illness, and geopolitical violence in her debut novel. Drawing from scholarship examining the relation among body, place, and the development of what Fanon calls a third-person consciousness, I analyze representations of location and dislocation in Pérez's book. In *Geographies of Home*, set in the late 1990s, Pérez depicts the seemingly endless hardships faced by a working-class Afro

Dominican American family living in a brutally inhospitable New York City. Aurelia, the family matriarch, is trying to take on more parental responsibility after having divested herself of such when suffering an emotional collapse upon her move to the United States. Her husband, Papito, is haunted by recollections of life under Rafael Leónidas Trujillo's reign of terror in the Dominican Republic. The trauma that Papito carries with him also follows from witnessing his first love, Anabelle, deliberately thrust herself into the eye of a hurricane. Years later, Papito and Aurelia's daughter Rebecca finds herself in her second abusive relationship, and Rebecca's children live in perpetual fear while their bodies waste away from hunger. Rebecca's sister Marina is diagnosed with bipolar disorder with symptoms of schizophrenia, is tormented by memories of being raped by an African American male psychic, has developed an externalized and internalized racism, and rapes her gender-bending sister Iliana. Iliana, the educated protagonist, is raped by Marina and is also sexually assaulted while in college. That none of the characters in the narrative is exempt from harm, and that there is so much harm, makes it difficult to read the novel as anything other than devastatingly tragic. Yet ethical imperatives are born from travesty. The idea of *rasquachismo*, or making the best out of less than ideal circumstances, with which Pérez ends her narrative suggests that activism and hope can exist even under the most dire conditions.

Chapter 3, "Madness's Material Consequences in Ana Castillo's *So Far from God*," takes to task critical dismissals of *So Far from God* as a primarily allegorical, magical realist, or *telenovela*-like novel. Concentrating on the text's juxtaposition of the extraordinary with the ordinary, I argue that this pairing provides a scathing commentary on the damage done to Mexican American women living on the U.S.-Mexico border during the Persian Gulf War. Castillo presents four daughters—Caridad, Loca, Esperanza, and Fe—and one mother, Sofi, who are viewed as anomalies by their community in Tome, New Mexico, and who undergo irreparable harm. Castillo positions the psychological and corporeal injury the sisters experience and the grief the mother faces against a backdrop of land appropriation and environmental genocide. Forming a tripartite crossroads of mental, physical, and environmental harm, Castillo highlights how the madness attributed to the four daughters has material consequences and cannot be separated from the damage done to their land and loved ones. Analyzing how Castillo casts these characters outside of society's norms and draws attention to their missing or mangled bodies, and building on the ecocritical and environmental justice work of Platt and Pulido, I explore how the corrosions of Castillo's characters must be read alongside both the corrosiveness of their surrounding environment and the female rebellion that forms a critical component of the narrative.

In chapter 4, "Artistic Aberrance and Liminal Geographies in Cristina García's *Dreaming in Cuban*," I examine the connections García posits among artistry, aberrance, and womanhood.[30] *Dreaming in Cuban* has a matrilineal, multigenerational focus, and its four main characters—Celia, Felicia, Lourdes, and Pilar—are labeled deviant, demonstrate defiance, and experience harm. Celia, the grandmother and matriarch of the novel, is institutionalized in a mental hospital at one point, plays the piano, writes secret love letters, enjoys poetry, and, as a judge, encourages artistic outlets as penance for crimes committed. Her daughter Felicia immerses herself in *santería*, an Afro Cuban religion that Felicia views as a type of poetry. Felicia is considered "crazy" because of her religious devotion, perceived hypersexuality, and injurious and sometimes murderous actions toward others, actions that arguably follow from the effects of the syphilis that she contracts from her adulterous and abusive first husband. Celia's daughter Lourdes flees Cuba after suffering a miscarriage and surviving a rape by a Cuban soldier, rebels against Celia through her staunch capitalism, develops an eating disorder, and finds creative outlets in the goods she makes for her Yankee Doodle Bakery. Lourdes's daughter, Pilar, rebels against her mother through her nostalgia for Cuba and uncanny attachment to her grandmother, fights against social injustice through her painting, finds solace in music, and, like her mother, is sexually assaulted. I explore how García situates such portrayals in a post-1959 context that forces family members to "call and wave from opposite shores."[31] Extending Kimberle López's analysis of female madness and revolution in *Dreaming in Cuban*, I situate the novel as following from Eurocentric and Anglocentric traditions of madwomen in literature and as linked to a complicated history of Spanish colonization. I also explore representations of race in the novel, relying on Toni Morrison's argument that race is always already embedded in language, and I examine how the gendered harm the characters experience at times is confounded by an ambiguous race politics. The chapter ultimately underscores the significance of revolution in the text, both with respect to the Cuban Revolution as well as to the female rebelliousness that casts the women characters as mad and allows them to defy the labels imposed on them.

Chapter 5, "Clamped Mouths and Muted Cries: Stifled Expression in Julia Alvarez's *How the García Girls Lost Their Accents*," reads

Alvarez's first novel through the lens of what Anzaldúa terms "linguistic terrorism," a concept that stems from the premise that certain languages are "right" and others are "wrong" and that accordingly relates to the racist, xenophobic, classist, and (hetero)sexist attempts to strip a people of its language. Describing the ways linguistic terrorism can instill a type of intimate terrorism through which bordered subjects are made to feel fear, shame, and illegitimacy and through which bordered subjects are effectively silenced, Anzaldúa emphasizes the connection between language and identity.[32] I analyze the representations of linguistic loss and search for, and acquisition of, voice in Alvarez's book. In the novel, set during and after Trujillo's dictatorship in the Dominican Republic and in a United States where schoolchildren hurl epithets at Dominican peers, the four García girls—Carla, Sandra, Yolanda, and Sofía—are silenced as they come of age. The four girls are characterized as rebellious, and they all are stifled in one way or another. This suppression manifests itself in various ways, including psychiatric hospitalization, imposed monolingualism, implicit and explicit acts of racism and sexism, and witnessed acts of sexual gratification that render two of the sisters mute in horror. Alvarez highlights how these examples of silencing are forms of traumatic violation. As in *Dreaming in Cuban*, in *How the García Girls Lost Their Accents,* the harm experienced by the female characters is sometimes also linked to artistic expression. Chapter 5 accordingly builds on the analyses provided in previous chapters and, in its focus on linguistic terrorism, compels readers to question where madness "really" lies.

What does it mean to position *The Ladies' Gallery, Impossible Motherhood, Geographies of Home, So Far From God, Dreaming in Cuban,* and *How the García Girls Lost Their Accents* together? *Intersections of Harm* takes two memoirs and four novels as its primary texts of analysis, puts multiple fields of study in dialogue with one another, and borrows heavily from a multigeneric work, *Borderlands,* to theorize the primary texts. In doing so, I illustrate how works of Latina fiction and nonfiction alike can speak to the same sets of issues. Even the writers whose works I analyze recognize the blurred lines distinguishing fiction from memoir. Vilar, for instance, invokes fictional references in her first memoir and intersperses these with her story and that of her mother and grandmother. In her second memoir, she refers to *The Ladies' Gallery* as "proof of the lie I have at times made of my life" and declares that her first memoir "was true, but it could have been truer."[33] In both books, she refers to herself and the people in her life as characters in a story.

Further confusing the distinctions between fiction and nonfiction, both *Dreaming in Cuban* and *How the García Girls Lost Their Accents*, works that have been marketed as fiction, are commonly referred to as semi-autobiographical novels. What is more, *Dreaming in Cuban, How the García Girls Lost Their Accents, Geographies of Home*, and *So Far from God* all incorporate actual historical events, arguably dabbling in what could be termed historical fiction.

The Latina protagonist who is vulnerable to psychic, physical, and geopolitical harm occupies a "real" and a symbolic role in these narratives. The subject of memoir, she is a tangible reminder of the harm done to Latinas over the course of history; as such, she compels readers to question her mistreatment and to reexamine the sociohistorical conditions that have contributed to the psychological and corporeal damage she experiences. This injury is not simply her individual condition with which she must deal; it is connected to the damaging, pathological sociohistorical forces surrounding her. In this respect, the representation of the harm she suffers in the form of memoir serves a metonymic purpose, depicting one woman's life story while simultaneously standing in for something larger than her individual narrative. As a literary device, the metonymic function provided here by memoir also lends itself to fiction writing. The Latina "madwoman's" portrayal, in fiction as in memoir, emphasizes that individual ascriptions of deviance form part of collective narratives about the residual effects of colonization, imperialism, dictatorship, and/or revolution and the concurrent effects of racism, xenophobia, (hetero)sexism, and classism. The similar position occupied by this Latina subject invites a comparative analysis of her representation across these genres.

In addition to examining texts across genres, *Intersections of Harm* embarks on a pan-Latina analysis that is illustrative of the pan-Latina/o direction in which the field of Latina/o studies is moving. The book is pan-Latina in its exploration of the gendered, sexualized, ethnicized, racialized, and classed harm depicted in texts by Puerto Rican, Dominican American, Xicana, and Cuban American writers from diverse racial and socioeconomic strata. I utilize the grassroots term *Latina/o* to invite important points of comparison among the writers of different ancestral-origin groups whose works I analyze. I am well aware of the different historicities of the various ancestral-origin groups that fall under the label Latina/o, and I examine how Vilar, Pérez, Castillo, García, and Alvarez incorporate the particular sociohistorical positionings of Puerto Ricans, Dominican Americans, Mexican Americans, and Cuban Americans in their texts. But I am also interested in the ways these narratives intersect and offer similar observations about the tripartite harm Latina subjects experience. Such comparative analysis is important because it highlights both shared and distinct experiences with oppression and resistance and because it can allow for the possibility of collective mobilization across differences for the sake of important social change. By placing *The Ladies' Gallery, Impossible Motherhood, Geographies of Home, So Far From God, Dreaming in Cuban,* and *How the García Girls Lost Their Accents* alongside one another, I am not trying to elide the differences among them, but neither am I suggesting that there is no place for comparative scholarship.

Pan-Latina/o analysis allows for recognition of the variations among Latinas/os and an acknowledgment of the connections that arise among those differences that can help forge what Caminero-Santangelo describes as a "commitment to solidarity."[34] Intersections can be shared spaces where multiple *latinidades* at times converge to depict similar histories of racialized, ethnicized, classed, gendered, and sexualized subjugation. Even though such spaces are shared only temporarily, it is important that they are ever shared at all. Despite the differences among Latinas/os across ancestral, racial, and socioeconomic origins (to name but a few variances), Latinas/os still often are lumped together from without by virtue of the intangible social construction sometimes referred to as *latinidad,* and Latinas/os often group together from within to address common interests. Looking to *latinidad* as allowing for the possibility of solidarity while recognizing the heterogeneous makeup of the groups that are uniting can foster social change based on both mutual and distinct concerns. Indeed, as Bhabha explains, an examination of ambivalence and ambiguity "affirm[s] a profound desire for social solidarity."[35] Solidarity underscores the relation between individual and collective, difference and similarity, and ambivalence and ambiguity. The intersections where these merge mark the location where social mobilization can take place. My emphasis on this location reveals the activist impulse undergirding *Intersections of Harm.*

An equally significant contribution this project makes is to position fields of study together that too often are examined separately in order to see how these fields (can) speak to each other and jointly (can) help speak to the various currents of thought affecting recent Latina literary production. I place Latina/o studies, literary studies, ethnic studies, feminist theory, psychology, pain theory, ecocriticism, environmental justice, geography, postcolonial studies, medical anthropology, and history in conversation with one another. Although there have been studies within these fields that have embarked on similar areas of inquiry as those investigated in this book, these studies have tended to be narrower in scope (for example, focusing on one form of harm) or wider in scope (for example, examining literary representations of "madwomen" across ethnicities and races that are readily recognized as distinct). I, however, explore connections among psychological, physical, and geopolitical harm and focus on one often homogenized, although by no means monolithic, pan-ethnic group: Latinas. *Intersections of Harm* ultimately argues that there is a need to view the individual in relation to the collective and that it is crucial to situate the multiple forms of harm Latina protagonists experience at the intersections where they simultaneously come together and split apart from one another. Despite the ways Western thought tends to render body, mind, and place separate from each other, *Intersections of Harm* underscores the importance of examining the junction of these entities. I take up Anzaldúa's call to develop "a tolerance for ambiguity"; I highlight multiple forms of harm experienced by Latina subjects in order to begin to uproot systems of oppression that contribute to such harm; and I aim to dismantle dichotomy.[36]

# 1 /    Rape's Shadow: Seized Freedoms in Irene Vilar's
##       *The Ladies' Gallery* and *Impossible Motherhood*

The history of U.S. intervention and industrialization in Puerto Rico, the mass sterilization of Puerto Rican women, and the oral contraceptive testing on Puerto Rican women in the name of medical progress and under the auspices of population control jointly form the critical backdrop to Irene Vilar's two memoirs, *The Ladies' Gallery: A Memoir of Family Secrets* (1996) and *Impossible Motherhood: Testimony of an Abortion Addict* (2009).[1] The national narratives are juxtaposed against the personal ones Vilar tells of her maternal grandmother (Lolita Lebrón), her mother (Gladys Mirna Vilar), and herself (Irene). Although thirteen years separate their initial publication, the two books complement one another to form a more complete snapshot of the three women's life stories and birthplaces. Writing that her grandmother's "personal tragedy was a moment in the collective epic," Vilar emphasizes the interconnectedness of the individual and collective.[2] Both memoirs are scathing social commentaries about the damage inflicted on Puerto Rican women and Puerto Rican land that extend beyond the life story of one individual and highlight broader patterns of psychological, physical, and geopolitical harm. What interests me is the juxtaposition of multiple forms of harm that are experienced at the individual and collective level. I analyze this multifaceted harm in tandem with the ideas of choice, constraint, and coercion, and I argue that Vilar's two memoirs center on the concept of seized freedom.

Some (admittedly abridged) background information about the history of U.S. involvement in Puerto Rico and the treatment of Puerto

Rican women might prove useful in contextualizing the legacies of harm and the manifestations of seized freedom portrayed in Vilar's memoirs. With the passage of the Foraker Bill (1900) and the Jones Act (1917), Puerto Rico was transferred from Spain to the United States, and Puerto Ricans were granted U.S. citizenship respectively. While this citizenship allowed Puerto Ricans to fight in World War I in droves, it did not allow them to vote for president of the United States—a right denied to this day. By 1930, U.S. corporations had displaced Puerto Ricans and usurped control of more than half of Puerto Rican land; by 1937, levels of unemployment on the island reached a staggering 37 percent, and the unemployed were considered "excess population."[3] With the implementation of the economic industrialization program "Operation Bootstrap" in the late 1940s, thousands more became unemployed and impoverished, creating the conditions for a mass migration to the U.S. mainland.[4] Upon naming Puerto Rico a commonwealth in 1952, the U.S. Congress effectively maintained territorial control of the island. For nearly sixty years after World War II, the U.S. Navy used the Puerto Rican island of Vieques as a testing site for nuclear weapons, leaving toxic waste in its wake. And after President Bill Clinton decided "to end tax breaks . . . that ensured the success of investments in manufacturing while decimating agriculture on the island," Puerto Rico witnessed an "abrupt decline of manufacturing," so that "Puerto Rico finds itself now with neither tax breaks, nor agriculture, nor half its population."[5]

Not only did U.S. involvement affect Puerto Rico's infrastructure, it also affected the treatment of women there. That treatment was integrally related to mainland attitudes toward Puerto Ricans, mainland ideas about "proper" sexuality, eugenic influences on health and population policy, and medical advances in the name of scientific "progress." Throughout the twentieth century, Puerto Rican women tended to be characterized as either dangerous or victimized, and ideas about (primarily working-class) Puerto Rican women's sexuality and reproduction were entwined with constructions of nationhood.[6] The positioning of Puerto Rican women in these ways scapegoated them as perpetuating "what was wrong in Puerto Rico" and arguably served as a convenient excuse for continued U.S. interference in the island.[7]

Acting as "benevolent protectors" of a population theoretically in need of aid, U.S. officials and medical researchers sought to address the "overpopulation problem" and poverty in Puerto Rico. They did so through the widespread dissemination of the birth control pill and the mass sterilization of Puerto Rican women.[8] Under "Operation Bootstrap," factories that had been established by U.S. corporations pressured Puerto Rican women "to limit their fertility."[9] From the 1940s to the 1960s, pharmaceutical companies based in the U.S. mainland experimented with Puerto Rican women's bodies to determine the appropriate hormonal dosage in the birth control pills they were developing. In 1956, "contraceptive pills twenty times as strong as the ones used today were first tested among Puerto Rican women who lived in government housing projects" without the women's knowledge that they were the first to receive these pills, and between 1968 and 1972, the U.S. Agency for International Development in Latin America "increased its budget for birth control programs by one hundred million," while "reducing sorely needed health care by the same amount."[10] Vilar herself describes the period between 1955 and 1969 as a time when "Puerto Rico was a human laboratory for the development of birth control technology and population control policies. Pills . . . with dangerous systemic side effects, including sterility, were tested on women by the U.S. government."[11]

It comes as no surprise, then, that while the use of the birth control pill was on the rise, so was the sterilization of Puerto Rican women. This was facilitated by the passage of Law Number 136 in 1937, legislation based on the principles of eugenics, "which included poverty as a legitimate reason for permitting sterilization." By 1974, over one third of Puerto Rican women had been permanently sterilized; by 1980, the rate of sterilizations in Puerto Rico surpassed that of every nation in the world.[12] Considering these statistics, the eugenic foundation of the law legalizing sterilization on the island, and the encouragement of sterilization and controlled reproduction from multiple sectors of the population, it is important to think about the rhetoric surrounding Puerto Rican women's sexuality—and the material consequences of this rhetoric—in terms of a paradoxical and incompatible juxtaposition of choice and coercion.

This juxtaposition is evident in *The Ladies' Gallery* and *Impossible Motherhood*. In both memoirs, Vilar highlights the relation among her nation's history of colonialism and repression of women's sexuality and reproductive liberties; her maternal family's history of mental illness, attempted suicide, sexual abuse, conflicted relationship with motherhood, and abandonment; and her paternal family's history of substance abuse.[13] The notion of individual choice in this context, while not entirely absent, is ironic at best. Yet it is impossible to read *Impossible Motherhood* in particular without thinking about choice, especially since the memoir chronicles what Vilar describes as her addiction to abortion. Although

*The Ladies' Gallery* does not instantly evoke the same idea of choice, its ghostly imprint can be detected; what is not explicitly articulated in the first memoir is brought to the fore in the second. What is readily apparent in both narratives is a focus on the notions of freedom, constrained freedom, and seized freedom.

## Barren Landscapes and Shifting Geographies

Vilar positions *The Ladies' Gallery* and *Impossible Motherhood* against a backdrop of geopolitical devastation, devoting substantial attention to a description of the political, historical, and geographic settings. She refers to Puerto Rico's double history of colonization with Spain and the United States and comments on the island's fraught relations with the U.S. mainland, noting the battles around the changing status of the island in her first memoir and condemning U.S. interference in Puerto Rican women's sexuality and reproductive liberties in her second. She also describes physical places and landscapes in detail, highlighting how the barrenness and fragility of those landscapes parallel the psychic and physical harm she, her mother, and her grandmother have experienced.

In *The Ladies' Gallery*, Vilar paints a landscape rife with poverty and contamination, yet infused with nationalist pride. Her portrait of place cannot be separated from her anticolonial stance.[14] Her depiction of place is marked by violence and loss. Her emphasis on the geographical is tied to her critique of U.S. interference in Puerto Rico, and both memoirs arguably entail a search for her (geographical) sense of self in the context of the U.S. appropriation of Puerto Rican land.

In her first memoir, Vilar recalls a nation once known for its production of sugarcane, aware that this yearning is directed toward a colonial past, when workers were exploited for the purposes of agricultural cultivation. She also references the agricultural decay following the industrialization efforts on the island. However, by stating that the past is "not completely lost, but grown into the ground," she suggests that there is a part of the preindustrialized landscape that still remains. She turns toward this stratum in what could be considered a type of archaeological excavation of this past, a psychological return to the past to make sense of the present, or a call to political action. Relying on patriotic, nationalist sentiment, Vilar reminds herself and us of *el grito de Lares*, the name given to the 1868 rebellion for independence, "with which Puerto Rico began its anticolonial struggle against Spain." She declares, "Lares is nationality," stressing how the city, as synecdoche, comes to embody the spirit of Puerto Rican resistance.[15] Relaying this particular history in this way, Vilar demonstrates that her grandmother's, her mother's, and her own battles are connected to this proud and resistant national consciousness.

This spirit of resistance is central to Vilar's writing and is immediately brought to the fore in *The Ladies' Gallery*, which opens with a description of Lolita firing on the U.S. Congress in the name of Puerto Rican freedom from U.S. governance.[16] Vilar's critique of U.S. policies in Puerto Rico in part can be found in her accounts of her conversations with her grandmother. In these, Lolita denounces the environmental destruction wreaked on the island, courtesy of the U.S. corporate and military presence there:

> The chemical-pollution horrors brought on by the tax exemption for American industries on the island are followed by the proposal to construct nuclear plants to generate electricity in areas of great human and environmental vulnerability, like the coastal towns of Manatí and Salinas, to which must be added the U.S. Navy's tests on the islands of Vieques and Culebra, their use of Agent Orange, which is contaminating the streams of the great forest reserve of El Yunque, the disastrous consequences of the petrochemical complex at Guayanilla, the workers poisoned (by mercury) at Beckton Dickinson, the workers poisoned at Puerto Rican Cement. And so on. . . .[17]

Adopting imagery akin to that found in Ana María García's documentary *La Operación* about the mass sterilization of Puerto Rican women, Vilar expounds upon the devastation to a land and its inhabitants under the ruse of economic "development." The phrase "and so on," followed by an ellipsis, underscores the seemingly never-ending nature of the horrific damage inflicted on the island from U.S. industrialization and militarization.

The colonization of Puerto Rico needs to be understood in relation to the harm inflicted on Puerto Rican women's bodies. In her foreword to *Impossible Motherhood*, Robin Morgan describes women as colonized subjects by virtue of their gender.[18] This claim is particularly salient for Puerto Rican women, who, as Morgan points out, have been "multiply colonized." Morgan asserts that Vilar's identity as a writer, a "prochoice feminist," "a Latina, a Puerto Rican American" creates "a tale of colonialism compounded by sexism."[19] But the ways Vilar presents issues of colonization and gender are more specific than is suggested by Morgan's analogy tying all women's bodies to the land. Morgan criticizes the decolonial scholars Frantz Fanon and Albert Memmi for failing to acknowledge gender oppression as a form of colonization, yet she neglects to emphasize that the denunciation of oppression at the heart of Vilar's writing *inseparably* links gender with nationality.

An intersectional approach to understanding Vilar's memoirs is key. Cherríe Moraga's writings can prove helpful in this regard. Like Morgan, Moraga underscores that women's bodies are connected to place and exposed to the same type of harm, highlighting how both women's bodies and lands are subject to colonization, exploitation, and rape.[20] Linking the geographical, political, and physical, Moraga asks:

> *How will our [women's] lands be free if our bodies aren't?*
> Land remains the common ground for all radical action.
> But land is more than the rocks and trees, the animal and plant
> life . . . land is also the factories where we work, the water our
> children drink, and the housing project where we live. For women,
> lesbians, and gay men, land is that physical mass called our
> bodies. Throughout las Américas, all these "lands" remain under
> occupation by an Anglo-centric, patriarchal, imperialist United
> States.[21]

Moraga broadens dominant perceptions of what counts as land, equating land with body, and she extends the idea of freedom that accompanies any anti-imperialist movement to encompass gender reform. She also implicates the United States for its imposition of patriarchy and imperialism and its corresponding suppression of freedom "throughout las Américas." In *The Ladies' Gallery* and *Impossible Motherhood*, Vilar provides a similar critique of U.S. policy; she implicitly asks the same question as that posed by Moraga—"how will our lands be free if our bodies aren't?"—and arguably asks the converse question too: How will (or can) our bodies be free if our lands aren't?

Likening Puerto Rican women's bodies to the land and highlighting the intersectionality of gender and geopolitical oppression, Vilar's "reclamation of flesh" articulates the type of "theory in the flesh" advanced by U.S. Third World feminists like Moraga who, according to the postcolonial studies scholar Chandra Mohanty, are united by a politics of resistance that includes the realm of the personal. Vilar's two memoirs adhere to the characteristics of Third World feminist writings articulated by Mohanty in Vilar's commentary on the damage caused by U.S. interference on the island and the Puerto Rican nationalist response to such intervention; in her attention to the gendered harm to which she, her mother, and her grandmother have been subjected; in her choice of genre to chronicle the events of her life and that of her family and nation; and in her recognition that she may have lost allies because of her fifteen abortions.[22]

As part of this project, Vilar positions her individual and collective tale against a national tale of environmental destruction, land appropriation, mass sterilization, and campaign for birth control, and she interweaves these narratives, placing herself, her mother, and her grandmother as part of the land that has been confiscated, contaminated, misused, and rendered fragile and barren. Vilar captures this sentiment when she writes, "Three generations of women. No, they were not women. They were part of the barren landscape seen at sunset from my window. . . ."[23] That the women form part of the desolate landscape, that this formation deprives them of their very womanhood, and that this landscape is seen at the day's end from an interior vantage point looking outward suggest a sense of resignation and closure, yet the ellipsis and placement of women in the external environment suggest possibility, open-endedness, and freedom from the confines of an interior domestic space.

In her second memoir, Vilar again describes the landscape as fragile and connected to its inhabitants, but she also repeatedly brings up the notions of home and homelessness in relation to place. Throughout *Impossible Motherhood*, she asks what it means to be countryless and homeless considering Puerto Rico's de facto status as a U.S. colony, her ever-shifting domiciles over the course of her childhood and adolescence, and her primary residence in upstate New York during her adult years.[24] She accordingly defines home as more than a set, singular physical location. This characterization resonates with the ideas of space advanced by Henri Lefebvre, Mary Pat Brady, and Doreen Massey, who argue against the notion that place and space are static constructs. By turning to the past in both memoirs and presenting an alternative version of the past in the second book by filling in the gaps present in the first, Vilar also speaks to Massey's contention that the past, like place and space, is something that is constructed.[25] Re-constructing her past, Vilar does not presuppose a fixedness to it, and one often romanticized at that. Rather, in retelling principal events that transpired in the past, she works against the nostalgic strain that can typify memoir in a manner similar to that of the Chicano scribe described by Moraga who "remembers, not out of nostalgia but out of hope. She remembers in order to envision. She looks backward in order to look forward to a world founded not on greed, but on respect for the sovereignty of nature. And in this, she suffers—to know that fertility is both possible and constantly interrupted."[26] For Vilar, this scripted look backward begins with a series of three snapshots: her grandmother's attack on Congress and subsequent incarceration; her mother's suicide; and her own psychiatric institutionalization.

## Lolita's Confinement and Rebellion

*The Ladies' Gallery* and *Impossible Motherhood* together highlight how the matrilineal cycle of abandonment, neglect, servitude, and mental illness that arguably starts with Lolita is connected to the history of the land and, more specifically, to the U.S. takeover of Puerto Rican land and displacement of islanders. Vilar ties these elements together by explaining the "choices" made for the sake of survival. She begins with Lolita's "decision" to sell herself to the owner of the coffee plantation where her father works. Lolita barters her body for rent at a time "when North American companies turned the island into a sugarcane monoculture," destroying the life opportunities available to many islanders and forcing many to "choose" between working under what basically amounted to a de facto sharecropping system or "shipping out" to New York. Sold to make ends meet and impregnated by the landowner who refuses to acknowledge his child, Lolita leaves Puerto Rico and her daughter, Gladys. She moves to New York, "the land that pushe[s] her out of her own to begin with," where she begins to fight to reclaim the land from which she feels obliged to flee.[27] It is in New York that Lolita gets involved with the Puerto Rican Nationalist Party, and it is on behalf of her homeland that she marches on Congress.

If woman is mother is nation, as the Puerto Rican Nationalist Party leader Pedro Albizu Campos would have us believe, then Lolita is the ultimate symbol of Puerto Rican motherhood and nationhood by virtue of her self-professed sacrificial offering in the fight for Puerto Rican independence from the United States. Vilar notes Albizu Campos's description of Lolita as his "transcendental woman" for these reasons.[28] As Puerto Rico's most (in)famous female political prisoner, Lolita is the paradoxical epitome of the deviant colonized subject and the antithesis of a subject who has been colonized. Despite her notoriety/fame, though, immediately following her attack on Congress, none of the public portrayals of Lolita by the politicians or the media grant her a voice with which to explain herself.

Instead, the ensuing characterizations of Lolita's act of political rebellion refuse to focus on her rationale for her actions, revealing a discrepancy between the media and politicians' representations of

Lolita's deviance and her self-expression of defiance. Describing the coverage of the shootings in the *New York Times*, Vilar comments on the newspaper's photo of Lolita the revolutionary with its simultaneous blatant omission of Lolita's words: "The front page of the *New York Times* would show the same woman [Lolita] wrapped in the revolutionary flag of Puerto Rico, her left fist raised high. What the *Times* would not quote were her words, 'I did not come here to kill. I came to die.' An old battle cry of Puerto Rican nationalism." With this portrayal, the *New York Times* renders Lolita an objectified symbol (via her visual display) devoid of subjectivity (via her silencing). Lolita is cast as insane in the public domain because of her actions. Vilar explains how Lolita, among others who have fought for Puerto Rican independence from the United States, is demonized by the media and dismissed by the governor of Puerto Rico as "crazy and savage" instead of recognized as a "freedom fighter" challenging the U.S. colonization of Puerto Rican land.[29] These representations reveal a conflation of Puerto Rican nationalism with insanity rather than a nuanced attention to the reasons for such extreme action, reasons stemming from an understandable frustration with U.S. involvement in Puerto Rico and a desire to be free from such intrusion, and reasons that implicate U.S. governmental policies for creating the conditions that lead to such action.

Because of the violent method Lolita adopts to display her political protest, she faces a fifty-seven-year prison sentence. While serving her sentence, she is committed as a mental patient to Saint Elizabeth's Hospital. Her turn to force, defiance of her subordination, and lack of compliance with the positionality thrust on her together make her threatening. Perceiving her as dangerous, the U.S. government transforms Lolita from national hero to madwoman via her institutionalization, effectively undermining her symbolic weight, minimizing any threat she could be considered to pose, and conveniently quelling any influence she might have over fellow Puerto Ricans.

Lolita's anticolonial struggle does not end while she is incarcerated or hospitalized, though, and Vilar's critique of the prison system, mental health care system, and U.S. industrialization and militarization in Puerto Rico is interlaced throughout her depiction of Lolita's time in jail and in a psychiatric institution. Vilar interweaves information about the environmental destruction wreaked on the island with the voices Lolita hears while she is imprisoned and the visions that appear to Lolita, visions that begin once she learns that her son, Félix, has drowned. In these visions, Lolita perceives herself as separate from her body, feeling like she "no longer inhabited her body" and sensing that while "she understood what was going on around her . . . it was happening to the other woman." Seeing her body as belonging to a different woman, Lolita dissociates her corporeality from her being and invokes the type of body-mind split corresponding to dominant Western systems of thought. The timing of this split corresponds with her grief over her son's death, but it also could be linked to her confinement, implicating the prison environment in its occurrence. Only upon envisioning Jesus before her does Lolita reunite body with mind and seemingly return to her former self. Yet she isn't quite the same. She now sees herself as a divine messenger who hears a voice that compels her to draft a document, "A Message from God in the Atomic Age." Recounting this time to her granddaughter years later, Lolita intersperses her account of her visions with her concerns over the geopolitical "problems of Puerto Rico and the world," problems consisting of "chemical-pollution horrors" and environmental devastation.[30] Immediately after noting the passion with which Lolita conveys her geopolitical worries, Vilar describes Lolita's institutionalization in Saint Elizabeth's Hospital, a hospitalization that comes a few days after President Dwight D. Eisenhower receives part of "A Message from God in the Atomic Age." Vilar conjoins the account of Lolita's incarceration, hospitalization, sense of separation from her physical self, and subsequent religious and ecocritical fervor, and she emphasizes Lolita's poetic mode of expression; she accordingly underscores the intersections of harm Lolita experiences and the intersectionality of issues that concern her. Vilar highlights the relation among body, mind, and place; connects different forms of institutional confinement; and positions Lolita's individual incarceration and hospitalization against a collective history of geopolitical destruction.

When detailing Lolita's transfer to Saint Elizabeth's Hospital from her jail cell, Vilar relates the gross mistreatment her grandmother experiences. She describes how Lolita is dragged and shoved by guards and orderlies. She comments on the physical scars still visible on her grandmother's body after nine months of being confined in a mental ward, scars induced "from the 'electric torture'" Lolita has undergone, and scars that show how Lolita's doctors treat her as if she were a lab rat subject to experimental procedures in the name of medical care. Vilar further recounts the psychological trauma her grandmother suffers *because of* her hospitalization: "[Lolita] told how they [the doctors] were trying to drive her crazy but hadn't succeeded. They were making her hear 'electronic voices,' injecting her, experimenting with her." Vilar elucidates how Lolita does not perceive herself to be insane when hospitalized but believes that her institutionalization is designed to make her *become* insane: "Ever since her arrival at the mental hospital she had fought for her sanity."[31] Although Lolita claims that the doctors do not succeed in their attempts to "drive her crazy," the information that Vilar provides readers nonetheless reveals that the very mechanisms supposedly put in place to help cure patients propel them toward mental instability and leave permanent imprints on their bodies and minds.[32]

Vilar also comments on the ambivalent treatment afforded to Lolita by fellow Puerto Ricans. Although Lolita is either revered as a national hero for her *independentista* politics and storming of the U.S. Capitol or denigrated for her political stance and actions, she is viewed in an ambiguous fashion upon her release from prison and the psychiatric hospital. Community members do not know how to interpret her newfound religiosity, which they perceive to be "seemingly so at odds with her political militancy." Other Puerto Ricans,

> who admired her once and still love her, feel obliged to accept her with a paternal attitude. . . .
> Or they'll say it's fine in a García Márquez novel, but not in Lolita the revolutionary.
> Or they simply treat her like a madwoman and do what the doctor-jailers of St. Elizabeth's Hospital did—devour her.[33]

What unites these disparate attitudes is that they are all dismissive. Even the positive reception of Lolita is qualified by a sense of obligation. Illustrating the hypocrisy in these reactions, Vilar demonstrates how behaviors considered redeemable in fiction are deemed unacceptable in "real world" revolutionaries. Vilar also underscores the malevolence behind the community's treatment of Lolita by comparing it to that bestowed by Lolita's doctors and jailers. Moreover, by hyphenating the terms *doctor* and *jailers* as if they formed one word and connecting them to Puerto Ricans' negative reception of Lolita's release from jail and the mental health facility, Vilar emphasizes the interchangeability of the different forms of confinement experienced by the island's renowned political prisoner.[34] Linking Lolita's imprisonment with her hospitalization, Vilar demonstrates that the notion of care needs to be scrutinized because of its association with confinement and control.

In her depiction of the wounds inflicted on Lolita by her doctors, jailers, and compatriots, Vilar paints a frightening picture of the treatment of those who defy the institutional (and colonial) apparatus that defines what is considered "normal." Like the colonized in Fanon's *The Wretched of the Earth* who undergo "a disintegration, dissolution or splitting of the personality, [that] plays a key regulating role in ensuring the stability of the colonized world," Lolita experiences a body-mind split during her confinement.[35] Only *while she is incarcerated* is she diagnosed as mentally ill. Even in Saint Elizabeth's Hospital, she is made to feel mentally unstable. That colonialism and confinement both can perpetuate a body-mind fissure, and that such a "splitting of the personality" arguably helps keep the colonial, prison, and mental health care systems intact, speaks to the ways these systems can function as structures of frightening control.

Yet Lolita resists her harsh treatment and diagnosis of mental illness.[36] Lolita acts hysterical to survive both her diagnosis as mentally ill and the trauma of her hospitalization. Sue Estroff and Vilma Santiago-Irizarry's ethnographic discussions of how patients "make it crazy" resonate with the ways Lolita takes on her "craziness." Estroff writes, "Clients may embellish this construction of reality." They may do so "by behaving, living, and thinking like crazy people (for they have nothing to lose). With other identities and roles cut off to them, they make the best of it. In a passively defiant way, they make it crazy."[37] Lolita demonstrates "passive defiance" by performing the madness thrust on her. She declares that "it was a circus, and it was [her] job to amuse" the guards and orderlies who questioned her upon her transfer to Saint Elizabeth's Hospital. She insinuates that her answers are crafted for the purposes of enlivening the spectacle where she is positioned center stage. During this same interrogation, the guards and orderlies actually "accuse her of putting on an act."[38]

Perhaps the most poignant way in which Lolita combats her characterization as mentally unsound is through a combination of the written and spoken word. When put on trial for opening fire on Congress, Lolita is advised to plead insanity to reduce her sentence, but she refuses to do so. Her lawyer explains: "It was unimaginable that she would let me use insanity . . . The only thing I could say was that what she did was an act of protest against the occupation of Puerto Rico, and that it was a statement in favor of the freedom of her country."[39] The lawyer's words underscore Lolita's unwillingness to have her actions marred or minimized in any way by an insanity plea. However, Lolita's decision not to plead insanity does not prevent her from being branded mentally unstable. Despite her self-representation as a political protester, she cannot escape her public representation as a madwoman on an insane mission.

This is not necessarily a case of the subaltern not being able to speak, though, as Marta Caminero-Santangelo or the postcolonial scholar, Gayatri Spivak, might have us believe. Lolita determinedly fights for her voice in her own self-representation, and she does so by writing. Her writing is a deliberate act of self-representation and evasion of the public representation imposed on her, her family, and her nation. She makes "a room of her own" out of her prison cell, refashioning the notion articulated by Virginia Woolf to suit her situation.[40] That Lolita writes out of survival and necessity no matter the location, even in the same place where she "withstand[s] torture," speaks to the urgency of writing for her.[41] Her writing keeps alive her spirit of revolt. It also serves as a gift she passes down to her granddaughter, who likewise takes up the pen to voice her own form of rebellion.

## Gladys: "The Almost Cliché Casualty of Colonialism"

What Gladys inherits from Lolita is a pattern of abandonment, sexual objectification, and physical and psychological harm. Abandoned by her birth mother and unacknowledged by her biological father, Gladys is raised by relatives. Among these are a sexually abusive uncle and sexually abusive town members, "some of her own blood, sneaking fumbling hands under her dress, thick fingers sliding up and down her thigh," with Gladys "watching the whole spectacle from a distance, as if she wasn't there."[42] Even as a teenager, Gladys learns to separate her self from her body as a coping mechanism that is to stay with her until her death by suicide years later. Just as Homi Bhabha links dislocation and colonization, Vilar frames Gladys's sexual mistreatment, sense of orphanhood, and unbelonging in terms of colonialism, describing her as colonialism's sacrificial offering: "Between the uncle who violated her, the rich father she didn't know, the mother who had abandoned her, and the town that just watched, she was the gift arranged even before she knew it, the almost cliché casualty of colonialism."[43] But she isn't a casualty of colonialism for these reasons alone: the U.S.-backed policies imposed on the island affect her in other profound ways.

At the age of fifteen, Gladys marries the man who will father her four children. Vilar portrays her parents' relationship as fraught, and she depicts her mother as engaging in a show of domesticity, devotedly performing household chores. But Gladys's compulsive and confining servility—which Vilar describes as a trait she herself inherits from her mother—does not keep her husband appreciative.[44] Instead, Vilar comments on her father's rampant adultery and the role this behavior, coupled with his alcoholism, plays in contributing to her mother's psychological distress.

Despite the damage inflicted on Gladys by her parents and husband, by virtue of their abandonment, indifference, and neglect, Vilar credits the U.S. exploitation of Puerto Rico with being the force par excellence that ultimately undoes her mother. Gladys takes "Enovid, the controversial 10-milligram birth control pill" disseminated throughout the island and subsequently found to have devastating side effects; her medical practitioners coerce her into having a tubal ligation following the birth of her third child in order to receive medical care; and she has a hysterectomy per her doctor's insistence upon discovering that she has a "nonmalignant, abnormal cell growth." Following her hysterectomy, her body and mind turn on her, causing her to suffer from depression, mood swings, migraines, bloating, weight gain, and shame.[45]

Vilar implicates the U.S.-backed sterilization program on the island, the eugenic impulse she ties to the program, and the medical system in Puerto Rico in her mother's physical and psychological pain: "What growing up poor and an orphan, the daughter of a woman imprisoned in the United States and being the wife for twenty-three years of a man unable to value her could not do, the U.S. mass-sterilization program and its racist population-control ideologies did. Self medicating with Valium and acting out a ransacked, frantic, if vacant, sexuality, my mother came undone while I watched."[46] With these charges, Vilar counters the biologization and feminization of mental illness to which she at other times ostensibly succumbs when emphasizing that mental illness is passed down from one matrilineal generation to the next. When Vilar blames institutional forces for undoing her mother, though—causing Gladys to turn to drugs, instilling a sense of shame and sadness within her, and ransacking her body and mind—she instead advances a social constructionist idea of mental illness that looks to how a pathological environment can create the conditions conducive to the development of individual pathology.[47] With this indictment and linkage of her mother to fellow Puerto Rican women who only have been privy to constrained choices because of the power of the institutional structures and ideologies surrounding them, Vilar underscores the relation between her mother's individual suffering and her nation's collective suffering.[48]

In *The Ladies' Gallery*, Vilar focuses on Gladys's deep sadness, detailing Gladys's fixation on her body image, depression, and self-alienation. Noting Gladys's preoccupation with her appearance, Vilar questions whether her mother's fascination with makeup and wigs really has to do with an attention to fashion as much as it has to do with creating a self-protective veneer behind which she can hide: "Makeup is all there is. She's in front of the mirror testing colors, blending them as if with this things come together." Vilar adds, "I wonder if making up and putting on wigs was a custom of the seventies or simply her way of protecting herself from all the women she carried inside her: the daughter, the wife, the mother, and, toward the end of her life, the Puerto Rican nationalist." Wondering whether Gladys is protecting herself from herself and the burden of the female legacy she has arguably inherited, Vilar describes Gladys as if she were a collection of disparate, fragmented personalities rather than one complete person, and she portrays these separate individual and collective personalities as a potential threat to her mother's sense of self. Grooming accordingly functions as a mode of escape and safety for Gladys and provides her with "structure to the days and to the growing restlessness that's coming over her."[49]

Elaine Showalter's observations about the relation between grooming and female madness provide a theoretical framework with which to analyze Gladys's excessive attention to her appearance. In her exploration of nineteenth- and twentieth-century constructions of female madness in England, Showalter notes that Victorian psychiatrists were preoccupied with their patients' grooming habits, viewing these as emblematic of their patients' mental health or illness. Although a general attention to appearance was considered healthy, "too much attention to dress and appearance was a sign of madness."[50] In *The Ladies' Gallery*, whereas grooming allows Gladys to exercise some measure of control over her restlessness, her extreme concern with her physical appearance locates her within a psychiatric tradition of women branded unstable for these same behaviors.

While Showalter's analysis of the historically feminized construction of madness is helpful, it is equally important to situate Gladys's preoccupation with her looks and self-abnegation against the neglect she endures throughout her life (by her parents and husband), the sexual attention she receives while growing up, and the U.S.-backed policies fixating on Puerto Rican women's bodies, sexuality, and reproduction. In this context, Gladys's mental instability needs to be understood just as much in relation to her gender as it should be in relation to her constant abandonment and neglect as well as to her status as a colonized subject. Gladys's bodily disenchantment while pregnant with Irene is only exacerbated by such forces and manifests itself when she inspects herself in the mirror: "Her belly was growing and . . . she'd cry every time she looked at herself in the mirror."[51] Gladys's despair and sense of separation from herself upon seeing her reflection indicates a lack of self-recognition, or at least a lack of recognition of self as she would like to appear. Unlike the infant in psychoanalyst Jacques Lacan's mirror stage who initially and ironically sees himself as an "I" upon looking at his reflection, or who at least sees the idealized image of who he would like to be, Gladys's self-gaze undoes her sense as an "I." Projecting a far from idealized image staring back at her, her gaze in the mirror triggers her despondency.

It would be apt to liken Gladys's self-alienation to the type of internalized oppression outlined by Ngugi wa Thiong'o in *Decolonising the Mind* or Gloria Anzaldúa in *Borderlands*. Gladys's self-dissociation, deprecation, and repulsion, positioned against the backdrop of her island's de facto colonial status, could be considered a manifestation of the type of colonial alienation outlined by Ngugi or the *Coatlicue* state articulated by Anzaldúa, for Gladys's geopolitical subjectivity (as a colonized Puerto Rican woman) affects her psychological and physical sense of self.[52] Gladys's self-alienation is so pervasive that she inflicts bodily harm upon herself during her pregnancy with Irene, bruising the part of her body that most obviously also would endanger the life of her unborn child: "She was bumping into everything, belly first, as if she wanted to get rid of the child. She had bruises from her navel to her waist. When she got it in her mind that it might be a girl, she finally accepted it. If only."[53] Only upon realizing that her baby might be a girl does she accept her impending motherhood. However, as her caretaker puts it, this acceptance is more of a resignation than an eagerness to be a mother for a fourth time. Adding the qualifying phrase *if only* and using the vague pronoun *it*, Vilar too questions Gladys's acceptance of her pregnancy, looming motherhood, and daughter. The link shown here among an unwanted, accidental pregnancy, soon-to-be-motherhood, self-inflicted harm, fetal harm, and depression foretells Irene's own subsequent struggles with the prospect of motherhood and reveals how Gladys's story is entwined with that of Irene.

Gladys's propensity to exact physical pain on herself operates in tandem with her mental anguish, and this predilection continues after giving birth to her daughter. Vilar ties her mother's pattern of self-imposed injury to Gladys's physical and mental health problems, specifically with the hysterectomy the doctor insists she have that renders her barren in the same way Vilar describes the Puerto Rican landscape. In *Impossible Motherhood*, Vilar critiques the health care system for removing her mother's uterus without sufficient cause while Gladys is still quite young and for denying her appropriate follow-up treatment. The corporeal damage seemingly within and beyond Gladys's control feed upon each other, exacting greater havoc on her body than either could do single-handedly. Indeed, Gladys's body as a whole begins to wither after the removal of her reproductive organ. Not only does she begin to grow thinner by the day, but she attempts suicide on more than one occasion. Desperately seeking love and attention from her adulterous husband and struggling with her own depression, Gladys practically drowns herself at one point, hovers at the precipice of a canyon at another, and swallows "a whole bottle of Equanil" at yet another.[54] She dies after throwing herself out of a moving automobile while her daughter sits in the backseat to witness the suicide.

## Irene's Remembrance

Like Gladys, Irene is abandoned by her mother, although Vilar doesn't frame Gladys's suicide as a form of abandonment until her second memoir. Vilar also describes herself as having inherited her mother's and grandmother's struggles with mental illness and *independentista* politics, her mother's servile disposition and self-deprecating attitude, and her grandmother's vocation for writing. In her first memoir, Vilar emphasizes the shared legacies among the three generations of women in her family by interweaving her account of her own psychiatric institutionalization with her grandmother's and mother's tales. In her second memoir, she is more introspective, as she focuses more on her own life experiences and delves into what is largely unspoken in *The Ladies' Gallery*, namely what she describes as her addiction to abortion. Both memoirs together highlight Irene's search for control over her own body and life decisions in environments where such control seems well beyond her grasp.

Throughout *The Ladies' Gallery*, Vilar chronicles her struggle with depression, suicide attempts, and internment in a mental health facility. She characterizes her depression as linked to her insecurity with and repugnance toward her body, yet she also describes her fascination with her body. Like her mother, who stares at her reflection in the mirror, Irene rushes to look at herself and "review the parts of [her] body," as if her reflection confirmed her material existence. Irene's gaze, however, unlike that of her mother, follows a curiosity about what others see when looking at her. These scenes tend to follow moments of sexual awakening or wonderment, depicted most prominently when Vilar describes a cruise she takes as a teenager. She explains how the gaze of male passengers aboard the ship prompts her to stare at her reflection and find temporary happiness in the image projected before her: "If I crossed paths with some passenger and he looked at me, I would run to the nearest bathroom and look at myself in the mirror. I liked what I saw." She elaborates, "[I'd] go up on deck, looking for myself out of the corner of my eye in the glass, happy with what I saw and felt."[55] Despite the temporary happiness from being noticed, instead of depicting these moments as ones of recognition of selfhood or of an idealized image of self, Vilar describes them in a manner reminiscent of that of Fanon sensing his triple existence for the first time. Just as a child's cry—pointing to Fanon and exclaiming, "Look, a Negro!"—leads to Fanon's introspection and awareness of his black body, the gaze of others most frequently precipitates Irene's self-gaze.[56] Although Irene is filled with a sense of awe and discovery when looking in the mirror, she views herself, her mother, and her grandmother as mirrors of one another, underscoring how their lives can never seem to escape the repetitive cycle of overwhelming sadness they each inherit. The mirror motif thus functions both as a sign of possibility (exemplified in the wonderment Irene feels while looking at her reflection) and despair (represented by the seemingly inescapable destiny of depression).

Throughout both memoirs, Vilar also expresses a profound ambivalence toward herself, one that is self-negating in much the same way as the third-person consciousness articulated by Fanon is. This psychological ambivalence is most visibly manifest in Irene's damaging actions toward her body. In The Ladies' Gallery, Vilar explains how her depression, coupled with her mother's and grandmother's histories of multifaceted harm, feeds into her injurious actions toward herself; in Impossible Motherhood, she contextualizes her self-inflicted harm in relation to her conflicted relationship with motherhood, issues with control, and compulsion toward servility while yearning for freedom. In the second memoir, she also positions her uneasiness toward her body against her nation's history of mistreatment of women's bodies and her mother's corporeal harm, highlighting connections among gendered intersections of bodily, psychological, and geopolitical harm.

The structure of The Ladies' Gallery itself emphasizes the links among Irene's physical and psychological anguish and her mother's and grandmother's psychological and political struggles, as Vilar intersperses her account of her hospitalization in every other chapter of her first memoir.[57] The bulk of Irene's narrative in The Ladies' Gallery centers on her mental illness, suicidal tendencies, and institutionalization, set against her maternal family's history. In *Impossible Motherhood*, she further implicates her *nation's* history in the damage she inflicts on herself. In *The Ladies' Gallery*, she mentions that her grandmother "felt that she . . . no longer inhabited her body," and earlier in that memoir, Vilar expressly states that she herself "wanted nothing to do with [her] body." Her rejection of her body can be associated with her description of her body as an object to be sacrificed to gain the love she desperately craves throughout her life: "I carried models, ways of offering the body as something given in exchange for something one wants: to be accepted, loved, the so-called 'love of some people.' At the university it was constantly necessary to choose classes, friends, lovers. The future. And the only thing I had to offer was a family history and my body."⁵⁸ Positioning her family history and body together as the only *thing* she can offer, Vilar underscores the inseparability of the two phenomena: her family history and body function as one sole possession. Describing them as a singular *object* that can be given away, Vilar detaches subjective meaning from herself.

One of the most obvious ways in which Irene sacrifices her body is in her seven suicide attempts. In *The Ladies' Gallery*, Vilar depicts the suicide attempt that leads to her mental institutionalization. She repeatedly mentions the smell of gas in the kitchen that triggers the idea that she can kill herself via asphyxiation. She shaves her legs and puts on clean underwear to appear to have taken good care of her body. She lies down on a towel on the kitchen floor, swallowing "the whole bottle of Tylenol and all the other pills," "down[ing] a full bottle of Popov vodka," and "clos[ing] [her] eyes and wait[ing] to pass out." She details the sensation of vertigo, sleepiness, and nausea she feels as the drugs, alcohol, and gas kick in; upon hearing the voice of her landlord outside her door crying out that he has a young daughter, she wakes up, avowedly out of fear and guilt for potentially jeopardizing the child's life as well as her own. She quickly turns off the gas and heads to a psychologist, who promptly hospitalizes her despite her protests that she isn't "crazy."⁵⁹

In the moments referenced just prior to this suicide attempt, Vilar repeatedly stresses her loneliness, bodily disgust, and feeling that she inhabits more than one self: "[I had] the clear idea that perhaps I should kill myself. I must have felt a repugnance for my body. I'd felt it before already, ever since I was a child, but then it was a vague, subterranean feeling. Lately it had become something else, and it was blossoming on the surface. Maybe I was looking for it now." She adds, "That same night I lay down in the bathtub with a book by Kierkegaard and a knife between my legs. . . ." Vilar likens her corporeal disavowal to Kierkegaard's perception of "himself as if he were someone else."[60] This description also ties her physical revulsion and thoughts of physical harm to her psychological disarray. Her encounter with the psychologist, however, does nothing but lead her to buy the bottle of Tylenol that she subsequently swallows in its entirety.

In these descriptions, Vilar connects body with mind and characterizes a mental health care system that cannot necessarily prevent patients from harming themselves. The literary critic Laura Kanost likewise comments on the inseparability of body and mind in *The Ladies' Gallery*: "By insisting upon the embodied nature of her own mental illness, Vilar resists the simple metaphorical reading of madwoman as rebellion. Physicality is salient in the memoir's opening paragraphs." Kanost explains, "This intense anguish of depression is a bodily experience as much as a mental and emotional one."[61] Positioning body and mind together, while highlighting how her bodily disavowal feeds into her suicidal desires, Vilar moves away from the distinction between body and mind drawn by Elaine Scarry and instead posits the sort of juxtaposition of body and mind put forth by Fanon, who emphasizes that "the body is not something opposed to what you call the mind."[62] Illustrating how her visit to a psychologist does nothing to alleviate her psychological distress, Vilar also signals that the mental health care system does not necessarily serve as the source of salvation some expect of it.

In her depiction of her institutionalization following her attempted suicide, Vilar provides a complicated portrait of a mental health care facility that theoretically is designed to help patients heal but at times functions as more of a jail than a hospital. By interspersing descriptions of her institutionalization with ones of her grandmother's imprisonment and hospitalization, Vilar only bolsters the connection between both forms of confinement. She highlights the paradoxes that surface in a mental health care system whose mission is to provide care to its patients but that instead dehumanizes them, acts as if they are invisible, deals with them as if they are prisoners, and tortures them. The staff at the psychiatric hospital treats the patients as inanimate objects when searching for potentially harmful objects on their persons. The dehumanization she and other patients experience is only heightened by the medical practitioners' expressed disgust toward them, which Vilar emphasizes when explaining how one of the nurses speaks to her "as if talking to some creature that causes him great revulsion." In passages resonant with those of Ralph Ellison in *Invisible Man*, Piri Thomas in *Down These Mean Streets*, and Fanon in *Black Skin, White Masks* that illustrate how the societies surrounding the protagonists ignore or dismiss the protagonists' needs because of their skin color, thereby making them feel invisible, Vilar recounts how the nurses where she is hospitalized "don't look at [her], or they look through [her] as if [she] were transparent, or just an idiot."[63] That she is not seen but *seen through* is heightened all the more by virtue of her reliance on others' gazes toward her.

In addition to echoing the motifs of unbelonging depicted by Ellison, Thomas, and Fanon, Vilar's account of her hospitalization speaks to the connections Michel Foucault and Thomas Szasz draw between imprisonment and institutionalization, for Vilar emphasizes the relation between physical and psychological place and details how much the built environment of the mental health facility physically and psychologically confines its patients. She notes the constructedness of the hospital, drawing attention to the "hermetic" and "enclosing" walls, the lack of windows in a type of interrogation room, the locks on windows and doors (in places where windows and doors are present), and the ubiquitous restraints throughout the facility. She also explicitly compares the hospital to a prison, explaining how it could have been "like jail for other people" and how, like "the school, the cloister, [and] the prison," it functions as a "closed house."[64] Her description of her own psychiatric institutionalization, juxtaposed with that of Lolita's incarceration and subsequent hospitalization, draws an inextricable link between the treatment of behavior deemed criminal and that diagnosed as mentally ill and ties together granddaughter's and grandmother's respective confinements.

However, Vilar's portrait moves beyond a straightforward, scathing critique of the mental health care system. In *Impossible Motherhood*, she admits that her characterization of her hospitalization in *The Ladies' Gallery* fails to provide a full picture of the reasons that led to her institutionalization and does not acknowledge that she actually "welcomed the medication a nurse brought into [her] room three times a day."[65] Even in her first memoir, her representation of the psychiatric hospital is complicated when she describes it as functioning as a prison for some, but also providing a place of respite for her, even if it is just a place to pass the time. In the same paragraph where she compares the hospital to a jail, she speculates whether her mother "could have been saved by something like this, an empty place, a 'peaceful house.'"[66] This question places a sense of purpose, hope, and faith in the institution, a sense that otherwise is conspicuously absent in the passages where she details her overwhelming feeling of containment. Although she refers to the hospital as an "empty place," she nonetheless characterizes it as a "peaceful house." Considering that throughout her second memoir Vilar describes herself as in constant search of a home, her word choice here significantly endows the hospital with a sense of belonging, a belonging situated against a backdrop of perpetual unbelonging.

This feeling of unbelonging is particularly palpable in *Impossible Motherhood*. Throughout her second memoir, Vilar contextualizes the struggles with depression and suicidal tendencies that she delineates in *The Ladies' Gallery*. She connects these to her fraught romantic relationship with one of her professors (a man thirty-four years her senior), a relationship that begins when she is a sixteen-year-old undergraduate at Syracuse University and that culminates in her first marriage and divorce. She repeatedly describes this professor, never mentioned by name in *Impossible Motherhood* and conspicuously absent from *The Ladies' Gallery*, as her "master," husband, or simply "he" or "him," and she underscores the control he has over her and the servile way she responds to him.[67] Nowhere in the narrative does she refer to this man as her partner. Instead, she describes a colonizing relationship, in which her colonized body stands in for her colonized birthplace.

Vilar repeatedly comments on the power differential in her relationship with her "master" and her tug of war with him regarding their dissonant ideas about freedom and control. Part of this power differential most obviously manifests itself in their different positions as professor and student when they first start seeing each other. With these different positions come dramatically disparate socioeconomic statuses. Throughout *Impossible Motherhood*, Vilar details the poverty in which she lives that leads to her constant hunger and emaciated body: "When I think of our first year together my stomach tightens. Such was the hunger I felt. Weighing 105 pounds at five foot six, pictures of me show a skeletal figure."[68] She regularly skips meals, pretending she isn't hungry to mask the shame she feels over not being able to afford food, and spends the little money she does have on books for herself or gifts for her professor instead of nourishment to sustain herself. She highlights her "master's" insistence that she pay her own way so as not to assume a type of parent-child relationship that would further exacerbate any power differential already existent between them and to maintain a partnership on independent and "equal" terms. Even during the decade they spend together, their marriage, and divorce settlement, he stipulates that they "equally" split expenditures without any acknowledgment of the blatantly unequal nature of this agreement.

*Controlling* is the word that best characterizes the relationship that Irene has with her "master"/professor/lover/husband. This control is apparent in the financial arrangement the two have and in the "master's" imposition of his ideas about freedom. According to Vilar, her first husband does not want to be tied down in any way; he wants to be able to travel at will without feeling shackled to any person or place. To preserve this freedom, he issues an ultimatum to Irene: that she remain childless and stay with him or that she have a child without him. "If you are with me," he tells her, "you have to endure the burden of freedom, and that requires, in part, remaining childless. If you are grown up enough to have a child, you are just as fit to be a single mother. But I will not be a victim of your displacement."[69] Yet his nomadic desires and his ultimatum displace *Irene*, or at least deny her the possibility of finding the type of physical or psychological home she desperately seeks. In this way, he renders Irene unhomely, as Bhabha or Fanon might call it, as he exacts a colonizing, estranging, and traumatic ambivalence on her by preventing her from having the home for which she yearns.[70] Denying her the possibility of being with him *and* becoming a mother at the same time, and relying on the rhetoric of women's liberation to support his stance, he positions independence outside the confines of the domestic sphere and positions potential fatherhood with victimhood.

Her first husband thus twists the platform of second wave feminism to suit his desires and assert control over her. Vilar writes, "He had told me that family kills desire, not to mention love. A child at my age would turn me into one more gender casualty. He was thinking of me, shielding me from a woman's fate and the shackles of domestic life we all took on when the challenge of freedom seemed too much a burden to bear."[71] In his push to keep Irene from having a baby, her "master" adopts a paternalistic mode of argumentation, and by imposing his views on her without granting her the respect of listening to her needs and wants, he ironically fosters the type of father-daughter relationship he so vociferously opposes when it comes to their finances.

The toll this not so benevolent care, or coercion, takes on Irene is extreme. Looking up to her "master," admiring his "brilliance" and "smooth[ness]," and seeing herself as "ignorant and uncultured" by contrast, Irene internalizes the sense of inferiority and infantilization implicit in his words of warning. What is more, she feels trapped by the "freedom" she and her first husband supposedly enjoy by virtue of having no physical or personal attachments. Indeed, she repeatedly refers to herself as living inside the "walls of [her] prison."[72] Controlled by her first husband and confined in this way makes her feel not only imprisoned but also insecure, illustrating how her emotional confinement causes her to feel physically constricted. That she regularly starves herself, physically wasting away while "he" watches and insists that she pay for her own meals, highlights just how skewed the power dynamic between them is and reveals just how vulnerable her first husband makes her feel. Referring to him as her "master" only underscores this inequity.

Internalizing the feeling of worthlessness that ensues from the psychological harm her first husband undoubtedly inflicts on her given his paternalistic, manipulative treatment of her, Irene exacts a tremendous amount of harm on her body: seven suicide attempts in the decade she spends with the man she calls her "master" and fifteen abortions in fifteen years, twelve of which she has while with him. Vilar admits that her initial sexual encounters with her "master" revolve around pleasuring him without any thought to using birth control, and throughout *Impossible Motherhood* she reiterates that she keeps "forgetting" to use birth control.[73] Only twice in the narrative does the responsibility of birth control fall on her first husband's shoulders. These moments occur in medical offices, as the doctors ask "the man [she] loved if he didn't know what a condom was" and suggest that he consider using a method of birth control rather than depend on Irene to take pills.[74] Nowhere else does Vilar explicitly place this responsibility on her first husband, even though he is so adamant about refusing to have children. Instead, she places full responsibility on herself.

In the process, Vilar simultaneously accomplishes two things. First, she absolves her first spouse of accountability for his actions and for the role he plays in her multiple pregnancies and repeated abortions. Second, by absolving him of accountability, she strips him of control over her body and her decisions, and she takes back some of this control for herself. Early in the second memoir, Vilar writes about not having a choice about whether to undergo an abortion if she wants to remain with her "master," but toward the end of *Impossible Motherhood* she reframes her analysis. Here, she claims that her "story is a perversion of both maternal desire and abortion, framed by a lawful procedure that [she] abused."[75] She ultimately states that she has had a choice about her abortions and that she has taken advantage of this right, conceding that her second memoir could be used to counter its very aims. Expressly advocating the importance of a woman's right to choose, she worries that her story of repeated abortions could be used by antichoice groups to justify their claims about the abuse of reproductive liberties that arguably can happen when abortions are legally sanctioned.[76] But her story also illustrates how the rhetoric of choice is far more complex than either side of the reproductive rights movement makes it out to be.

Choice goes hand in hand with control and power, and these are not readily abundant or available to all, despite claims to the contrary espoused by philosophers like Foucault, who declares, "Power is everywhere; not because it embraces everything, but because it comes from everywhere."[77] Although Vilar admits that she has abused her right to choose, she explains that her choices have been framed by constraint after constraint, including "family trauma, self-inflicted wounds, compulsive patterns, and . . . moral clarity and moral confusion." She accordingly undermines neoliberal ideas of individual agency, explaining that the "language of choice invokes free will based on individual freedom, obscuring the dynamics between social constraints and human activity. Choices are framed by larger institutional structures and ideological messages."[78] The accumulation of so many constraints—individual, familial, institutional, and ideological—highlights the flaws surrounding the very concept of choice and beckons us to question whether we really can regard circumscribed choice—or "constrained choice," as Iris López would describe it—as choice at all or whether we should conceive of a fundamentally different vocabulary with which to address these questions (more) aptly.[79]

After all, control and power, or lack thereof, are key determinants in the actions Irene takes. Toward the end of *Impossible Motherhood*, Vilar suggests as much. She links her emotions to her body and her notions of motherhood. Finding the prospect of motherhood, no matter how impossible she considers it, as something that takes her out of her sadness relates to her desire to have some sort of control over her body, a control not readily available to her in other facets of her life:

> I never craved that moment when I clenched my vibrating abdomen, feet high up on cold stirrups, and told myself never again. There was no high that came with that. . . . At times the high took place before pregnancy, waiting for a missed period, my body basking in the promise of being in control. At other times it was the pregnancy itself, the control I embodied if only for a couple of months, and still other times it was leaving the abortion clinic, feeling that once again I had succeeded in a narrow escape. The time of my drama was my

time, no one could interrupt it, and what was more important, I could not interrupt it to meet others' needs.[80]

The language of addiction (highlighted through terms like *craved* and *high*) notwithstanding, what is striking here is Vilar's emphasis on her "body basking in the promise of being in control." That this control is phrased as a promise, and that the abortions refer to the abandonment, deferral, and/or possibility of such promise, underscores the ephemeral and complicated nature of the control Irene can enjoy. The assertion that her drama is *her* time indicates that her multiple pregnancies and abortions at least temporarily allow her to put herself and her needs first. Given that motherhood is a phenomenon that seems impossible to Irene—because of the demands imposed on her by her first husband, her own struggles with self-worth, her fears, and her abandonment by her mother when just a child—and considering that she casts aside her own desires in her yearning for lasting affection, the positioning of her drama as something that belongs to her significantly but paradoxically endows her with a certain amount of power and corresponding sense of dignity.

Yet Vilar also refers to her abortions as a mode of self-injury, and she does not refrain from highlighting the tremendous amount of physical and psychological harm exacted on her body in tandem with them. Throughout *Impossible Motherhood*, she repeatedly mentions the physical pain that follows from her pregnancies and abortions, recounting the jabbing in her abdomen, bleeding, hemorrhaging, nausea, dizziness, headaches, and "ravaged cervix."[81] In *The Ladies' Gallery* too, she details the bodily pain accompanying her suicide attempts and provides a rather cryptic narration of her multiple pregnancies and her ambivalence regarding them. In one such narration, she describes the physical and psychological pain she endures while experiencing an induced late-term "miscarriage": the "invasion in [her] stomach," her visceral and affective response to such an invasion, her inability to "repress [her] disgust," her feelings of incomprehensible "rancor," and her desire to "wipe the slate clean and start all over." Vilar ends the portion of *The Ladies' Gallery* prior to the epilogue by chronicling the pain that precipitates this medically labeled miscarriage. She writes about wavering in her decision to undergo another abortion, taking "an overdose of a cathartic," and subsequently experiencing "a very sharp pain in [her] abdomen, a jab, and [she] was only able to cry out when the flow of blood came on as though something had broken open inside [her]."[82] Here, as when she recounts her abortions throughout *Impossible*

*Motherhood*, Vilar emphasizes the corporeal pain and the psychological harm that accompany her preempted motherhood. Indeed, the sensation that "something had broken open inside" attests to the broken insides of her body and mind alike.

Ending her memoir that chronicles the three generations of mental illness on the matrilineal side of her family with a paragraph-length sketch of her "miscarriage" and feelings of detachment from her physical self, Vilar illustrates the extent to which her corporeal distress and psychological distress are entwined, and she sets the stage for her second memoir. She describes her body according to disparate parts—eyes, forearm, face, and legs—adding, "Down below, between my legs, I thought I felt cold pinches and everything began to turn into a dialogue between the needles and my body, and the operating table might just as easily have been a dissection table. Was there a sewing machine nearby?" She writes of pain and time disappearing: "I no longer felt myself rooted to anything on earth. My only links were to the metal railings on the gurney . . . time, the hands on the clock flowed on, the memory of something that had ceased to exist. I was able foggily to make out a body, someone with glassy eyes pushing the gurney along the hall."[83] Likening the operating table to a dissection table, Vilar underscores how her body functions as a collection of components subject to examination. The reference to a sewing machine, meanwhile, evokes images of *la operación* that so many of her compatriots have undergone as well as images of the forced tubal ligation her own mother had, linking Irene's "miscarriage" and psychic disarray with her family's and nation's histories of "constrained choice" regarding women's reproductive liberties. Her self-characterization as uprooted speaks to the constant search for home she invokes throughout her second memoir. Stating that her "only links were to the metal railings on the gurney," she suggests that it is her hospitalization alone that grounds her to anything at all, tying her existence to the multiple ways she is medicalized. In this way, Vilar here ironically puts forward an essentialized construction of identity in which she defines herself via her medicalization.[84] Where she possibly elides such a move is in her arguable depiction of herself as the "something that had ceased to exist," relegating her medicalized self to the realm of the past. By subtitling her second memoir *Testimony of an Abortion Addict*, though, she (re)casts her medicalization front and center.

It is impossible to read *The Ladies' Gallery* or *Impossible Motherhood* for that matter without noting the centrality of medicalization to the formation of identity in both texts, even while both narratives simultaneously critique the rampant medicalization of Puerto Ricans for the sake of scientific advancement or for the patients' "own good." For these reasons, the medicalization of identity in Vilar's two memoirs paradoxically is presented as essentialized and constructed *at once*. Whether this medicalization takes place at a collective level (through Puerto Rico's history of mass sterilization and oral contraceptive testing, the history of the reproductive rights movement in the U.S. mainland and Puerto Rico, Vilar's matrilineal family's history of mental illness, or Vilar's patrilineal family's history of substance abuse) or at an individual level (through Vilar's depression, suicide attempts, institutionalization, or repeated abortions), medicalization functions as the thread that weaves the two memoirs, and the multiple strands within each memoir, together. Vilar's individual tale is connected to the collective ones she references.

Just as medicalization ties together the strands of both memoirs, so does the motif of female sacrifice, whether this sacrifice is self-inflicted or externally inflicted. Irene's bodily sacrifice through her multiple suicide attempts and arguably through her repeated abortions can be likened to, and ostensibly follows from, Lolita's self-sacrifice in the name of Puerto Rican independence, with both Irene's and Lolita's sacrifices plausibly serving as forms of protest over the unbearable conditions under which they each live. Even Vilar's description of herself throughout *Impossible Motherhood* as regularly "forgetting" to take her birth control pills needs to be understood beyond the framework she advances when she refers to herself as an "abortion addict" who has "abused" her legal right to "choose" whether to terminate her pregnancies. After all, even this seemingly simple act of "forgetting," which Vilar herself puts in scare quotes, is not that simple. It follows from her mother having been subjected to a birth control pill "twenty times stronger than those used today," having had her tubes forcibly tied together, and having had her uterus ripped out, and it follows from her mother's psychological demise after having undergone such corporeal invasions.[85] Although Vilar nowhere expressly links forgetting to take her pills to everything that Gladys has undergone, she begins and ends *Impossible Motherhood* with a reference to the harm her mother has experienced that explicitly originates from U.S.-backed policies fixating on Puerto Rican women's sexuality and reproduction. Beginning and ending her second memoir in this way, Vilar demonstrates the extent to which her collective family's and nation's histories feed into her own, and she implicates these collective forms of externally imposed harm in the harm she inflicts on herself.

## On Rape and Solitude

Toward the beginning of *The Ladies' Gallery*, Vilar writes, "Where I come from, rape, metaphorical and literal rape, is considered the spark of our history, and solitude its human consequence." She goes on to describe how the motif of rape resonates throughout literature (particularly Latin American literature that references the creation of what she terms bastard, *mestizo* subjects) and comments on how women are notably rendered absent in such depictions.[86] Speaking back to masculinist interpretations of the aftermath of the conquest of the Americas, arguably to those advanced by writers like Octavio Paz in *The Labyrinth of Solitude* who similarly unpacks the motifs of rape and solitude but who does so in a manner that privileges the colonial legacy left to male subjects, Vilar explicitly positions women at the center of her analysis, concentrating on the effects of colonialism on female subjects.

When critiquing masculinist interpretations of the conquest of the Americas, Vilar pointedly asks, "Where was *she* all this time? Woman is either inexplicable or . . . a gothic spinster, weaving . . . her own death shroud."[87] She then mentions her mother and grandmother. Vilar accordingly reframes the way history is narrated. She does so by calling attention to the invisibilized and marginalized *mestiza* subjects who inherit a colonial legacy *along with* the mother and grandmother figures who form part of this history, and she does so by illustrating how the personal and the historical are entwined, such that history is *historia* (story/history) and *historia* is history. In this way, Vilar aligns herself with U.S. Third World feminist writers like Anzaldúa, Moraga, and Norma Alarcón, who write about La Malinche (the iconic mother figure of colonialism whom writers like Paz objectify in elaborating at length about how she is "the fucked one"), who unpack La Malinche's potential rationale for having acted as mistress and translator for the Spanish conqueror Hernán Cortés, and who bestow La Malinche with an agency that has been stripped from her in dominant masculinist accounts. Kanost comments on the ways Vilar emphasizes female subjectivity and agency: "By explicitly comparing herself to both literary characters and writers, including profound identification with a feminine tradition, Vilar flouts the marginality of women's writing within the literary canon as well as the objectification of people with mental illnesses."[88] In writing her life story and entwining it with that of her mother, grandmother, and nation, Vilar challenges the prevalent masculinist literature about conquest, rape, and solitude; moves women out of the periphery of such dominant narratives; bestows subjectivity on those grappling with mental illness; and demonstrates how rape and solitude together highlight the layers of individual and collective physical, psychological, gender, and geopolitical violence she presents in her *historia*.

The language she deploys in both memoirs to illustrate the harm done to her mother, her grandmother, herself, her fellow (female) compatriots, and her island of birth centers on the idea of seized freedom. Coercion and violence permeate the two memoirs. Vilar emphasizes how these are felt at the national level in her depiction of the environmental devastation wreaked on Puerto Rico in the wake of widespread U.S. industrialization and militarization there, in her commentary about the U.S. appropriation of Puerto Rican land, and in her criticism of the mechanisms of control over Puerto Rican women's sexuality and reproductive liberties. She highlights how these are felt at the familial level in her portrayal of her grandmother—who is sold to a man so her family can survive and who later is subject to what Vilar describes as "torture" during her confinement—and also her mother, who is sexually abused while growing up and who becomes "undone" following the medical treatment that seeks to restrict her reproductive abilities. Vilar elucidates how the concept of seized freedom manifests itself at the individual level through her self-characterization as someone who yearns for control over herself and her life after being abandoned by her mother and while in an emotionally abusive relationship with a man who imposes his desires on her. In all these ways, she underscores that the harm and corresponding sense of solitude experienced by the individuals whose stories she narrates need to be contextualized in relation to the collective histories of aggression against their communities.

Harm fosters harm. Despite drawing this bleak causal relationship, despite emphasizing the interconnection among the damages inflicted on body, mind, and place, and despite providing harrowing accounts that admittedly are difficult to read, Vilar nonetheless does not necessarily leave readers with an utter sense of despair or futility.[89] Some certainly could interpret the multiple constraints Vilar presents and the repeated cycles of abandonment, neglect, and physical, psychological, and geopolitical injury that she paints as falling in line with Caminero-Santangelo's contention that there is nothing about madness, or the violence and silencing accompanying it, that can be empowering. Indeed, through Vilar's emphasis on repetition and inheritance, there is a way in which she herself at times succumbs to a rhetoric of essentialization and predetermination that precludes the possibility of any form of agency that would allow for such painful cycles ever to be broken.

However, writing serves as a potential venue for change. Just as Lolita writes to survive her confinement and to keep her political activism alive, Vilar's writing serves as a mode of rebellion in which she elucidates and comments on the multiple types of harm imposed on her community, family, and self. Admittedly, Vilar details how much her first husband encourages her writing and shapes what she has to say in *The Ladies' Gallery*. Although she grants him authorial voice in the ending of her first memoir when she states that "the idea was his" and claims that she "was writing for him," I argue that she gains an authorial voice of her own in the process of narrating and renarrating her own *historia* and that of her family and nation. Writing is a mode of control for Vilar, as evidenced in her "remembering" to take her birth control pills while doing so.[90] Kanost similarly speaks to this power of writing, asserting that *The Ladies' Gallery* "boldly affirms her [Vilar's] capacity to speak."[91] Benigno Trigo likewise concedes that writing and remembering in the context of Vilar's first memoir "transform both the process of subject formation and the abject, opening the possibility to a less violent world."[92] Putting her "shame" and pain on display for others to read and situating such individual feelings against externally imposed forms of harm, Vilar not only refuses to be silenced or controlled, but she engages in an activist project that seeks to find a way to break free from the type of gender and geopolitical violence surrounding her, her family, and her compatriots. In this way, she certainly opens "the possibility to a less violent world."

Toward the end of her second memoir, Vilar acknowledges the power of the written word. A mother of one at the time *Impossible Motherhood* was written (now a mother of two), Vilar concludes the book with a series of diary entries in large part directed toward her firstborn daughter: "I . . . search for all the ways I can protect you from me. . . . I don't want you to live the anguish of feeling trapped in the wrong body. I don't want you to ever succumb to the dismembered life of a false self. I don't want you ever to lie on a stretcher at an abortion clinic, your feet propped up on cold, steel stirrups. Your fate depends, a great deal, on me. Writing this down, in part, is my own fantasy of shielding you from my history."[93] Relying on repetition (reiterating the phrase "I don't want") to refer to patterns she hopes her daughter will not repeat, and describing her writing as a fantasized mode of protecting her daughter from potentially repeating such patterns, Vilar emphasizes the overwhelming power of the cycles of harm that neither she, her family, nor her compatriots have been able to escape. Even though the reference here to an abortion clinic explicitly relates to her own experiences, her individual history of repeated abortions forms part of a collective history of reproductive, psychological, physical, and geopolitical violence. Writing, however, is a deliberate and active attempt to free her daughter from such cycles of harm. Vilar ends *Impossible Motherhood* by directly addressing her daughter: "You are becoming my origins."[94] With the locational and temporal shift elicited in these words, in which origins move between selves and between past and future, Vilar underscores the possibility of renewal, rebirth, and hope.

## 2 /  Violated Bodies and Assaulting Landscapes in Loida Maritza Pérez's *Geographies of Home*

*The very meaning of "home" changes with [the] experience of
decolonization, of radicalization. At times, home is nowhere. At times,
one knows only extreme estrangement and alienation. Then home is no
longer just one place. It is locations.*
—BELL HOOKS, *YEARNING: RACE, GENDER, AND CULTURAL POLITICS*

Loida Maritza Pérez's debut novel, *Geographies of Home*, just as easily
could be titled *Geographies of Harm*, as the narrative portrays multiple
types of harm in relation to the constructs of geography and home.
Jumping across characters, time, place, and space, *Geographies of Home*
depicts various forms of psychological, physical, and geopolitical damage, including mental instability, environmental inhospitableness,
incest, intimate partner abuse, sexual assault, and political and structural violence. Pérez situates such overwhelming harm against the backdrop of "home" as an ever-shifting site that corresponds with selfhood
and state of mind. Like bell hooks, who presents home as connected to
multiple places and as fostering a sense of estrangement and dispersal,
Pérez depicts home as a paradoxical space of identification, alienation,
and fragmentation. Like Irene Vilar, Pérez ties together home, self,
belonging, and memory. Central to *Geographies of Home* is the idea of
remembering as a way to recall the past, as an imperative "that does not
demand forgetting," and as an attempt to bring together what has been
dismembered.[1]

Focusing the bulk of her narrative on the lives of a working-class Afro
Dominican American family in 1990s New York City, Pérez links the
physical and psychological harm the characters experience to the physical, social, and mental spaces they inhabit. Aurelia, the family matriarch,
is traumatized upon her arrival in the United States, and her husband,
Papito, is haunted by memories of Raphael Leónidas Trujillo's thirty-
year dictatorship in the Dominican Republic. Anabelle, Papito's former

love interest, hurls herself into the eye of a hurricane. Rebecca, Aurelia and Papito's eldest daughter, is married to an abusive man and neglects her starving children. Struggling with memories of being raped and an internalized racism, Rebecca's sister Marina is diagnosed with bipolar disorder with symptoms of schizophrenia. Rebecca's youngest sister, Iliana, is also assaulted. All of the harm the characters undergo could be read through the lens of assault or violation.

In part, Pérez depicts assault and violation in the manner in which we are apt to think of them, as instances of physical, emotional, and/or sexual violence imparted and felt on a one-to-one basis, but she moves beyond such an understanding and additionally highlights how assault and violation can transpire as a result of systemic forces. The family in *Geographies of Home* deals with the detrimental effects of poverty and, to varying degrees, grapples with the destructive effects of patriarchy and racism. Although the novel does not explicitly reference racism in the Dominican Republic, the country's history of rampant racism implicitly pervades the text. Under Trujillo's dictatorship, the racism against Haitians (constructed as black in contradistinction to the construction of Dominicans as white) led to their widespread massacre in 1937. Dominican nationalism, in turn, has revolved around a denial of African roots. This racial denial has not existed exclusively in the Dominican Republic. In Pérez's novel, it can also be detected in the United States, most explicitly in and through the characterization of Marina, who clings to dominant Dominican and U.S. racialized ideas of beauty. Pérez emphasizes that such pervasive structural ideologies can be just as hurtful as the individually imparted forms of assault and violation inflicted on the characters. Illustrating how assault and violation can be individually and collectively imposed and experienced at once, Pérez underscores the association between individual and collective harm. Highlighting how the recipients of such harm subsequently mete out harm to others and themselves, she demonstrates that the damage imposed from without does not end there.

The juxtaposition of individual and collective violence falls in line with my argument that the psychological and physical harm experienced by individuals cannot be separated from the geopolitical harm felt by collectives. Individual and structural forces alike can be damaging, and they feed into one another. That these modes of harm affect subject formation—whether this happens through identification or alienation—hearkens back to hooks's formulations about home as a place that changes with the experience of decolonization and that can create fragmentation. Home and harm are entwined. Embedded within each lie powerful ideas of location and dis-location. That home consists of plural locations, and that Pérez situates her characters in the spaces "between and among" such places, reveals the primacy of the interstices, especially for U.S. Third World subjects. I accordingly turn therein, to the intersections where place, space, body, and mind come together and depart from one another to analyze Pérez's depictions of harm, home, memory, and selfhood.

## Re-locating Aurelia

Pérez presents the novel's matriarch, Aurelia, in relation to her familial and geographic positioning, depicting her as a mother trying to bring stability to a family that feels like it is coming apart before her eyes. But Aurelia hasn't always been the pillar of strength she now strives to be. Upon migrating to the United States, she struggles with debilitating health issues. Although she remembers her life in Trujillo's Dominican Republic as filled with poverty and fear, she recalls her move to the United States as instilling an even greater terror within her, causing her to "deteriorate to a skeletal eighty-one pounds." Aurelia's physical dis-location from her birth country, re-location in the alienating urban setting of New York City, and positioning toward the lower rungs of the socioeconomic ladder and racial and ethnic hierarchy in the United States affect her sense of social and mental space. Pérez underscores the overpowering harshness of the urban environment, as she personifies the buildings as "looming" and threatening, and she utilizes sensory language to depict images of dirt and blood, a cacophony of sounds, and a feeling of being closed in. Her description of the buildings as "assault[ing]" and rendering Aurelia "vulnerable" emphasizes the power of places to inflict damage; for Aurelia, the effects of this power surpass those of the most brutal dictatorial regimes.[2]

Such a portrayal of New York City falls in line with the observations of urban environments put forth by the social studies scholar Elizabeth Wilson, who "writes of the way in which the big city . . . has produced in many a feeling of fear; fear of the disorder, the uncontrollable complexity; the chaos."[3] Presenting Aurelia as the character most visibly terrified and confined by her urban milieu, Pérez counters Wilson's contention that cities can be paranoiac spaces for men and liberatory spaces for women.[4] Instead, Pérez's depiction of the terror that the city instills in Aurelia elucidates the postmodern urban sensibility that Wilson affiliates with "disorientation, meaninglessness, and fragmentation" and a "schizoid world [that] anaesthetizes us" and makes us "all become hysterics."[5] Aurelia's dis-location and physical emaciation in an urban setting brings about her psychological breakdown, showing how physical place and psychological space meet and how the former has the power to destabilize the latter.

The notion that the postmodern urban world can lead us all to "become hysterics" and fragmented, disoriented subjects illustrates the extreme psychological alienation that can follow from being positioned in a city environment. The violence of Aurelia's surrounding setting instills in her what Ngugi wa Thiong'o might call a type of colonial alienation. Ngugi defines colonial alienation as a type of internalized colonization in which the colonized subject experiences an alienating disjuncture between the environment in which she or he was raised and the one created by colonizing forces.[6] Although Aurelia is not a colonized subject in the strict sense of the term, she experiences a traumatizing disjuncture between the environment where she was raised and the one where she has migrated. Her dis-location leads her "willingly [to bring] herself to the brink of death" and causes her to be hospitalized for a nine-month stay.[7] The psychic disarray and terror she experiences could also be explained as a form of intimate terrorism, or a sensation of alienation and immobilizing fear brought about by an internalization of social forces that depict and make women of color feel inferior.[8] Yet Aurelia refuses to remain permanently immobilized, defiantly recovering from her collapse for the sake of her children. Whereas Aurelia lacks confidence and trust in herself at the beginning of the narrative, by the end, she takes charge of her life and that of her family by refusing to be a passive onlooker to the damage she and her family endure. She is ultimately able to break free from the psychological constraints her physical environment places on her.

Raúl Homero Villa's analysis of Helena María Viramontes's short story "Neighbors"—and his attention to the story's protagonist, Aura—can prove helpful in understanding the colonial alienation and intimate terrorism that Pérez's Aurelia experiences in the United States.[9] If we explore the similarities in the characters' names (Aurelia and Aura), then Villa's analysis of the word *aura* could prove illuminating. Villa explains that *The American Heritage Dictionary* defines *aura* as "Pathology. A sensation, as of a cold breeze, preceding the onset of certain nervous disorders." He applies this definition to Viramontes's story: "The pathological meaning of *aura* as a premonitory sensation, like a cold breeze anticipating a nervous disorder, foreshadows Aura's imminent breakdown under the aggravated and aggravating conditions of her multiple social, physical, and psychological containments."[10] That the word is defined in part as pathology resonates with Pérez's preoccupation with pathology, regardless of whether we view Aurelia's name as an elongated moniker for *aura*. Like Aura, Aurelia undergoes a breakdown that follows from the "aggravating conditions" of her surrounding environment. Moreover, Pérez pays just as much attention to ghostliness and the supernatural as she does to pathology, and the character through whom she most notably does so is Aurelia.

Aurelia is one of three characters in *Geographies of Home* to have "premonitory sensation[s]," a trait that she inherited from her mother, Bienvenida, and passed down to her daughter Iliana. She has the uncanny ability to know things she should not know according to the rules of rationality. Throughout the bulk of her life, Aurelia dismisses her supernatural senses and abilities, putting her faith in the Seventh Day Adventism that would allow her "to believe in a death that laid spirits out to rest and in a God who would one day reward those who had suffered. She did not want to consider that after dying she too might continue yearning or seeking answers to what she did not understand."[11] Despite her piety, though, Aurelia cannot escape the supernatural insight she possesses.

Eventually Aurelia realizes that she can use her supernatural powers to protect her daughter (Rebecca) and grandchildren (Esperanza, Rubén, and Soledad) from the abuse meted out by Rebecca's husband, Pasión. Trying to strip Pasión of his control of Rebecca, and mindful that only his death will keep Rebecca from returning to him, Aurelia decides to take matters into her own hands. She relies on her supernatural powers to do so, using her preparation of Christmas dinner both to make a meal for her family and to ensure that Pasión can never harm Rebecca again. She knows that Pasión's apartment is filled with chickens that he keeps but does not maintain. He relies on Rebecca to care for them, partly because the down from the chickens triggers his asthma. When Aurelia purchases the chickens for her meal, she requests that the butcher let her pluck them herself. Aurelia focuses all her attention on Pasión as she removes the feathers. She relies on her inner powers so that she can improbably appear before Pasión and so that her release of feathers in her kitchen can trigger a parallel release of feathers in Pasión's apartment:

> She wanted him to know that what was about to occur was
> not mere chance but had been purposefully willed by her. The
> strength of her desires jerked his head up as if it were attached to

> her hand by strings. . . . He saw her clearly then, saw her despite
> the improbability of her having materialized from air. . . . Pasión
> stumbled. . . . Aurelia plucked and released more feathers. She did
> this again and then again, her hands moving at a dizzying speed,
> the air thickening with dust and feathers that choked Pasión.[12]

Thanks to Aurelia's powers, the chickens that Pasión leaves rotting in his apartment undo him, suffocating him and sending him to a supernaturally constructed, and yet materially gruesome, death. Aurelia's most violent and horrific act allows her to see her inner strength. Pasión's death marks a shift in Aurelia, bringing about a self-awareness within her and a sense of rootedness for the first time since her arrival in the United States.

The invincibility Aurelia feels toward the end of the narrative is not permanent, though, as she is unable to protect all of her children from further experiencing unspeakable harm. With all of the pain she and her family have survived, however, Aurelia ultimately realizes that the best way to cope with the "legacy of woe" that she believes she has inherited is to remember it and speak about it. As she learns from her mother, "the future will hurt worse if you deny the past."[13] These words emblematize what could be considered Pérez's primary message (and a central argument in *Intersections of Harm* as well), as Pérez compels us to closely scrutinize the environments in which we live and to know our past to be able to move forward. This look backward in order to move forward, or what Homi Bhabha might call a "'projective' past," emphasizes the crucial roles of memory and history in creating a world with a little less hurt.[14]

### Haunted by the Past: Papito and Anabelle

In the middle of *Geographies of Home*, Pérez takes us on a journey back in time, detailing Papito's traumatic recollection of his distant past in the Dominican Republic when he was in love with a woman named Anabelle. Throughout the novel, Papito has recurrent nightmares about the Dominican Republic. These come after moments of terror that he feels in the United States, particularly ones associated with his daughter Marina. Marina forces him to confront the Seventh Day Adventism he believes saved him during Trujillo's dictatorship, the religion "he had wielded . . . as sword and shield in [his daughter's] defense" and the religion that does anything but defend Marina. Indeed, upon experiencing a delirium in church and claiming she has "seen God's face," Marina is promptly thrown out of the church.[15] She returns home, only to try to kill herself. After Marina is released from the hospital following her failed suicide attempt, Papito reflects on past events.

Seeing Marina's body convulse in church and hearing her voice insist that she is a medium for a divine force releases a flood of memories for Papito: "He had suddenly been thrust back to the Dominican Republic." He remembers that "pagan rituals were transpiring and bodies swaying to achieve the delirium necessary for demons to possess souls. It was this delirium which his daughter had exhibited, this delirium which had made him forget her mental state and persuaded him that all he'd done to protect his family from evil had been to no avail."[16] In Papito's temporal flux, he draws parallels between the horrors observed during Trujillo's reign of terror and his fright at witnessing Marina's spasms and transfixion in church. That Papito likens his daughter's delirium to the demonic one associated with the Trujillo regime connects individual pathology to dictatorial pathology, taking pathology outside of a strictly intrapsychic framework and also positioning pathology in the environment.

With this move, Pérez could be seen to build on Frantz Fanon's writings linking colonialism with hysteria.[17] Fanon explains, "A disintegration, dissolution or splitting of the personality, plays a key regulating role in ensuring the stability of the colonized world."[18] If a personality split is tied to the ensured "stability of the colonized world," and if hysteria is the label applied to colonized subjects whose "psyche[s] retract" due to their colonization, then it is important to consider what is defined as pathological and who is defining behavior as such. If hysteria is a mode of surviving colonialism, as Fanon suggests, and if Marina is a type of colonized subject whose "affectivity is kept on edge," then the "madness" Marina exhibits needs to be considered a survival mechanism for the multiple forms of oppression she experiences.[19] That Papito likens Marina to the "demonic" "pagans" in a Trujillo-fearing Dominican Republic positions Marina as the type of hysterical, colonized subject delineated by Fanon and contextualizes why her delirium is the portal that transports Papito to his haunted past.[20]

As Papito remembers his life in the Dominican Republic, he reflects on the time after his father's death, when he is orphaned and alone. Yearning for companionship, he sets his sights on a young woman named Anabelle. Seeing her for the first time, Papito notes her external features: "bronzed skin," "woolly hair," and "chiseled face." He dreams about her, eroticizing and exoticizing her, imagining her "enchanting" voice and "untamed" passion, and picturing her naked image sucking on a tropical mango.[21] He envisions a life with her, going as far as to set up a home for the two of them.

This fantasy is shattered, however, when a hurricane hits the island and the woman he has been idealizing appears before him as a disheveled apparition on the brink of death. In the fury of the storm characterized as an "unprovoked assault," Papito is taken aback when he spots Anabelle intently walking directly into the middle of it.[22] What arguably startles him most is seeing her as a thing rather than a person. His immediate reaction is to dismiss her actual existence and instead view her as a ghostly figure cloaked in white. The literary critic Lyn Di Iorio Sandín notes that Anabelle's portrayal as a specter likens her to Annabel Lee, the title figure of Edgar Allan Poe's poem based on his deceased wife, who is the object of the speaker's love, is killed by "a wind [that] blew out of a cloud," and is buried in a tomb by the sea.[23] Apart from bearing the same name as this doubly ghostly poetic predecessor (albeit with an altered spelling), Pérez's Anabelle shares the same dire fate. Considering Poe's preoccupation with racism, colonialism, and imperialism, his "centrality . . . to 'American Africanism,'" and his associations of the sea with death, Pérez's intertextual invocation here is noteworthy.[24] Pérez engages with the same discourses as Poe, but with a twist, or as David Eng might say, with a (postcolonial) difference.[25] Her Anabelle is rendered otherworldly, fragmented, and animalized, and Pérez implicates patriarchal violence in this characterization.

Along with seeing Anabelle as otherworldly, Papito refers to her by using the object pronoun *it* instead of the subject pronoun *she* or even the third-person object pronoun *her.* Viewing the figure before him as "the apparition posing as Anabelle," Papito attaches subjectivity to the ghostliness of Anabelle, since that is the *thing* performing the posing action, and he relegates Anabelle to an object position. In the process, he separates Anabelle from her body, as if they were two distinct entities. This dissociation is further elucidated in Pérez's depiction of Anabelle's demise: "Her tangled hair whipped her face. . . . Her arms flew up and her torso bent forward at a precarious angle. In defiance of gravity, she sustained this position and offered herself to the wind. When moments passed and her offering was spurned, her arms plummeted back down. It then appeared that her body grew heavy and her height diminished, as if she were being sucked into soil."[26] Only at one point in this passage does Pérez use the pronoun *she* in conjunction with the active voice. But after Anabelle offers herself to the wind in vain, it is as if she loses any active subjectivity. For the most part, the actions Anabelle takes here are described as being performed by her disparate body parts—hair, face, arms, torso, body—rather than by her *self*. Anabelle thus is stripped of subjectivity and agency even in her own suicide attempt.

Pérez's characterization of Anabelle and her death not only hearkens back to Poe's depiction of Annabel Lee, but it also recalls the strikingly similar "endings" (or foreshadowed "endings") by or in a body of water of other iconic female literary figures, including William Shakespeare's Ophelia (*Hamlet*), Alfred Lord Tennyson's Lady of Shalott ("The Lady of Shalott"), Kate Chopin's Edna Pontellier (*The Awakening*), and Cristina García's Celia (*Dreaming in Cuban*).[27] By inviting such intertextual readings, Pérez situates Anabelle within literary traditions that are preoccupied with the figure of the archetypal madwoman who dies by drowning. The notably similar word choice and imagery Pérez deploys to that used by Shakespeare, Tennyson, Chopin, García, and even Poe lend themselves to such an interpretation. That Anabelle initially is clad in a white dress (the same color as that worn by Ophelia and the Lady of Shalott) evokes further literary connotations. In *The Madwoman in the Attic*, Sandra Gilbert and Susan Gubar analyze the color white and point out its literary associations with "enigma, paradox, and irony," creative energy and loneliness, "the Victorian ideal of feminine purity," and "virginal vulnerability and virginal power." Gilbert and Gubar emphasize the significance of the ready portrayal of literary *madwomen* as wearing white. They also underscore the nineteenth-century preoccupation with whiteness as ghostliness.[28] Such understandings of the significance of the color white help contextualize the portrayal of Anabelle, who embodies the paradoxes undergirding these gendered literary associations. Pérez certainly emphasizes Anabelle's solitude, vulnerability, "madness" (in that she knowingly endangers her life), and ghostliness. Anabelle's ghostliness is manifest and manifold: she is ghostly in her resemblance to her female literary predecessors, in her characterization as otherworldly, and in the way she haunts Papito decades after her death. Unlike these other literary "madwomen," though, Anabelle by and large remains silent. Readers never really hear Anabelle's voice, heightening her ghostliness and objectification and illustrating her suppression.

Anabelle's surrender to the storm finally allows Papito to see her not as an idealized image but in her material corporeality. This corporeality only underscores the paradox of purity and virginity associated with her, for when Papito finally sees Anabelle the woman instead of Anabelle the fantasy, he realizes the thing too horrible to name: that Anabelle is carrying her father's child. "Only now, confronted with the evidence of

Anabelle's belly protruding against the soaked fabric of her dress, did Papito understand why his friends had warned him to find himself another girl. Only now did he understand as well why she had hidden in shapeless garments throughout the previous months." Pérez never explicitly states that Anabelle's pregnancy is the product of incest and rape, but she, like the Barahona townspeople, hints at it in her description of Papito's reaction to the "evidence" confronting him. Noticing Anabelle's "protruding belly" causes Papito to ruminate about why Anabelle's now obvious pregnancy had been kept hidden, why she had been kept secluded, why her father hadn't searched for the man who impregnated her and why he hadn't forced the man to marry his daughter according to the town's conventions. As Papito realizes the unfathomable answers to his questions, "something inside Papito snapped."[29]

At this point, Papito tries to save Anabelle, causing her to "emit a sound" for the first and only time in the narrative; yet it is a sound without words, one that could hardly be considered a voice, and one that is animalized, likened to "that of a rabbit caught in the claws of its prey and swooped into the air."[30] The moment Anabelle is granted any agency by virtue of being materially seen and heard, her subjectivity as a woman is denied to her as she is bestialized. Indeed, upon hearing Anabelle "emit a sound," Papito remembers a childhood story of a donkey that is beaten by its owner and speaks back to him, telling him of its determination to die rather than continue to be beaten. Papito's recollection of this story upon hearing Anabelle's animalized utterance likens Anabelle to this donkey. In her analysis of this scene, Sandín explains that it draws from the repertoire of Zora Neale Hurston's works that have centered on the same figure of the abused donkey. Not only does Pérez liken Anabelle to this iconic animal in African American literature used to represent the indignities endured by African American women, but she describes Anabelle as possessing "bronzed skin" and "woolly hair," arguably characterizing Anabelle as an Afro Dominican woman.[31] Pérez thus emphasizes the intersectional forms of harm Anabelle suffers as a racialized Dominican woman who is robbed of her humanity but who rejects her dehumanization. She resists this positionality in part through the sound accompanying her animalization. Admittedly it is only via analogous parable, solely through her comparison to and positioning as a donkey, that Anabelle (can) speak(s). That the sound Anabelle emits holds "no words" and cannot be described as an identifiable form of human language speaks to Elaine Scarry's observations about the impossibility of describing pain through language and to postcolonial and feminist scholarship that suggests that voice is not available to all.[32] Considering that the sound Anabelle (finally) utters is at once submissive and insolent, and that it is likened to the donkey's assertion, "I am tired and will lay myself down to die. Your beating me has no power to change my mind," nonetheless signals a resignation to die *and* a defiance against future physical harm.[33] As such, it could be construed as falling in line with Suzanne Bost's claim that pain is not the incommunicable phenomenon Scarry makes it out to be, but that pain allows for movement and change.[34]

Anabelle's sole utterance in the narrative could be viewed as a mode of resignation and an act of resistance, locating her in an ambiguous, interstitial space. At the crossroads between life and death, voice and silence, power and powerlessness, she inhabits the type of *Coatlicue* state articulated by Gloria Anzaldúa in *Borderlands,* for Pérez's depiction of Anabelle elucidates a third perspective that moves beyond dualistic understanding.[35] In Anabelle's animalization and defiance, she possesses characteristics similar to Anzaldúa's rebellious Shadow-Beast "that refuses to take orders from outside authorities. It refuses to take orders from my conscious will, it threatens the sovereignty of my rulership. It is that part of me that hates constraints of any kind, even those self-imposed. At the least hint of limitations on my time or space by others, it kicks out with both feet. Bolts."[36] Just as the Shadow-Beast stubbornly rejects any impositions hurled in its direction, drawing strength from this revolt, the donkey that is likened to the dying Anabelle and the Anabelle who is likened to the dying donkey rebel against the harm imposed on them by others and alternatively opt for self-inflicted deaths. My comparison of Anabelle with Anzaldúa's Shadow-Beast cannot ignore the Jungian shadow concept underlying Anzaldúa's theorizations.[37] According to Carl Jung, the shadow represents "the 'negative' side of the personality" and tends to be associated with the "dark-skinned, alien, or primitive."[38] In Anabelle's positioning as a donkey (associated with an African American literary tradition), depiction as alienated from her community, and characterization as the subject of Papito's repeated nightmare, she ostensibly represents key elements of Jung's shadow concept. However, as with Anzaldúa who embraces the Shadow-Beast—notably gendered female—instead of rejecting it because of its perceived negativity, Pérez underscores the formidable patriarchal violence imposed on Anabelle and emphasizes her attempt to "kick out with both feet [and] bolt."

## "Placing Herself Directly in Harm's Way": Rebecca's Abusive Relationships

Just as Anabelle "plac[es] herself directly in harm's way," so does Pap-ito's daughter Rebecca. However, whereas Anabelle knowingly hurls her-self into the eye of a hurricane arguably to *escape* the patriarchal harm to which she has been subjected, Rebecca, like Irene in *The Ladies' Gallery* and *Impossible Motherhood*, knowingly and repeatedly puts herself *in the way of* patriarchal harm. Indeed, Rebecca cannot seem to have a rela-tionship with a man that isn't abusive. The only two men with whom she has had a relationship are Samuel and Pasión, both of whom harm her physically and emotionally. Although Rebecca does not passively take the abuse without defending herself, it is as if she defines herself solely through her relations with men who mistreat her.

That Rebecca finds herself in more than one abusive relationship needs to be understood in the context of her paradoxical desire to receive attention and love from others and her general lack of attention to herself. Even as an adolescent, she exposes herself in public, "heedless of the dangers existing for a girl her age," and even while living under a dictatorial regime where it was commonplace for people to go missing, she lets her sexual yearnings dictate her actions without regard for the potential harm she could experience.[39] *Unguarded* might well be the word that best describes her.

Just as Rebecca leaves herself unguarded from puberty onward, she increasingly fails to care for her surroundings, herself, her appearance, and her children. When she marries Pasión, she believes that she finally has made it, has achieved the American Dream for which she has longed, and has found a safe haven after having come out of an abusive relationship with her first love. After all, as a U.S. citizen and homeowner, Pasión brings with him the promise of the American Dream in all its glory. As such, he also supposedly brings with him a sense of security; unlike Samuel, he is not with Rebecca in a futile attempt to attain a green card. As a homeowner, he theoretically can provide Rebecca with a physical place where she can retreat and that she can call hers, thereby granting her the psychological belonging she craves. Upon seeing Pasión's house for the first time after marrying him, though, Rebecca realizes that the dream she thought she had attained by virtue of becoming Pasión's wife is anything but the idealized life for which she had hoped.

As she enters Pasión's house for the first time, Rebecca's dreams are promptly shattered. Pérez illustrates just how far Pasión's brownstone deviates from the sought-after house with white picket fence, 2.5 children, and dog that epitomize the American Dream.[40] Pasión's place is claustrophobic, and Pérez relies on imagery of trash and clutter to describe its interior: "garbage," "stained," "gutted," "only inches of cleared space," "cluttered," "shabby," "mismatched," "collapsed," and "junk." Pasión's brownstone is crowded with chickens and animal feces, and the bathtub therein is used as a trough, illustrating the inhabitability of the place for *humans* and calling attention to the animalization tied to the portrayal of Rebecca. Pérez emphasizes the literal coldness of the abode, noting that "the gas [is] cut off" and that even the frostiness of the city streets is welcoming in contrast to the "numbing cold" of the brownstone; she also emphasizes the figurative coldness of the house that is absented of happiness. Moreover, Pérez describes Rebecca as living amid "filth" in a "pigsty" in a crime-ridden, poverty-ridden, black and Latina/o neighborhood.[41]

Dirt metaphorically represents Rebecca, and the environment surrounding her is depicted as unyielding, highlighting how Rebecca embodies her physical surroundings. The dilapidated neighborhood populated with people of color could be seen to succumb to ready, essentialized constructions of people of color as belonging to a "culture of poverty." The portrayal of this neighborhood as "ailing" also arguably medicalizes space in the manner against which Henri Lefebvre warns, for Lefebvre claims that the pathologization of space fails to recognize that space is *produced*.[42] Alternatively, Pérez's portrait of the environment and Rebecca's internalization of the environment's despondency could be considered a scathing critique of the hostile conditions under which so many people of color live. Highlighting the power of institutionalized oppression in the formation of her setting, Pérez reveals the actual constructedness of this space.

Rebecca internalizes her wretched surroundings. She initially tries to prettify Pasión's house, cleaning it and "deplet[ing] the savings from her former job in a garment factory" to buy items to decorate it. At first, she publicly feigns happiness, believing that faith and hard work will allow her to acquire the happiness she dons for others and will give Pasión the time he needs to modify his behavior. Like her father, who turns to religion after witnessing dictatorial madness, Rebecca turns to Seventh Day Adventism to explain the miracles she observed when those who had disappeared under Trujillo's regime suddenly returned to their homes. Her faith causes her to think that "anything was possible," including Pasión's transformation. Eventually, though, Rebecca gives up trying to make her house a livable home, especially since "Pasión continued to haul in junk."[43] Nevertheless, she remains in the house, holding steadfast to her belief in the possibility, no matter how remote, of change.

Determined to stay with Pasión despite his mistreatment of her, and resolute in her religiosity, Rebecca generally fails to care for her surroundings, herself, and her children. She stops cleaning the house and comes to embody the mess that surrounds her. She pays attention to her looks only when she returns to Pasión (following the fleeting moments when she temporarily leaves him) and when she applies makeup to conceal the bruises and scars visible on her body from the abuse suffered at his hands. Rebecca's general failure to bathe or to groom herself arguably positions her as the type of "madwoman" about whom Elaine Showalter writes in *The Female Malady*. Showalter notes that in the nineteenth century, Victorian psychiatrists associated "appropriate" attention to feminine dress with sanity and linked women's lack of concern with their appearance with insanity, and she explains that these notions existed well into the twentieth century. That Rebecca takes pains to groom herself when returning to her abusive husband, however, destabilizes such medicalizing gendered ideologies. It could well be argued that it is when she chooses to leave Pasión, if only temporarily, that she is her most "sane" self, and that it is when she attempts to return to him—with an *attention* to her appearance—that she relinquishes reason. At least, this is the perspective her family members adopt.

Rebecca's self-neglect is connected to her self-image as anything but whole. After surviving a particularly violent beating by Pasión, she gazes at herself in the mirror, only to notice her splintered reflection. Rather than view herself in her entirety, she sees the different pieces of her battered body: "lips bruised purple," "dry skin flaking off," "prematurely wrinkled face" with "dirt embedded deep" within it, "the nose bent beyond recognition," bleeding nostrils, "swollen tongue," "split lips," "cavity-rotted teeth," and "greying hair." Not only does she see herself as an assortment of fragmented parts, but she observes how these parts are deformed as a result of physical harm or are decaying due to premature aging. Believing that the fractured image before her "was what Pasión had seen, what others regularly saw whenever she stepped outside, what her mother and sister had noticed too," Rebecca shows how she internalizes others' views of her.[44] That she does not see herself as whole highlights the Lacanian nature of her gaze, for Rebecca, like Gladys in *The Ladies' Gallery*, sees herself as anything but the idealized image of an "I" that she would like to be. In this sense, Rebecca's mirror scene counters that of the infant in Lacan's mirror stage who initially sees a fantasized image of a unified "I" staring back at him. However, by emphasizing the fractured reflection Rebecca sees before her in the mirror, Pérez, like Vilar, portrays a character typified by her lack of unity and who therefore emblematizes the actual junction of loss and selfhood at the core of Lacan's theories. Indeed, Rebecca represents the type of Lacanian divided subject described by Antonio Viego in *Dead Subjects*, an image sustained by the distorted reflection she finds gazing back at her in the *cracked* mirror.

Like her mother, Rebecca is subject to the type of intimate terrorism articulated by Anzaldúa. Whereas Aurelia experiences this intimate terrorism from her environment, Rebecca most visibly experiences it from her husband, even while the physical place where Rebecca lives, like that surrounding Aurelia, harms her psychological sense of self. The lack of safety, alienation, and sense of betrayal that characterize intimate terrorism all are felt by Rebecca. Just as Anzaldúa describes the seeming impossibility of returning home and the importance of carving out a new space after the wounds and silences, Rebecca finds herself in similar interstices, between a house with an abusive husband and a house with a disapproving family. Like the "battered and bruised" woman described by Anzaldúa, Rebecca finds her rebellion *en su propria soledad*.[45]

In her defiance, however, Rebecca is the recipient and perpetrator of harm, highlighting how harm can be self-propagating and continual. Not only does Rebecca generally fail to care for herself, but she also neglects to prioritize the needs of her three young children, significantly named Esperanza, Soledad, and Rubén. Esperanza means hope, Soledad means solitude, and Rubén is the Spanish spelling of a biblical name that refers to the self-professed affliction Leah suffered as a hated woman. According to the Bible, "Leah conceived and bore a son, and she called his name Reuben, for she said, 'Because the LORD has looked upon my affliction; for now my husband will love me.'"[46] The children's names reveal Rebecca's shifting attitude toward her situation. Rebecca's first-born is named Esperanza, underscoring the hope Rebecca initially has upon marrying Pasión; her second-born is named Rubén, revealing her desire to be wanted by her husband; and her third-born is named Soledad, illustrating her resignation toward her solitude.

Esperanza, Rubén, and Soledad witness the habitual harm inflicted on Rebecca and suffer the verbal violence she spews at them when she blames them for the pain she endures, as she repeatedly asserts that if it weren't for them, Pasión would not treat her as violently as he does. The children are subject to more than verbal and psychological abuse, however. They suffer from neglect. Neither sufficiently nourished nor bathed, their physical and social health is jeopardized. Rebecca purportedly does not bathe them because of the lack of hot water in the household, claiming that the cold water would endanger them more than not paying attention to their hygiene. But her children smell so bad that Rubén's teacher sends a note to Rebecca urging her to bathe him and clean his clothes. Because the family lives in poverty, as Pasión fails to provide them with enough money for food, and as he asserts his patriarchal privilege by demanding that Rebecca's gendered duty is to stay at home with the kids, the children become emaciated and learn to hide and horde whatever bits of food they can scrape together. Meanwhile, Rebecca appears oblivious to the child abuse she herself perpetuates.

Rebecca's family members do not understand why she "chooses" to remain in such a situation. Considering her "insane" for "getting herself into" more than one abusive relationship and staying with Pasión, they adopt a psychiatric, patriarchal, and racialized rhetoric of rationality to denounce her "decisions." Their condemnation of her suggests that if Rebecca only had enough willpower and made better choices, she would be able to leave her abusive husband. But this attitude fails to recognize that the cycle of abuse in which Rebecca finds herself, like that in which Irene finds herself in *Impossible Motherhood*, is not that easy to escape: there is a reason it's called a *cycle*. Instead, Rebecca's sister Iliana insists that Rebecca needs to seek psychiatric treatment for her pattern of abusive relationships, and Iliana encourages her parents to take custody of Esperanza, Rubén, and Soledad to protect the children from the abuse they endure in their household. Rebecca's parents, meanwhile, insist that Rebecca be held responsible for her own actions, and they threaten to call Social Services and take her children from her if she will not leave Pasión. Although Aurelia and Papito never actually phone Social Services, toward the end of the novel they take Rebecca's children and inform her that she can decide whether she wishes to join them. By threatening to appeal to the government to gain legal custody of their grandchildren, Aurelia and Papito contemplate turning to the very source that regularly strips women of color from making their own child-rearing decisions. By removing Rebecca's children from their home, Aurelia and Papito mirror the ways the U.S. government historically has interfered in the lives of women of color in the name of safety.[47] Since Iliana functions as the educated protagonist of the novel, and since her mother acts as the glue holding the family together (despite Aurelia's threat to Rebecca to tear her family apart), the reader is likely to align herself with either Iliana's or Aurelia's ideologies.

These ideologies, however, rely on a rhetoric of individual responsibility that echoes the rhetoric prevalent in psychological and psychiatric institutions in this country and resembles dominant neoliberal discourses that privilege a Horatio Alger "pull yourself up by your bootstraps" mentality. Although such ideologies would seem to bestow survivors of domestic violence with a certain amount of agency by placing responsibility in their hands, the danger in such approaches is that survivors ultimately are blamed for their suffering without regard for the surrounding circumstances or conditions that contribute to their pain. The individual is absented from her environment.[48]

Rebecca's family members' emphasis on choice fails to see that leaving an abusive situation is not as simple as they make it out to be, nor does it recognize that in this context the term *choice* itself is paradoxical. As I emphasize throughout *Intersections of Harm* and underscore in chapter 1, the concept of choice cannot be separated from that of power or even survival. Rebecca's family's rhetoric of individual responsibility and Iliana's repeated insistence that Rebecca seek therapy refuse to acknowledge that the "choice" to leave an abusive household is a luxury not available to all.[49] The poverty in which Rebecca lives, the racism to which she and her family are subject, and the internalized oppression she feels help explain why she remains steadfast in her allegiance to Pasión despite the abuse she experiences under his roof. Yet none of Rebecca's family members ever listen to her, let alone comprehend why she would stay with her husband. Perhaps this is because they are acculturated to believe in the ideology of free will commonplace in dominant U.S. society, and/or perhaps it is because they rely on the Latina/o philosophy that stresses the importance of "*sobreponerse* (to overcome), a[n] . . . active cognitive coping that allows for working through or overcoming adversity."[50] Rebecca's family accordingly only contributes to her sense of shame. Emphasizing her individual responsibility and believing that "genuine power originated from a soul resilient enough to persevere against all odds," Rebecca's family downplays the societal forces and images that rigidly codify gender and race roles, relegating women of color to the societal and psychic edge.[51] As Ana Castillo alternatively asserts, "The sense of submission and docility that we see is . . . about survival."[52]

## Rape and Repulsion: Marina's and Iliana's Webs of Violence

Like Rebecca, Marina and Iliana are ensnared in their own webs of violence. The structural violence that most evidently affects Marina is the institutionalized racism she internalizes and externalizes. Although Iliana is also affected by institutionalized racism, the structural violence with which she most evidently grapples is (hetero)sexism, as she defies gender norms in her behavior, aspirations, educational achievement, attire, and birth order that dictated she should have been born a boy. Although neither Marina nor Iliana is subject to intimate partner violence as Rebecca is, they experience sexualized harm, as both are raped.

Like Rebecca, Marina is viewed as mentally imbalanced by her family. Nevertheless, the family treats the sisters differently because Marina is diagnosed with a mental illness while Rebecca is not. Marina's family members for the most part condone the majority of her actions since a psychiatrist has diagnosed her with a known disease, whereas they condemn Rebecca's actions because they believe she can and should determine what she does of her own accord. The family members therefore consider Marina's conduct to be beyond her control for biological reasons, whereas they treat Rebecca's circumscribed decisions as if they could be altered by sheer willpower. In the process, they define Marina via her medicalization, while they denounce Rebecca because of her refusal to be medicalized. At no point does the family recognize the roles the sociopolitical environment might well play in the development of Rebecca's and Marina's identities or in the actions Rebecca and Marina do or do not take.

Despite these disparate attitudes toward the two siblings, there are notable similarities between Rebecca and Marina. Both are harmed by others and harm themselves or put themselves in situations that make them susceptible to being hurt. Both also inflict the type of harm they receive on others they supposedly love. The sisters internalize others' perceptions of them; in turn, both come to see themselves as split subjects. The two also bear the Europeanized and Christianized names of iconic female figures of conquest, connecting them to their namesakes. Rebecca is the baptized name of the indigenous woman born Pocahontas, and Marina is the Spaniards' name for the indigenous woman born Malintzín/Malinalli and commonly known as La Malinche.[53]

Giving Rebecca and Marina these particular names, Pérez situates them within a (post)colonial trajectory of gendered and racialized deviance and subjugation. According to Rayna Green, the author of "The

Pocahontas Perplex," Pocahontas traditionally has been painted as a romanticized figure, the "good Indian" who put aside racial differences in pursuit of her love for the British colonizer John Rolfe; she generally has been hailed an "American" icon for aiding the British in their colonization of indigenous peoples. Like Pocahontas, who aligned herself with the Europeans in their invasion of indigenous lands, La Malinche sided with the Spaniards during their conquest of the Americas, serving as Hernán Cortés's mistress and translator. Unlike Pocahontas, who has been depicted as a heroine in the mainstream U.S. imaginary, La Malinche has been portrayed as a whore and traitor to her people in the dominant Mexican imaginary.

Although Pérez does not portray Rebecca as a heroine or characterize Marina as a whore in their family's eyes, she paints them in ways not altogether different from these dominant constructions of Pocahontas and La Malinche. Just as Pocahontas saved the life of the colonizer John Smith, although his people pillaged the territory of hers, Rebecca defends her violent husband to the end. Just as Pocahontas is viewed as having turned against her people for love, Rebecca turns against her family, or at least is at odds with them, because of her professed love for Pasión. Likewise, just as La Malinche typically has been perceived as a traitor to her people, Marina can be regarded in the same way, since she betrays her sister Iliana by raping her. Like La Malinche, whom some Chicana feminists have reclaimed and portrayed as a rape survivor, or at least a survivor of conquest, Marina too is a rape survivor. Moreover, La Malinche's nominal multiplicity could be interpreted as virtually schizophrenic in a manner paralleling Marina's diagnosis of schizophrenic symptoms. Although the context of *Geographies of Home* is neither American Indian nor Mexican American, Pérez's decision to name Rebecca and Marina as she does situates her novel within a broader postcolonial, or decolonial, context. Giving the two characters in the family who most readily are cast as deviant in others' eyes the Christianized and Europeanized names of these indigenous women predecessors, Pérez links individual struggles with physical and psychological harm with collective histories of gendered and racialized oppression and geographic dispossession.

In her portrayal of Marina, Pérez illustrates the overwhelming power of oppression, especially in relation to Marina's own racial consciousness—or racial rejection—as Marina turns the institutionalized racism directed toward blacks against herself. Sandín comments on Marina's obsession with whiteness, "Marina demonstrates that she has internalized the general Hispanic Caribbean tendency toward lactification."[54] Marina has so vehemently internalized societal racism that she comes to loathe and deny her own Afro Latina features. In a disagreement with Iliana, she reveals her internalization of socially constructed beauty myths. Marina insists that blue-eyed white men are to be desired, maintains that black men are "lazy as shit and undependable," and claims that she is "Hispanic, not black."[55] Sandín explains that this conversation highlights the rift between the way Caribbean migrants are identified from without in the United States and the way they self-identify. Jorge Duany, a Caribbean studies scholar, similarly observes, "Whereas North Americans classify most Caribbean immigrants as black, Dominicans tend to perceive themselves as white, Hispanic, or other."[56] In her self-identification as "Hispanic, not black," Marina rejects the racial ideology of hypodescent that frames dominant constructions of race in the United States in black and white terms. She adheres instead to the construction of race along a continuum prevalent in Latin America and the Caribbean while ascribing to the ready vilification of blackness in U.S. Anglo culture. Iliana's insistence that Marina acknowledge her blackness *along with* her *latinidad*, meanwhile, both destabilizes the ideology of pigmentocracy to which Marina adamantly clings and subverts the monolithic racialization of *latinidad* in the United States by illustrating that Latinas/os come in all races, shapes, and colors. Marina is not persuaded by Iliana, though. In her assertion of her *latinidad* and "rejection of [her] own negritude," Marina refuses to recognize that she can be both "Hispanic" *and* black.[57] Not only does she adamantly hold fast to readily available ideologies that position blacks as ugly and dangerous, but she also "distrust[s] what is black in [her], that is, the whole of [her] being."[58]

Marina's racial denial needs to be understood in relation to her harrowing recollection of her rape by an African American male psychic. She is so haunted by her assault that she continues to have visions of her attacker after the rape has taken place. We readers are privy only to Marina's visions and memories of her violation (instead of reading about the assault as it transpires), and we are expected to regularly question the reliability of her claims. The narration encourages skepticism toward any of Marina's assertions since she sees things no one else seems to see. Even in the moment prior to the most vivid vision of Marina's attack, Pérez encourages readers to question its veracity: "[Marina] knew that if she screamed her parents would claim that she was crazy, that no one else was there."[59] The idea of the absent presence that Pérez introduces here can be understood in relation to Bhabha's analysis of the "rememoration" of the "not there" (which he borrows from Morrison), invocation of Lacan's *extimité*, and reconceptualization of Freud's *unheimlich* space.[60] What unites these concepts is a haunting and traumatic unveiling of something that has been kept hidden. Despite illustrating the unreliability of Marina's narrative, Pérez emphasizes the destructive power of the haunt, and she provides a remarkably detailed account of Marina's relived rape. In addition, after Marina is hospitalized upon attempting suicide, Papito links Marina's mental illness to her rape, implying that the former follows from the latter. Pérez accordingly compels us to view Marina's assault not as the dream sequence Sandín suggests, but as the very real, horrific event it is to Marina.[61] Even if the only version readers have of the attack is called into doubt as "actually" existing at the time in question, textual evidence supports the idea that the assault transpired at a prior point.

The language Pérez deploys to describe Marina's reconstructed rape is so graphically charged that readers can see the tangible effects the assault has on Marina. Upon sensing her rapist's presence in her bedroom, Marina "recognized the shape" and could not forget the smell of "the man who'd raped her," positioning the rape as something that already has occurred and setting up the new attack as the type of relived experience of trauma not uncommon for rape survivors, or survivors of other forms of trauma, to undergo.[62] Recognizing her attacker as the man who raped her, Marina remains "paralyzed by fear." In her description of this reconstructed assault, Pérez mostly strips Marina of subjectivity and power by emphasizing the majority of the actions that are performed *on* her. Even the bulk of the subjects performing the action of the verbs are not readily identifiable subjects, but objects. Instead of Marina dissolving, collapsing, recoiling, or convulsing, her will, body, limbs, and stomach do. Likewise, instead of positioning Marina's attacker as the subject of the majority of the sentences, Pérez writes that his "hand clamped onto her mouth.... The cold steel of his zipper cut into Marina's hips. His penis found an entry." This is not to say that neither Marina nor her rapist is devoid of subjectivity. Marina's attacker speaks during the assault, imposing his voice and body onto her and forcing her to face him. Pérez also uses the third-person singular male subject pronoun more than once in her description of the attack: "he had asked," "he yelled," and "he would exit."[63] Pérez uses the third-person singular female subject pronoun to describe Marina only when she musters whatever strength she has left after the rape has transpired. Inserting these pronouns where she does, Pérez underscores the frightening amount of force and power

Marina's rapist exerts over her and Marina's inability to wrest herself from her attacker's clutches, but Pérez also emphasizes Marina's efforts to fight back.

Highlighting Marina's determination to reclaim herself after her assault, Pérez writes:

> No flat-nosed, wide-lipped nigger would claim her soul. No savage with beads dangling from his neck. She would survive all this. There was nothing else to lose. Nothing else to fear.
>
> . . .
>
> Her destiny could still be changed. . . . Her body might be snatched, but not her soul. And her body was merely dust. It did not consist of who she was.[64]

Emphasizing Marina's resolve to move forward in the wake of her violation, Pérez relies on a rhetoric of willpower and resilience. Pérez also notes Marina's appeal to God to help her move on with her life. Marina's turn to religion as a source of comfort in a time of distress parallels that of her sister Rebecca and her father, who similarly find solace in their religiosity. Yet just as religion is not the source of salvation for which either Rebecca or Papito hopes, neither does it protect Marina from sustaining further harm.

In Marina's focus on self-survival, she draws on two coping mechanisms. The first is to detach her body from her soul as if they were distinct entities. In doing so, she adheres to dominant Manichaean discourses dissociating body from mind also prevalent in Seventh Day Adventist theology. Her second coping mechanism is to attempt to strip her rapist of subjectivity by defining him according to a host of racist stereotypes. Viewing her attacker as a "flat-nosed, wide-lipped nigger" and a "savage with beads" who reeked of "rotting greens," and subsequently mistrusting *all* black men, Marina then projects her hatred and fear of blackness onto herself.[65]

Marina cannot escape her own Afrocentric features that, in their resemblance to those of the man who raped her, serve as regular reminders of her attacker and reflect his image when she sees her own. In the scene immediately following the one described above, Marina enters the bathroom to try desperately to rid herself of any trace of her attacker on her person. Like Rebecca staring at her cracked reflection after one of Pasión's beatings, Marina here stands before a mirror. It is as if the moments of extreme violence to which these characters are subjected precipitate their gazes at themselves to affirm their selfhood.

As with Gladys in *The Ladies' Gallery*, Rebecca's and Marina's gazes in the mirror highlight a desired unity yet actual disjunction of self, and they reveal the "irreducible force" of the "real yet unreal" images reflected in the mirror.[66] Just as Rebecca sees a fragmented image staring back at her, Marina sees her mutilated body parts, the "blood congealed on her lower lip" and the bruises staining her body. Repulsed by the image before her, Marina grows suddenly aware of her own distinctly Afrocentric features, features that she had heretofore not noticed (or willfully ignored), given her yellowish skin "shades lighter than any of her sisters"; now, however, she sees "her kinky, dirt-red hair, her sprawling nose, her wide, long lips" that "appeared magnified, conveying to her eyes that she was not who she'd believed."[67] Not only does her gaze in the mirror mark a moment of misrecognition, newfound recognition, or "willed unknowability," but it causes Marina to conflate her image with that of the rapist of her nightmares, instilling her with a deep and abject "self-loathing."[68] Waiting for the "steam [to] obliterate her image in the mirror," she then undergoes an intensive posttraumatic cleansing ritual, scrubbing herself with Brillo pads and shaving her pubic hair in a frantic attempt to return to a state of childlike innocence.[69] She asserts that proof of her rape lies in her visibly violated body; she therefore exposes herself to her family to convince them of the ordeal she has survived. Her scarred body, though, reveals the extent of the harm she can inflict on herself, shows the long-lasting psychological effects of sexual assault that extend well after the violent incident, and serves as an alarming reminder of the trauma induced by an external(ized) and internalized racism, such that her scarred psyche is etched onto her body.

The only time Marina looks at herself in the mirror and sees herself as whole is when she imagines herself as such, hearkening back to Lacan's observations that the subject's recognition of herself or himself in the mirror as an idealized "I" is just that, *idealized*, and correspondingly fictitious. Walking in a formerly middle-class (presumably white) neighborhood, Marina pictures herself inside the attic room of one of these houses looking at herself in a mirror.[70] Here she projects an image of herself as she *would like* to appear, fixating on her dramatically changed bodily appearance: "Gone were the ninety-two pounds which had bloated her body to its massive two hundred and seventeen. Not only had her weight decreased: her hair had grown straight enough to billow with the slightest breeze."[71] Constructing her body image in such an altered manner, Marina positions herself in control of her body in ways seemingly impossible in her life.

Marina here inserts and asserts her presence in a place of her choosing. Envisioning this house as her home, she "imagine[s] herself looking out of one of its windows rather than trying to see in," and she sees "her own history twin[ing] with theirs [the owners of the house], forming an extensive web of roots that assured her she too belonged as surely as did the oak outside."[72] Marina's desire to belong somewhere is striking here and resonates with Vilar's yearning for a place to call home in her memoirs. In Marina's case, it is no coincidence that she finds a sense of belonging only in a fantasized place free from traumatic memories. There are telling ironies, though, in the description of the place she dreams of as providing her with such a powerful sense of belonging.

These ironies are connected to the intertextual invocations Pérez arguably draws in this scene to Charlotte Brontë's *Jane Eyre*, Jean Rhys's *Wide Sargasso Sea*, and Charlotte Perkins Stetson Gilman's "The Yellow Wallpaper." Situating Marina's dreams in the attic of the house, Pérez likely gestures to one of the most famous attics in literature: the one that imprisons the iconic "madwoman in the attic," Bertha Mason, born Antoinette Cosway. Marina shares Bertha's "madness." (Un)like Bertha, who is cast as Jane Eyre's racial "other" as a Caribbean creole in contrast to Jane (who is characterized as a white British woman), Marina acts as her own racial "other," as she comes to hate and fear her own blackness. Like Bertha, who sets fire to the Rochester mansion, Marina sets fire to her family's house and to the attorney's papers in the firm where she works to protest his mistreatment of her. Despite such similarities, whereas Bertha does all she can to escape her confinement in an attic, Marina fervently wishes she could belong there.

In addition to situating Marina's dream sequence in an attic, Pérez draws attention to the "yellowed sheets of paper" found in one of the trunks there.[73] This descriptor conjures the central image of Gilman's short story. Pérez's decision to incorporate the detail of the "yellowed sheets of paper" in a scene where the only character in her novel who is diagnosed with a mental illness sees her idealized reflection staring back at her resonates with Gilman's tale. After all, in Gilman's story, the female protagonist, who likewise is struggling with a mental disorder, is confined in a space surrounded by a suffocating and ghostly yellow wallpaper, and she sees a woman/herself/her double in this same wallpaper. That Marina's skin color is described as yellowish bolsters the connection to Gilman's tale. The intertextual invocations that Pérez draws in Marina's fantasy scene thus position Marina within a trajectory of literary "madwomen"; however, unlike Brontë, Rhys, or Gilman, Pérez foregrounds the debilitating role dominant *racial* ideologies play in struggles with mental illness.

Pérez's attention to the centrality of race in constructions of mental health and illness in her depiction of Marina could be considered to engage with Freudian psychoanalysis in terms that the performance studies scholar José Esteban Muñoz might describe as disidentificatory. Pérez arguably works within the framework of Freudian psychoanalysis while calling it into question, for her construction of an Afro Latina character as possessing "primitive" and "savage" traits could seem to succumb to Freud's characterization of those who are "dark-skinned" as "maldeveloped," "undeveloped," "undevelopable," and, in turn, pathological. However, by portraying the overwhelming harm inflicted on and by Marina because of dominant racist ideologies, Pérez could be deploying this psychoanalytic discourse to challenge its essentializing premises and to "broaden . . . the psychoanalytic project to encompass a serious analysis of racial difference" in the same way that David Eng, David Kazanjian, Anne Cheng, and Ranjanna Khanna do.[74]

Pérez emphasizes the degree to which Marina absorbs the societal racism directed toward her. In her fantasy scene, Marina ultimately realizes that her imagined vision of herself before a mirror is illusory; rather than run her fingers through strands of billowy hair, she finds her "fingers tangled in knots of kinky hair."[75] At this moment, when her fantasy is disrupted with the reminder of her Afrocentric features, a car swerves to avoid hitting her. As a black man steps out of the vehicle, Marina runs away in fear.

Haunted by the trauma of her rape, Marina channels her hatred toward her attacker onto herself and others. She justifies the violent actions she takes against others by aligning herself with a type of martyrdom. She sardonically stresses the beginnings of her suffering as a child, when she and her siblings Beatriz and Gabriel were left behind in the Dominican Republic under the custody of their aunt, to be neglected, "barely clothed or fed," and kept "in a chicken coop," in a manner similar to that of Rebecca years later.[76] In the face of adversity as an adult, Marina, like her father and sister Rebecca turns to religion. And like Anzaldúa, who describes herself as "the mutant stoned out of the herd," Marina compares herself to "the faithful who, in times of old, had been stoned, cast into a lion's den or burned alive for acknowledging God's influence in their lives."[77] Unlike Anzaldúa, though, who relies on such imagery to comment on the destructive power of dominant ideologies, Marina wields Seventh Day Adventism to accommodate her viewpoints. Rather than see Cain as immoral or traitorous for having slain his brother, Abel, she considers his actions "inadvertent," stemming from *madness*.[78] Through this interpretation, she takes the biblical figure whom the Ku Klux Klan has appropriated as the emblem of evil, envy, and blackness and transforms him into an empathetic figure who lashes out against his sibling because he cannot control his actions.[79] Implicit in Marina's reading lies a foreshadowing of her own later actions and a self-exoneration of any culpability for her behavior, since she (too) is diagnosed as mad, is symbolically doomed to wander without a home, and is deemed an outcast. Marina's devout fervor propels her to wreak devastation around her. Apart from resorting to arson, she tries to kill herself by swallowing her mother's heart medicine. Once she gains enough strength after surviving this suicide attempt, she secretly refuses to take her pills since they numb her senses, which she perceives to be her reason for existing.[80]

As she lets her primal impulses take control, Marina turns against her sister Iliana and rapes her twice in the same night. Only now, when Marina inflicts the same type of violence on her sister that has already been imposed on her, do her parents finally realize they no longer can provide the sort of care Marina needs at home. When the harm Marina inflicts is directed toward herself alone, her parents (especially Aurelia) feel that the best place for her to receive care is not in a hospital but in her home.[81] When Marina hurts her sister, though, they resign themselves to interning Marina in a mental institution. All the while, Aurelia insists that her daughter "couldn't have known what she was doing," absolving Marina of culpability for her actions.[82] Yet since Aurelia repeats the phrase, the reader is left to wonder whether she actually believes that Marina has no control over her actions, or whether Aurelia cannot let herself fathom that a daughter of hers knowingly could sexually violate her own sister.

Iliana, however, is certain of Marina's cognizance, and she holds Marina accountable for assaulting her. But this certainty is not immediate. In the moments just prior to her rapes, Iliana senses that she is not safe with her sister. She is "unnerved" by the darkness of the basement room she shares with Marina (notably the antithesis of Marina's attic fantasy); she struggles with "the forebodings that had accompanied her to bed"; she "could not shake the certainty that her sister equated her with the devil and had some wicked plan in store"; she finds that her "senses [are] preternaturally alert," "yet she no longer knew if her senses could be trusted." Like her mother, Iliana dismisses her sensory knowledge, even though her senses warn her that she is in peril, and even though she is suddenly "assailed by a memory of . . . [Marina] barging into the bathroom to see between [Iliana's] thighs."[83] The timing and description of this recollection suggest that Iliana somehow knows her sister will assault her but that she refuses to believe Marina will harm her in such a horrific way. Instead, Iliana chooses to rely on reason and logic (a.k.a. "white rationality") to assure herself that she is safe with Marina, and she dangerously silences what Anzaldúa might label her "other mode of consciousness" (one that "facilitates images from the soul and the unconscious through dreams and imagination") or her *facultad* ("an instant 'sensing,'" or "an acute awareness").[84]

Even when Marina rapes Iliana the first time, Iliana still refuses to listen to her *facultad*, repeating that "nothing happened" and that she is "fine." Positioning her rape as something unreal that did not happen, or could not have happened, to cope with the unfathomable harm she has experienced, Iliana dissociates herself from her body and the trauma inflicted on it. She sees her body "only as part of the darkness that concealed it from her eyes," and she views "the body that had been violated" as "a mere fraction of her existence," as she considers herself to be "far more than the sum of her spilled blood and her flesh that had been pierced." Iliana's use of the definite article *the* rather than the third-person possessive adjective *her* to describe her violated body reveals her need to distance herself from her corporeality to survive the trauma of her rape; her view of herself as more than a collection of parts illustrates her reliance on a rhetoric of willpower and resilience to move on after her assault. Iliana also adopts a medicalized discourse of rationality to explain the rape. Conceding that this reasoning protects her from going insane, she, like Aurelia, initially attributes the rape to Marina's mental illness; she believes, or tries to convince herself, that "her sister had not meant her any harm. It was her madness which had lashed out—a destructive madness incapable of making distinctions and as likely to be turned on Marina herself."[85]

When Marina assaults Iliana for a second time, however, Iliana no longer credits Marina's violence to her mental illness. Even in the moments that immediately precede the second attack, the narrative voice (inflected through Iliana) asserts, "There was no trace of sleep or madness in [Marina's] voice. Yet there was malice in her eyes." After the second violation, Iliana thinks, "Her sister knew. Her sister knew precisely what it was she'd done. She knew and was pleased that no one else would ever detect what it was she had destroyed. She knew and depended on shame to silence Iliana and to efface whatever self she'd been."[86] The repetition of the phrase *she knew* highlights Iliana's shift away from a medicalized rhetoric that would absolve Marina of accountability for her actions to one that holds Marina responsible for the harm she perpetrates on Iliana. Only after being violated twice does Iliana realize the dangers of treating medicalization as an excuse to condone Marina's violence.

In her depiction of Iliana's two rapes, Pérez deploys imagery and language that parallel the scene describing Marina's reimagining of her own rape. In so doing, Pérez relies on an uncanny doubling, as Sandín explains when commenting on the narrative's doubling of incestuous rape (that of Iliana by Marina and Anabelle by her father), one that Bhabha might claim to effect a displacement by virtue of its repetition.[87] Pérez also provides a type of Derridean doubling of a doubling, underscoring the ghostliness, cyclicality, and (re)production of harm. More important than an originary or individual moment of harm is its continual and collective repetition. Such repetition is only heightened by the analogous images and language Pérez uses to describe Marina's reconstructed rape and Iliana's rapes by Marina. Pérez marks these sequences with seeping blood; she describes Marina's "searing pain" and Iliana's "raging pain"; she details the "zipper cut[ting] into Marina's hips" and the "pubic hairs prick[ing] Iliana's shins," while painting Iliana's pain as "incisive as a blade"; she portrays Marina's recoiling limbs and Iliana's forsaking limbs; she describes Marina's attacker "thrust[ing] himself deeper into her womb" and Marina's "fist crash[ing] against Iliana's womb"; and she emphasizes the nausea both Marina and Iliana feel after their respective assaults. Even Iliana's self-loathing after the rape—"this blood in my veins which my sister has made me despise just as she has despised her own"— resembles Marina's internalized hatred following her rape.[88] Likewise, Iliana's resolve in the aftermath of her violation that she is more than the sum of her parts echoes Marina's belief after being raped that "her body might be snatched, but not her soul." The strikingly similar language, images, and character reactions position these moments together, despite the ways they bookend the narrative.

Marina's rape of her sister is doubled in the sense that she attacks Iliana twice in the same night, that it mirrors Marina's own (relived) assault, and that it echoes Anabelle's implied rape by her father; it is also doubled in that it hearkens back to Iliana's sexual assault while she is away at college. Although Pérez does not provide much information regarding Iliana's earlier assault, she includes telling details about the attack and the place where it transpires. In the novel's opening image,

Pérez immediately makes clear that the college environment is not "the ideal place of escape" Iliana had envisioned it to be. Instead, Pérez emphasizes the racial and geographic violence therein. She calls attention to the epithet "nigger" posted on the door to Iliana's dorm room, and she paints even the natural world as threatening, such that Iliana has no safe haven where she can retreat. In her fleeting descriptions of the college town, Pérez underscores its collective "hidden violence," connecting the racist and anti-Semitic slurs and images with the sexual assaults against women therein.[89] A recipient of "the town's hidden violence," Iliana is stalked and attacked by a fellow student while there.

Iliana recalls this assault twice in the narrative. The first time is when she distinguishes herself from Rebecca, who stands by Pasión. By contrast, Iliana remembers successfully having fought back against her attacker in college and determines that Rebecca should see a psychiatrist for staying with the man who beats her. The second time is just prior to the moment Marina rapes her. Iliana's recollection of her attack at these particular times links the violence the three sisters experience, such that the individual harm the three undergo forms part of a pattern of collective harm. Iliana views her own ability to fight back against the student who had forced himself on her as testament to a woman's ability to fight back against male-inflicted violence; this helps explain her reaction to Rebecca's refusal to leave Pasión. That Iliana fears Marina just as she had feared the stranger (although her fear of her sister is less "conspicuous") highlights a tragic irony, for it is Marina, not the male stranger, who is able to impose herself on Iliana without Iliana's having the strength to hurl Marina off her.[90]

The amount of harm inflicted on women's bodies positions the novel as a feminist text that exposes the damage done to "the geography closest in—the body."[91] As the feminist critic Adrienne Rich points out, the female body is just as much a geographical site as the external environment is. Highlighting the devastation wreaked on women's bodies, and juxtaposing this with an attention to the built environment, Pérez locates geographies within and outside the self. With this move, she "situate[s] the politics of women's experience[s] first and foremost in the core of the geographies of their own bodies" and connects these to "the violated bodies of [their] *antepasadas* (forebears)."[92] Despite Sandín's assertion that "incest is the supreme signifier of patriarchal violence in the book," Pérez's inclusion of multiple forms of gendered violence suggests that the commentary she provides about incest and violence more broadly defined extends beyond a critique of patriarchy.[93] Pérez also criticizes *other* modes of structural violence. This multilayered critique speaks to the intersectional concerns central to U.S. Third World feminism.

Indeed, in her portrayal of Marina, Pérez emphasizes the devastation exacted by institutionalized racism coupled with that inflicted by rape. Describing Marina's reimagined rape and Marina's rape of Iliana in such similar terms, Pérez links Marina with her own attacker, depicting her as recipient and perpetrator of mirroring assaults. Given Marina's racist fears of and assumptions about her rapist, the analogous language used to narrate her reconstructed violation and that of Iliana suggests that Marina has these same racial anxieties and presuppositions about herself. During her attack against Iliana, "hatred was visible in Marina's eyes: raw, unadulterated hatred that confirmed those times Iliana had detected glimmers of it but had dismissed it, times when her sister had said, 'You're so beautiful, so smart, so cool.' Hatred that now conveyed: *You think you're so special, so goddamn smart and cute! Let's see what you think of yourself after I'm through!*"[94] The repetition of the term *hatred* illustrates the degree to which Marina has developed the type of negating third-person consciousness outlined by Fanon in *Black Skin, White Masks*, an awareness of the self through the hateful and frightful eyes of others and an awareness that triggers shame and self-contempt.[95] Although Marina here projects this hatred onto Iliana, her transference of hate onto a relative underscores Marina's envy of her sister who, unlike Marina, does not give in to societal dictates that demand that women be relegated to the domestic sphere or that equate blackness with ugliness. Likewise, Marina's focus on Iliana's beauty here recalls the conversation between the two about men they find attractive, and it indicates how Marina's internalization of beauty myths not only perpetuates her self-imposed racial erasure but also causes her to hate those who manage to disavow or elide such myths. Marina's rape of her sister therefore can be read as an attempt at least to gain control over the body of someone else, especially since she feels as if the overwhelming institutional structures surrounding her prevent her from controlling her own.

It is impossible to understand the psychological and physical harm to which Marina is subjected and the harm she then inflicts on herself and her sister without considering the forms of harm meted out by structural forces. Attributing her actions to her mental illness, as Marina's parents do, strips Marina of agency and naturalizes her behavior without regard for the powerfully oppressive structures around her. This biologization and individualization of violence only perpetuates stereotypes that historically have pathologized women of color in this country. Instead, it is crucial to examine the societal forces that have implanted a lack of self-worth in Marina *in conjunction with* her mental illness—and the many variables that have contributed to her mental disorder—to begin to understand both Marina's pain and the actions to which it gives rise.

## Re-envisioning Power

To excuse Marina for being powerless because of her mental illness and to criticize Rebecca for not taking control of her life and leaving an abusive marriage, as Aurelia and Papito do, fails to account for the ways in which power is limited for impoverished women of color. This does not mean that such women have no access to power; it means that power cannot take on the same meaning for them as it does for those with (greater) racial, ethnic, socioeconomic, gender, or sexual privilege. Resiliency and perseverance, the two key concepts that the narrative voice insists are integral to "genuine power," sometimes are not enough to combat the ready sense of overwhelming shame.[96] To fight such shame, the oppressive structures at play need to be critically examined and revealed for the harm they themselves impose.

The novel's emphasis on responsibility and resilience in the wake of horrific harm can be linked to the Latina/o ideology of *sobreponerse* (overcoming adversity) and the Chicana/o concept of *rasquachismo*: "Tomás Ybarra-Frausto has described *rasquachismo* as practical inventiveness motivated by limited material conditions. . . . it originated and had its most organic manifestations in the expressive practices and ethos of the poor and working classes. . . . one of its fundamental premises . . . [is] the way in which 'resilience and resourcefulness spring from making do with what's at hand.'"[97] Rather than view the repeated stress on resilience in relation to dominant ideologies that foster the types of conditions conducive to keeping cycles of harm intact for impoverished communities of color, it is possible to view Pérez's final message in tandem with the ideas of *sobreponerse* and *rasquachismo*. The Latina/o philosophy of *sobreponerse* resonates with African American civil rights protest rhetoric of overcoming, and the Chicana/o philosophy of *rasquachismo* has activist roots, stemming from impoverished Latina/o (specifically Chicana/o) communities. Given the activist impulse undergirding these ideas, Pérez's ultimate emphasis on making the best out of the worst of situations and being able to adjust in turn accordingly can be seen as a call to political action and a cry for social change.

The language surrounding neoliberal principles of "pulling oneself up by one's bootstraps" is eerily similar to that of overcoming and "making do" that is associated with *sobreponerse* and *rasquachismo*, respectively, potentially (and problematically) making it difficult to discern Pérez's final message. Ending her novel with Iliana's realization that she possesses the strength to take "full responsibility for her life," that "any difficulties she encountered from then on would be hers to work out on her own," and that "her soul had transformed into a complex and resilient thing able to accommodate the best and the worst," Pérez could be considered to conclude her text with a neoliberal emphasis on individual responsibility and perseverance.[98] Indeed, Iliana's final determination that she needs to leave her parents' house to move forward with her life falls dangerously close to espousing an individualist, neoconservative ethos in which the individual places her needs above all else. However, the context undergirding Pérez's ultimate message proves critical in ascertaining its impulse.

Bringing racism, poverty, and (hetero)sexist ideologies to the fore of her text and highlighting their devastating effects, Pérez positions individual struggles and responsibilities in relation to collective, institutional forces. Through her subtle invocation of Rebecca's and Marina's Christianized names of conquest and her depiction of the horrors Papito, Anabelle, and Aurelia experience in Trujillo's Dominican Republic and in a hostile New York City environment respectively, Pérez underscores that the harm she depicts and the resilience that she emphasizes are multilayered and need to be understood within the geopolitical contexts from which they emanate. Even Iliana's decision to leave her house and realization that she alone is accountable for her life are set against her recognition that she will always be connected to her family: "Everything she had experienced; everything she continued to feel for those whose lives would be inextricably bound with hers; everything she had inherited from her parents and had gleaned from her siblings would aid her in her passage through the world."[99] With this juxtaposition, Pérez moves away from an individualist emphasis and alternatively underscores that the individual is tied to the collective. This does not mean that the individual is exclusively defined by the collective. It means that the two are entwined, such that while Iliana might need to be apart from her family, she still will always be a part of it, as it will always be a part of her. Reading the ending of *Geographies of Home* as invoking a neoliberal ideology therefore would fail to recognize the attention that Pérez devotes to the ways individuals and communities (need to) shape one another.

It is significant that Pérez provides this message through Iliana, the educated protagonist and arguable ethical voice of the narrative. She is her family's (and the narrative's) anomaly and hope. She is the anomaly from the moment she is born female, defying her siblings' alternating sexed birth order; she is the anomaly by virtue of her college education; she is the anomaly by being able to seek this elite education upstate, away from her family; and she is the anomaly by repeatedly insisting that there are ways out of the difficult situations her family faces and by finding ways out for herself in order to move on with her life. For these reasons, Iliana also represents her family's hope, as the one who is most likely to be able to escape the cycle of poverty in which the rest of her family lives and as the one who encourages her family members to believe that they too can escape the cycles of harm in which they find themselves. As a type of insider-outsider vis-à-vis her family, Iliana is positioned in an ambiguous space.

This ambiguity resembles the type of ambiguous subjectivity in Anzaldúa's *Borderlands* and that emphasized throughout *Intersections of Harm*; it also is paralleled in the characterization of home as fluid in *Geographies of Home*. Pérez bookends her novel by positioning Iliana in relation to the geographies of home she carries with her. At the narrative's start, a "disembodied voice" disrupts Iliana's sleep to tell her of her family's difficulties at home, correspondingly calling her there; at the narrative's close, Iliana realizes upon leaving her family's house that "she would leave no memories behind. All of them were her self. All of them were home."[100] Pérez accordingly underscores both the powerful hold and the mobility of home. Equating memories, self, and home, Pérez invokes notions of place as constructed and (U.S. Third World) feminist ideas of home as a plural site that is carried on one's back and never forgotten. More than being drawn to a physical site, Iliana is pulled toward the *idea* of home throughout the narrative, ultimately determining that home is something she will forever carry inside of her. That Iliana wishes to return home after being assaulted by Marina only to realize that "she was already there" elucidates the ambiguity of home; it speaks both to the observations by the Chicana/o studies scholar Richard Griswold del Castillo about the *barrio* as instilling "a feeling of being at home" *and* creating a sense of "despair" and to Doreen Massey's explanation that "home may be as much a place of conflict . . . as of repose."[101] Pérez's emphasis on the fluidity and constructedness of home additionally falls in line with feminist critiques of the idea of space as bounded and gendered. Ending her novel with Iliana's realization that she can no longer stay in her family's house but that she still will carry home with her, Pérez reveals Iliana's need to move away from the domestic sphere that is readily coded female while also demonstrating that home is about self and community. Much like the protagonist Esperanza in *The House on Mango Street,* who realizes that she *is* Mango Street and cannot and should not forget her roots once she is able to leave her neighborhood, Iliana recognizes the integral relationships among herself, her family, her home, and her community.[102] Even if home isn't the pretty place portrayed in Dick and Jane books, it still is home.

# 3 /  Madness's Material Consequences
in Ana Castillo's *So Far from God*

*For subaltern actors it is their land and* their *bodies that are at risk.*
—LAURA PULIDO, *ENVIRONMENTALISM AND ECONOMIC JUSTICE*

Ana Castillo's 1993 novel, *So Far from God,* is set in the predominantly Mexican American town of Tome, New Mexico, and focuses on subaltern communities whose lands and bodies are at risk.[1] The narrative revolves around one family in particular: that of Sofi (or Sofia), her largely absent husband, Domingo, and their daughters, Caridad, Loca, Esperanza, and Fe.[2] All of the female characters in the family experience some form of harm. To varying degrees, they are considered deviants by their own community, and each of the daughters dies by the novel's close. Castillo situates the injury to which her characters are subjected against a backdrop of land appropriation, environmental genocide, and war. Because of this backdrop, the individual devastation the characters experience acts as a microcosm for a larger sociopolitical and geopolitical commentary. Highlighting an integral connection between individual and collective harm, and portraying *so much* deadly harm, Castillo emphasizes the material consequences of sociopolitical oppression and geopolitical dispossession and underscores the frightening impact of political, patriarchal, and environmental corrosiveness on the individual characters and collective communities she depicts.

The harm that the protagonists experience needs to be contextualized in relation to their deviation from communal norms, for Castillo links their deviance, defiance, disease, and distress. Community members view Sofi and her daughters as deviant because they do not adhere to behaviors that the community deems morally acceptable or to which it can readily relate. Caridad defies gendered and (hetero)sexist norms through her initial promiscuity and subsequent love for a woman, and she isolates herself in a cave for a year. Loca, sometimes called La Loca or La Loca Santa, wears her aberrance in her very name; she shuns human contact, knows things she should not rationally know, and aligns herself with the natural and supernatural worlds. Esperanza expresses her defiance through her staunch feminist and *Raza* politics that lead her to pursue a college education and leave her hometown. Fe is so distraught after her fiancé Tom leaves her that she wails to the point that even her family describes her as "out of [her] mind."[3] And Sofi transgresses gender norms through her take-charge attitude and community activism.

Just as the female protagonists are branded aberrant by their community, they undergo irreparable and often inexplicable harm. Caridad is completely mangled from an assault by a supernatural force, only to be miraculously restored, and she dies by hurling herself off a cliff while fleeing from a male stalker. Loca dies at the age of three, is resurrected at her funeral, is subsequently diagnosed with epilepsy, and dies for the second and last time after she inexplicably is diagnosed with HIV and AIDS and after none of the medical treatments she receives works. Esperanza dies after being taken hostage while stationed in the Persian Gulf during the Persian Gulf War. Fe permanently damages her vocal chords from her incessant hollering after being dumped by her fiancé, and she dies after a gruesome struggle with cancer. Unlike her children, Sofi does not experience irreparable bodily injury. Her suffering stems from the grief of outliving all of her daughters.

Because the narrative is set in the U.S. Southwest during the Persian Gulf War, in an area that once belonged to Mexico and a region devastated by environmental destruction, the harm that the main characters undergo needs to be examined as more than just individual and more than fantastical or outrageous. Despite Castillo's use of tongue-in-cheek humor and exaggeration, and despite her inclusion of extraordinary happenings, reading *So Far from God* primarily as a *telenovela*, comedy, romance, allegory, or work of magical realism fails to (sufficiently) recognize the materiality of the body central to the text and the scathing sociopolitical and geopolitical commentary therein.[4] Castillo does not present the type of feminist politics that examines women's bodies through an exclusively discursive lens; she emphasizes the body's *corporeality*, calling for the type of material feminist reading put forth by the feminist critic Stacy Alaimo, who underscores the ethical importance of understanding human bodies in relation to the environment.[5] This is not to say that Castillo in no way deploys soap-operatic, comedic, romantic, allegorical, or magical elements; when she uses these, though, she does so to advance a politicized, U.S. Third World feminist, material feminist, and ecofeminist agenda.

This results in a blend that can be difficult to classify under one stylistic rubric. Even more confusing is the frequently paradoxical juxtaposition of content and tone. Although many of the events are horrific, the tone used to narrate these is sometimes humorous or bitingly caustic, leading to a variety of contradictory scholarly interpretations of this novel. To describe this text as either humorous or devastating, without explaining how it simultaneously is both, does not adequately attend to the book's central polemics. It is precisely the contradictory mix of the two that allows Castillo to comment on the intersectional types of harm faced by Mexican American women in the Southwest.

The confusion generated by the disconnect that often exists between what is depicted and how this material is depicted is purposefully defiant. The text's stylistic defiance of conventional understandings of literary form parallels the characters' defiance. Like the protagonists who are dismissed as deviant by their own communities, *So Far from God* itself is readily characterized as "wacky," branded as such on the back of its paperback cover. These parallel contradictions elucidate the type of ambiguity for which Castillo calls. Castillo relies on interstitiality and hybridity to delineate the type of third space articulated by Anzaldúa in *Borderlands*. I accordingly adopt an interstitial and intersectional approach to my analysis of *So Far from God*, relying on U.S. Third World feminism, material feminism, ecofeminism, and environmental and social justice theories and highlighting the intersections of environmental, bodily, and psychological harm.

## *Hijas de la* Malinche: Caridad's and Loca's Sexualized Harm

Caridad and Loca inherit La Malinche's legacy of sexualized harm.[6] Like La Malinche, whom writers like Gloria Anzaldúa, Cherríe Moraga, and Norma Alarcón have described as the raped indigenous mother of the Spanish conquest of the Americas, Caridad and Loca are both cast as deviant and worshipped by their community. Their bodies are also the sites of astonishing sexualized violence. Although neither character is construed as a traitor to her race in the same way that La Malinche has been depicted in the dominant Mexican (American) imaginary, Caridad and Loca occupy an ambiguous interstitial space as insider-outsiders in their communities, as both are shunned and revered at different points.

Town members read Caridad according to the ways she displays her body, much like Sofía's family in *How the García Girls Lost Their Accents* reads Sofía based on her presentation of herself as a woman with sexual desires. The reactions of the town members in *So Far from God*, like that of Sofía's father in Julia Alvarez's novel, play into gendered and racialized expectations of Mexican American (and Latina) women's docility and virginity and reveal the power of the virgin/whore dichotomy that Castillo challenges in her representation of Caridad. Castillo destabilizes this binary ideology by positioning Caridad as *both* virgin and whore. As Caridad's body undergoes intense transformations, the community members' attitudes toward Caridad shift. Before her body suffers its first major transmutation, she is dismissed by her community and viewed as a whore for flaunting herself in front of men and drawing excess attention to her body.

Caridad's control of her body is temporarily stripped from her when she experiences an assault by a supernatural force that leaves her utterly deformed. The description of her distorted appearance here elucidates her body's animalization and fragmentation. Likening her to a stray cat, cattle, and "a run-down rabbit," Castillo renders Caridad akin to one animal that wanders the streets without a home, another branded for the purposes of consumption, and another prey to larger beasts and vehicles. By comparing Caridad to a stray cat, Castillo emphasizes the dis-location that Caridad experiences upon being assaulted. Her corporeal fragmentation stems from her torn nipples and stabbed throat, causing her to undergo a tracheotomy to repair the damage. The loss of her nipples represents more than just the loss of a body part. Given that breasts are coded as defining features of female sexuality in Western thought, Caridad's mangled breasts arguably signify the loss of her female sexuality, a central marker of her self prior to her attack. Enduring a tracheotomy, meanwhile, affects her literal voice, impairing her ability to speak. Just as Loida Maritza Pérez highlights Anabelle's speechlessness, animalization, and objectification in *Geographies of Home*, Castillo portrays Caridad on her return home from the hospital as more of a thing, or a remnant of a thing, than a person: she describes Caridad as "what was left of her" rather than a woman character in her own right.[7]

Depicting Caridad's assault in such a gruesome manner, Castillo underscores the overwhelming violence to which Caridad is subject. This violence presents itself in the form of the attack itself and its material effects on the body, as well as the community's response to the assault. Although a supernatural force ultimately is understood to be responsible for the attack, Castillo does not shy away from emphasizing the tremendous harm that emanates from this supernatural force. While Castillo invokes supernatural elements here, it is critical not to downplay this event as a magical realist occurrence.[8] As Marta Caminero-Santangelo argues, *So Far from God* does not present magical elements under the rubric of magical realism: the characters construe the magical moments as extraordinary, not ordinary.[9] The shock elicited by the damage inflicted on Caridad by the supernatural force and the extremity of this damage underscore this point.

Before the characters determine that Caridad has been attacked by a supernatural thing, they believe that an individual harmed her. Yet not much effort is put into finding the attacker. Highlighting how the police do little to find the assailant, largely because they condemn how Caridad carries herself sexually, and emphasizing how the community forgets that the assault had ever transpired after some months go by, Castillo offers a scathing gender commentary about institutionalized power and community apathy and antipathy. The harm that Caridad undergoes extends beyond the assault that leaves her mutilated; it also consists of the gendered judgment and neglect she faces at the hands of the police and community.

In the same abrupt and astonishing manner in which Caridad is hurt, she later abruptly and astonishingly recovers, restored to her former physical appearance. She is not the same Caridad by any means, though. Before the attack, she delights in the company of men; afterward, she keeps to herself, emblematized through her year-long self-imposed isolation in a cave. When she leaves the cave, community members suddenly revere her, believing that she now has miraculous healing powers. Caridad decides to study under Doña Felicia, one of the town healers, and become a healer in her own right. Only after living like a hermit and hiding herself *and her body* from the world is Caridad worshipped, revealing the community's adherence to a strict virgin/whore dichotomy. When she displays her body to others, she is denigrated; when she conceals her body, she is venerated.

The community's shifting attitude toward Caridad relates to the sexualized ways they read her. After Caridad's isolation, she receives the nickname La Armitaña, or La Santa Armitaña, and she is likened to la Virgen de Guadalupe and the ghost of Lozen. The appositive Armitaña arguably is a feminization of the Spanish word *ermitaño* (hermit), and the *santa* (saint) stems from the divine powers community members think Caridad now possesses. These perceived powers stem from the herculean strength she has developed after her lengthy isolation from human contact. Eventually, however, the *santa* is dropped from her nickname. That Caridad ever is labeled a saint, though, speaks to the mythical martyr figure Saint Charity whom she could be considered to allegorize.[10] When she is worshipped as a saint, Caridad is also compared to La Virgen de Guadalupe. This analogy is significant because La Virgen de Guadalupe is a symbol of moral good and cultural and religious hybridity.[11] Like her, Caridad occupies a both/and positioning. The historical association of La Virgen de Guadalupe with rebellion also ties into Caridad's rumored incarnated spirit of the ghost of Lozen, a woman warrior and "sister of the great chief Victorio who had vowed 'to make war against the white man forever'" and "who alerted others when the enemy approached."[12] That Caridad is likened to La Malinche and La Virgen de Guadalupe, referred to as La (Santa) Armitaña, and thought of as the ghost of Lozen situates her alongside mystical and powerful women dismissed or worshipped because of their defiance, revered for their faith and spiritual guidance, or admired for their revolutionary prowess. She thus stands for more than the charity symbolized by her birth name. She embodies the ambiguity and interstitiality characteristic of the type of borderlands, *mestiza* consciousness articulated by Anzaldúa and the ambiguity and interstitiality that lie at the intersections of psychological, physical, and geopolitical harm that Latina protagonists experience.

Caridad occupies a third space in the multiple names she possesses and the many ways she is constructed by others as well as the sexual binaries she challenges. She cannot remain in this in-between space in the living world for very long, however. After her uncanny recuperation from her assault, she falls in love with a woman, defying traditional heterosexist gender ideologies, this time not because of her promiscuity but because of her romantic feelings for a woman named Esmeralda. Although Esmeralda is in a relationship with another woman (María) and is an unattainable love interest for Caridad, she and Caridad become close. But even the platonic intimacy they share is perceived as a threat to the patriarchal power and institutionalized religion that Caridad's stalker, Francisco el Penitente, personifies. Obsessed with Caridad, Francisco closely follows her and Esmeralda, eventually and mysteriously abducting Esmeralda outside of the rape crisis center where she works, and ultimately pursuing the two women by car. Like the end of the cult classic feminist film *Thelma and Louise,* when Thelma and Louise are being chased by the police and drive off a cliff presumably to their deaths, Caridad and Esmeralda hold hands as they run from Francisco and jump off a cliff to their untimely demise.[13]

It is possible to read this scene through an indigenist, romantic, or even feminist lens that would destabilize an interpretation of Caridad's and Esmeralda's deaths as tragic, as the literary critics Theresa Delgadillo and Ralph Rodriguez do. Although Delgadillo does not dismiss the harm that Caridad or Esmeralda suffers at the hands of Francisco, she maintains that this scene evokes indigenous images of birth and rebirth, such that the deaths need not be viewed as an "end" in the manner in which death tends to be construed in Western thought. Rodriguez similarly focuses on Castillo's mention of the spirit god Tsichtinako calling Caridad and Esmeralda to the earth, "guiding the two women back . . . down, deep within the soft, moist dark earth where Esmeralda and Caridad would be safe and live forever."[14] That Castillo invokes the notion of eternal life in this passage and has the two characters return to the earth to be part of it feeds into Rodriguez's analysis of this scene as romantic, just as it ties into Castillo's ecocritical commentary that we all are part of the earth and need to respect it. Likewise, Castillo's prioritization of indigenist elements in this scene highlights the disparate religiosities embodied by Caridad and Esmeralda and those embodied by Francisco. As Delgadillo notes, this scene offers a critique of the patriarchy associated with the institutionalized religion Francisco represents: Caridad and Esmeralda's jump off a cliff can be seen as a literal and figurative flight from the patriarchy and religiosity associated with Francisco. Reading this scene in these ways, with particular attention to Castillo's invocation of Tsichtinako and insinuation that death is not necessarily a marker of tragedy but instead a marker of safety and eternal life, corresponds with my assertion that *So Far from God* advances a hybrid, interstitial, feminist, and ecocritical ideology.[15]

However, *exclusively* analyzing Caridad's and Esmeralda's deaths through an indigenist lens and interpreting this scene as romantic instead of tragic fails to fully recognize the devastating harm to which both female characters are subjected. Even if their bodies are swallowed whole by the earth, leaving them physically intact, "There weren't even whole bodies lying peaceful. There was nothing."[16] Whereas Caridad is described according to her residual fragments after she is assaulted, she is depicted by the contrasting lack thereof in her death. But the lack does not mean that she has been exempt from experiencing unspeakable injury: she and Esmeralda have been stalked; Esmeralda has been abducted (and who knows what else) by a zealot; and both characters throw themselves off a cliff while running from this same fanatic. Even if Caridad and Esmeralda "live forever" in their deaths, their bodies vanish from the face of the earth, so that there is nothing left for their families to bury. Castillo's emphasis on the word *nothing* underscores the profound emptiness that follows from Caridad's and Esmeralda's deaths.[17]

Like Caridad, Loca is subject to mysterious, sexualized, and premature deathly harm. Caridad and Loca are the only family members to possess clairvoyant and healing powers, and they are the only sisters to practice folkloric medicine. They also are the two characters most readily dismissed as deviant by their community and the two most readily revered by this same community. Loca is even positioned as a Jesus-like figure who is cast aside and subsequently worshipped. Both Caridad and Loca are accordingly depicted as anything but ordinary.

From the beginning of the narrative, Castillo shows just how unusual Loca is by describing how she, like Jesus and Saint Christina the Astonishing, is resurrected. Like Christina the Astonishing, Loca comes from poverty, suffers from seizures, travels to hell while her family grieves for her, flies to the roof during her own funeral, avoids human contact, and is repulsed by human smells.[18] Both are viewed by others as "crazy" iconoclasts who are later revered. And like Christina the Astonishing, considered the patron saint of the mentally ill, Loca wears her perceived saintliness and madness in her very name. Indeed, after she comes back from the dead during her own funeral, Loca's birth name is replaced with her moniker: La Loca Santa, La Loca, or simply Loca. Like the inhabitants of Tome, the reader too knows this character only by her appositives. Neither the community members, readers, Loca's family, nor even Loca herself remembers or knows of Loca as anyone other than the permanent bearer of madness and occasional bearer of saintliness, as the *santa* is only sometimes included as part of her name.[19] The absence of any name other than Loca by which to call or recall her emphasizes the extent to which she is identified by others' perceptions of her behavior as well as the degree to which she has so internalized these perceptions that she responds only when called crazy.

Just as Loca's name is tied to saintliness and madness, the term *loca* is associated with sexuality and deviance.[20] According to the Latina/o studies scholar Lourdes Torres, "['loca'] is one of the many names used for Lesbians in Hispanic and Latina contexts." Torres elaborates, "Although these words are often used in derogatory ways, Hispanic and Latina lesbians have reappropriated many of them as affirming identity markers."[21] Loca's sexual orientation is never discussed in the novel; if anything, her aversion to human contact positions her as asexual. Yet toward the end of *So Far from God,* she is puzzlingly diagnosed with the human immunodeficiency virus and later said to have contracted AIDS. That she receives this diagnosis medicalizes and sexualizes her, as HIV and AIDS historically have been (mis)construed as diseases primarily contracted by "overly sexual" individuals. Portraying Loca as a virgin who contracts a disease associated with hypersexuality in the popular imagination, Castillo highlights how Loca, like Caridad, destabilizes the virgin/whore dichotomy prevalent in Mexican American thought. What is more, Loca's sexualized medicalization locates her in a liminal space and further punctuates her deviance, especially since HIV and AIDS have been linked to "deviant" behavior in the popular imagination. Mainstream society perpetuates a culture of fear by readily labeling HIV-positive individuals and individuals with AIDS "irresponsible" for making sexual choices that have put them in harm's way and suggesting that these individuals potentially endanger their communities as well. Within these dominant discourses, HIV and AIDS thus stand at the crossroads where individual and collective meet.[22]

Apart from its link to sexuality and deviance, the word *loca*, in the context of Castillo's narrative, can also be tied to suffering or ghostliness. Naming Loca as she does, Castillo arguably nods to Alice Walker's *In Search of Our Mothers' Gardens* and Moraga's "Pesadilla" in *Loving in the War Years.* In her compilation of essays, Walker explains that black women in the 1920s experienced tremendous bodily harm and were described as "crazy Saints" who were absented from their personhood and whose "bodies became shrines."[23] The similar language and characterization in Castillo's and Walker's texts are striking. Not only does Castillo translate the "crazy Saint" into Spanish in her name choice, but she highlights how both her crazy saint and Caridad are treated as objects of religious worship who likewise undergo unfathomable harm. Walker's and Castillo's analogous depictions of "crazy Saints" suggest that parallels potentially can be drawn between the historical (mis) treatment of black and brown women, despite the groups' differences. This similarity across difference locates *So Far from God* within a collective tradition of writings about women of color.

Castillo's choice to name her character La Loca also undoubtedly invokes Moraga's character of the same name, La Loca, of "Pesadilla." Although it is not uncommon to refer to a character as *loca*, it is unusual to *name* one Loca; it is even more unusual to place the Spanish definite article *la* before it. That the *la* is capitalized marks it as part of the characters' names, but it also highlights the objectification of the characters since articles generally are used before common nouns, not proper ones. Considering the rarity of the name, Moraga's "canonicity" in Chicana literature and feminist theory, and Castillo's explicit references to *Loving in the War Years* in her work *Massacre of the Dreamers*, it seems likely that Castillo is referencing Moraga's La Loca through her own La Loca. Moraga mentions her La Loca in only three paragraphs of "Pesadilla"; however, as Christina Sharpe remarks, La Loca haunts the entire story. Castillo's Loca is ever-present in *So Far from God*, as her role is overtly central to the narrative and as her deaths bookend the text. That Castillo arguably is alluding to Moraga's character of the same name only bolsters the ghostliness associated with *So Far from God*'s La Loca Santa.

The ghostliness tied to Las Locas in Moraga's and Castillo's stories is magnified by their associations with the Mexican (American) folkloric figure La Llorona, the weeping woman who allegedly drowned her children to run off with a man. According to popular legend, La Llorona is a type of boogie woman who wanders by bodies of water at night howling for her lost children; young children accordingly are warned to steer clear of her and the bodies of water she supposedly haunts. In much the same way in which Chicana feminists have reclaimed La Malinche, they also have reclaimed La Llorona, arguing against her ready construction as a deviant woman and instead suggesting that she is a resistant figure who has been the recipient of manifold forms of harm. The Latina/o studies scholar Domino Renee Pérez points out that what unites the disparate portrayals of La Llorona is an association of her with "physical and communal loss."[24]

The relationship between La Llorona and loss is evident in both Moraga's and Castillo's depictions of their Las Locas. In her reading of "Pesadilla," Sharpe maintains, "La Loca is La Llorona."[25] If Moraga's La Loca is La Llorona, and if Castillo's La Loca is tied to her literary namesake, then it follows that Castillo's Loca also is La Llorona, or at least is connected to her in some way. That *So Far from God*'s Loca knows of La Llorona without having had anyone tell her about the figure's legend, and that La Llorona appears to Loca regularly by the irrigation ditch, informing her of her sister Esperanza's death, links Loca to La Llorona and destabilizes the ready characterization of La Llorona as a woman to be feared. La Llorona here functions as a truth bearer, not a monster to be avoided. As María DeGuzmán asserts, "In Anzaldúan fashion, *So Far from God* transvalues La Llorona from a Lilith-like monster to a long-suffering heroine."[26] La Llorona's transvaluation aside, the lament and sorrow that typify her are connected to the suffering associated with Moraga's and Castillo's Las Locas.

Both Las Locas are described as suffering women. Moraga writes, "¿Quién sabe la pena que sufría esa mujer?"[27] With this question, Moraga highlights La Loca's pain, sorrow, and suffering, but the question is also rhetorical, as Moraga never pinpoints the cause of her La Loca's *pena* or *sufrimiento*. All Moraga includes is a glimpse of La Loca's pain and rage, so powerful that they seep into her surrounding environment and permanently remain even after she has left. Castillo's Loca's individual suffering, meanwhile, most evidently is made manifest in the corporeal damage that befalls her: her body withers, and she ultimately dies after a presumed battle with AIDS. But the suffering Castillo's Loca endures is more than just physical or individual, as she outlives each of her sisters, witnesses the harm each of them undergoes, and forms part of a community plagued by environmental genocide.

When *So Far from God*'s Loca sees Caridad and Fe experience seemingly irreparable harm, she helps them heal, much as Christina the Astonishing is said to have devoted her life to healing others. When Esperanza is a prisoner of war in the Persian Gulf, Loca is the first to learn that her sister has died. Despite Loca's lack of formal education, she somehow possesses detailed knowledge about women's bodies and holistic medicine, demonstrating that the ability to care for and heal others need not stem from scientific training alone. Loca's innate gynecological knowledge enables her to perform three abortions on Caridad (before Caridad's isolation in a cave), and her connection to La Llorona puts her in a position to let her family know that Esperanza has died, finally allowing them to grieve. When Fe neglects herself after her fiancé Tom leaves her, Loca cleans and feeds her. Immediately after Caridad's body returns to its former physical state prior to its mutilation by a supernatural force and after Fe's incessant wails upon being abandoned by Tom cease, Loca states that she had prayed for both sisters. The emphasis given to Loca's prayers positions them as potentially responsible for her sisters' miraculous recoveries, and the ways Loca cares for her sisters highlight her curative and spiritual powers.

Although Loca is able to care for her sisters and help them heal, she is unable to do the same for herself. Despite her immunity to infirmities throughout most of her years, the beginning and end of her life are framed by illness and death. Upon returning from her proclaimed death at the age of three, she is subsequently diagnosed with epilepsy, this time by a different medical practitioner than the one who previously declared her dead. Although her diagnosis explains her seizures according to modern medicinal labeling theory, it neither accounts for her apparent death as a toddler nor does it consider alternative explanations for the seizures, which may have nothing at all to do with illness. For instance, according to *curandería* (or *curanderismo*), a healing practice common in Mexican American cultures and prevalent in the community depicted in *So Far from God*, seizures do not necessarily correspond to a recognizable illness. Instead, they may represent a connection with a divine force of some kind—the thrashing movements sometimes are seen as a sign that a divine force has possessed the person. Understanding Loca's seizures through the framework of *curandería* then would establish a link between Loca's seizures and resurrection that mainstream medical thought would likely dismiss. By positing Loca's death as a toddler as something that *actually* occurred (as Sofi does years later), Castillo emphasizes that certain things just cannot be explained according to the dictates of rationality or scientific reasoning upon which mainstream medical thought is built. Indeed, the novel's emphasis on the supernatural and deviation from rationality reveals the importance of acknowledging the "other mode[s] of consciousness" readily branded "pagan superstition" that Anzaldúa prioritizes in *Borderlands*.[28]

At the end of *So Far from God*, the inexplicable recurs, as Loca is told that she has HIV, even though "there was no way Loca could have gotten it."[29] Here Castillo again provides an ambiguous portrait of mainstream medicine, and she reveals the benefits of what Delgadillo might term a hybrid practice, whereby mainstream and folkloric medicine inform one another.[30] When Sofi notices that Loca seems to lose interest in the things for which she previously cared and begins to undergo dramatic physical changes, Sofi decides to phone Doctor Tolentino, the family doctor. Castillo describes the doctor and his wife in notable detail; she comments on the doctor's long-standing role in the community; and she mentions his familiarity with the community at large and Sofi's family in particular, having delivered all of Sofi's children as well as Sofi herself. Castillo also distinguishes Doctor Tolentino from the modern mainstream medical system that no longer accommodates home visits. Just as he is part of this medical system by virtue of his training, yet distanced from it since he is an "old-fashioned" doctor, he and his wife occupy an in-between insider-outsider status in the Tome community. Castillo illustrates this ambiguous positioning in her characterization of Doctor Tolentino as a Filipino in a predominantly Mexican American township, her emphasis on the fact that he "was not a native to the area," and her description of his Anglo wife as having deep roots in the area.[31] The doctor and his wife lead private lives, setting them apart from the Mexican American community for whom collective knowledge is a marker of community membership. Yet despite the Tolentinos' separation from the Tome community, community members still view them as belonging therein, partly because of their proficiency in Spanish and partly because of the doctor's belief in old-school medicine and willingness to treat patients in their homes.

The Tolentinos are portrayed in an even more ambiguous fashion when they visit Loca prior to her ultimate death. Sofi phones the doctor to determine what is ailing Loca because, "aside from the unexplainable weight loss, Loca also had a sore throat all the time, not to mention that she couldn't stay awake or do nothing no more. She just plain did not seem to care much about nothing." Loca's symptoms suggest a literal and figurative loss of voice; her characterization at this point markedly contrasts with earlier ones of her active caring for others and her previous fascination with nature and its elements. Given such a shift in Loca's mental and physical state, Sofi assumes that her daughter is suffering from depression, especially since by now all three of Loca's sisters have died. However, when Sofi asks the doctor whether her daughter is depressed, both Tolentinos dismiss her, and the doctor hastily claims that Loca has HIV. Sofi's immediate reaction is to draw on her knowledge of the virus and question the diagnosis. How could her reclusive, virginal daughter, who has avoided human contact at all costs and who has kept herself isolated in her home and the neighboring irrigation ditch throughout her entire life, have contracted the virus? Readers too are likely to ask this question given common knowledge about how HIV can spread. Castillo also places doubts in readers' minds about Doctor Tolentino's abilities—"by the time he came to see Loca . . . his eyes were not what they used to be. And there was something particularly disturbing about that cough of his, especially since he smoked those smelly cigars all the time"—even though immediately after listing these misgivings she states that the doctor still "looked as able as" he had way back when.[32] For all of these reasons, Castillo here calls the doctor's credibility into question.

Sofi, however, quickly silences herself and defers to the doctor's authority, dismissing her own common sense knowledge and privileging his assertions by virtue of his vocation: "Doctor Tolentino was a doctor so he couldn't be wrong and she said nothing." Although Sofi thinks about getting a second opinion and running tests to figure out what is wrong with her daughter, the doctor "stop[s] her thoughts" and appeals to her sense of faith to trust in both him, as a "devotee of the Lord," and God, who he claims is the only one who really has any power to help Loca. The doctor's actions here echo those found in the epigraph to *Intersections of Harm*, in which the dentist in *Borderlands* tries to control the female patient's wild tongue. Just as the dentist tries to tame his patient's tongue, Doctor Tolentino suppresses Sofi's tongue. He goes beyond silencing Sofi's words and silences her *thoughts*, imposing his authority as medical practitioner over her power as Loca's mother. His wife too asserts her position of strength as "La Mrs. Doctor" and reiterates her husband's fatalistic plea, invoking prayer as the necessary course of action.[33] But her face is caked with powder, underscoring her artificiality and undermining the sincerity of her and her husband's words.

Just after mentioning the wife's heavily powdered face, though, Castillo again illustrates how Doctor Tolentino occupies an interstitial space, and she arguably repositions him as a figure of trust. In this way, he differs from Anzaldúa's dentist, who in no way is situated in an interstitial space. Although Doctor Tolentino went to the same medical school as his father, he learned some of his healing techniques from his mother (who at no point is said to have received school training for the treatments she passed down to her son). The doctor's inheritance of patriarchal *and* matriarchal methods of caring for others locates him in an in-between, hybrid space. His use of one of the treatments that he learned from his mother on Loca upon diagnosing her with HIV also reveals how modern and folkloric medicine complement one another, and it troubles his otherwise gendered silencing of Sofi's thoughts.

Even the description of the procedure and the characters' reactions to it are complicated. Castillo highlights the invasiveness and futility of the surgery performed on Loca, but she also comments on Loca's fascination with the surgery that does nothing to help her heal. Castillo details the blood clot, cystic fibroids, and ovarian tumor that have been wreaking damage on Loca's body and that Doctor Tolentino removes. The lasting physical effects of the procedure itself are evident in the visible "red mark across Loca's belly"; the intangible, psychological imprint left on her is noticeable in that "La Loca wasn't the same Loca no more." Just as Doctor Tolentino sticks his hand into Loca's body to remove the dangerous growths, it is "as if [he] had stuck his hand into [Sofi's] head and pulled out her thoughts" to warn her not to "forget [her] faith."[34] The repetition of the gesture, even if it is phrased as unreal (through the use of "as if" followed by the past perfect subjunctive verb tense), situates them together and underscores the invasiveness of both moves. Using the term *warned* rather than *encouraged* in relation to the doctor's summoning Sofi to be faithful, Castillo implies that he is forcefully implanting religiosity within her rather than suggesting that she might want to turn to religion of her own accord to help her cope with her last living daughter's impending death. The harm here is thus manifold: it presents itself in the corporeal devastation theoretically inflicted by AIDS on Loca's body, the permanent scars left on Loca's body following her surgery, and the imposition of power the doctor and his wife wield over Sofi.[35] Loca, however, responds with wonder instead of dread to the procedure Doctor Tolentino performs on her. Although she is alert during the "psychic surgery," Loca is said to be "fascinated" and feeling "no pain," suggesting that the damage her body inflicts on itself far surpasses the harm she otherwise would experience during the medical procedure.[36] Describing the procedure as a "psychic surgery," even though the doctor is operating on Loca's *body*, Castillo also highlights the type of material feminist conflation of body with mind, negating the ready dissociation of the two in dominant Western thought. By inflicting harm and instilling wonder, the surgery accordingly is indicative of the complex and contradictory portrait of the Tolentinos.

The surgery is not the only treatment Loca receives. Doña Felicia and a few other town healers visit Loca to impart their own forms of folkloric medicine. By the time they try to help alleviate some of Loca's symptoms, Sofi's aforementioned questions regarding Loca's diagnosis seem to have vanished, as all accept the AIDS diagnosis as fact. Just as Doctor Tolentino cannot save Loca from imminent death, neither can Doña Felicia nor the other *curanderas*. Despite their different training and treatment practices, both Doctor Tolentino and Doña Felicia invoke prayer as part of their healing methods. And while Castillo points out that faith can be problematic in its own right—exemplified in her portrayal of Francisco el Penitente, whose devotion turns into obsession, and her depiction of the Tolentinos as implanting religiosity in Sofi—she nonetheless emphasizes the benefits of prayer in times of need. Castillo's characterization of Doctor Tolentino's and Doña Felicia's similar turns to prayer prior to treating Loca corresponds with the centrality of prayer in *curandería*, and it effectively reinforces Doctor Tolentino's interstitial positioning and underscores the importance of hybrid modes of care.[37] Although neither mainstream medicine nor folkloric medicine—emblematized through Doctor Tolentino and Doña Felicia, respectively—can cure Loca, Castillo emphasizes that the two modes of care need to operate together. Indeed, after pointing out that Doctor Tolentino and Doña Felicia alike perform prayer rituals before treating others, Castillo describes how the two collegially converse about remedies they know and bond over their non-native status in Tome, writing, "It may be said in the end that they did have much in common."[38] Ending the chapter prior to Loca's death in such a way, Castillo emphasizes the importance of hybrid practices for the sake of holistic care.

## The Nothing That Remains: Esperanza's and Fe's Absent(ed) Bodies

Whereas Castillo positions Caridad and Loca in an interstitial space, she highlights Esperanza's and Fe's contrasting lack of ambiguity. Rather than illustrate how Esperanza and Fe are read, reread, and misread by fellow town members, as Caridad and Loca are, Castillo provides a more straightforward portrait of these two siblings. Like their sisters, though, Esperanza and Fe are depicted as deviant in their own ways. Castillo draws particular attention to their absent(ed) and tortured bodies: Esperanza's body is declared missing when she goes to report on the Persian Gulf War, and it is never recovered; Fe's body is ravaged after a battle against more than one form of cancer. While Caridad and Loca undergo a harm that could be construed as sexualized, Esperanza and Fe experience a harm that is more explicitly racialized. Castillo implicates the U.S. government and institutionalized structures of power in the harm that befalls Esperanza's and Fe, and she reveals how Esperanza and Fe's fatalities are connected to the deadly damage affecting communities of color in general and Mexican American women more specifically.

Esperanza's deviance manifests itself through her feminist and *Raza* politics. Like Iliana in *Geographies of Home*, Esperanza defies gender norms that relegate women to the domestic sphere, pursuing a college education and fighting for the development of a Chicano studies curriculum there. She in turn is labeled "revolutionary" by Tome community members and by her sister Fe, who, in many ways, is her opposite in Fe's rigid adherence to conventional gender roles. Unlike Fe, Esperanza continues her activism and becomes a news broadcaster. Her interest in her professional advancement and her need "to get [far] away" from her family cause her to go to Saudi Arabia to cover the Persian Gulf War for a major television network. Yet her ethnicity implicitly plays a major role in her *station's* decision to send her to report on the war. As her father points out, it is not as if the station is sending the reporter with the most experience, someone "like la Diana Sawyer," to the Middle East.

By sending Esperanza, the station instead is arguably suggesting that a reporter *like* Esperanza is dispensable. When Esperanza informs her family about the assignment, "she saw in their eyes that despite their naïveté about the things that happened in the world, they were well aware of what that assignment meant. So many men and women throughout the state had been shipped off in the last months because of the imminent global crisis."[39] Signaling the large number of New Mexicans serving in the war, and considering the sizable Latina/o (and specifically Mexican American) population in that state, Castillo illustrates how the bodies and lives of people of color are the ones most notably sacrificed in times of war.[40]

While stationed in the Persian Gulf, Esperanza becomes a prisoner of war, and her photograph becomes a regular fixture on the nightly news. Once the war ends, though, "people seemed to be losing interest, and in the meantime Sofi's girl was still missing." Admittedly her family has already learned that Esperanza died, thanks to the visitations Loca receives informing her that Esperanza "got killed over there. Tor . . . tured." The ellipsis splitting the word *tortured* draws attention to the dis-location Esperanza's body undergoes. By representing something so horrific that it cannot be named, but rather, as a type of gasp, disrupts utterance, the ellipsis emphasizes the extremity of the torment to which Esperanza is subject before dying. When army officials confirm that Esperanza has died, the family still does not have a corpse to bury, for the army officials "claimed to not be able to locate her body so as to send it home." In death, Esperanza's body undergoes a dis-location that parallels her missing state prior to her demise. Earlier in the narrative, Castillo similarly describes Esperanza as "still missing in the Persian Gulf." The repetition of the phrase *still missing* that evokes a doubling, or at least a continuation, of its own through the adverb *still* illustrates just how long Esperanza's family is left in limbo wondering whether Esperanza is dead or alive. Castillo highlights the degree to which Esperanza has been absented from her body by describing her last "traces" as displaced onto material objects or ghostly footprints: "The last traces of her . . . were [her] abandoned jeep, six thousand dollars in cash, camera equipment, and footsteps in the sand leading toward enemy lines."[41] Although the college-educated protagonist who arguably signifies hope (considering the literal translation of her name) returns to visit her family ectoplasmically, she, like her sister Caridad, leaves her family without a corpse to bury. Showing how all that remains of Esperanza are material objects and ephemeral footprints, Castillo underscores Esperanza's profound dis-location and emphasizes the overwhelming harm to which she has been subject.

The U.S. Army's proclamation of Esperanza as "an American hero" and conferral of a posthumous medal do nothing to minimize the loss or downplay the family's frustration with the army or the government. After all, Castillo suggests that the army and the government, by extension, are keeping information from Esperanza's family about the circumstances surrounding her disappearance and death. Sofi and Domingo go to Washington, D.C., multiple times while Esperanza is missing to see if any official can help them. Instead of receiving aid, "they were sent to one office, then to another. Everyone in Washington seemed sympathetic to them, but no one had an answer. Each time Esperanza's parents returned more frustrated and sadder than when they left."[42] Sofi and Domingo do not receive any answers because they do not have the insider status needed to access the information they desperately seek. Through her portrayal of the surreptitious army and government officials and through Esperanza's rants about President George H. W. Bush and the Persian Gulf War during her ectoplasmic visits with her family, Castillo provides a staunch critique of U.S. governmental policies.

This critique carries over into Castillo's depiction of Fe and the multifaceted harm that Fe experiences. At one level, this harm presents itself through Fe's internalization of dominant Western ideas about self and society, an internalization similar to that of Rebecca in *Geographies of Home*. Although Fe's name translates as *faith*, the faith she has is not in a deity but in an allegiance to pervasive patriarchal and neoliberal ideologies about gender, individualism, and success. Unlike her defiant sister Esperanza, Fe has absorbed the societal myths that dictate what women's lot in life should be. She is consumed with the idea that she must marry and abide by gendered grooming norms. As with Pérez's Rebecca, only when Fe is attempting to capture the attention of a man is she concerned with her looks. When Fe's fiancé Tom leaves her, she no longer bothers to notice these elements that had been so important to her beforehand, and she neglects to care for herself. Her fixation on her image for the sake of male attention and utter disregard for her appearance upon being abandoned by Tom speaks to Elaine Showalter's observations about the relations among femininity, grooming, and madness. Like Showalter, who notes that "proper" grooming was linked to ideas of female normalcy and that excess grooming was associated with female madness during the Victorian age, Castillo reveals the relations among dress, (in)sanity, and control in her portrayal of Fe. That Fe is excessively concerned with her looks when she is dating Tom and excessively unconcerned with her looks when she is suddenly single situates her alongside a trajectory of women deemed mad. Indeed, once Tom leaves her, Fe completely lets herself go: "Now it was Sofi and her daughters who took turns feeding, cleaning, and dressing poor Fe, who was truly a mess and who—if she were in any way capable of realizing it—would have been horrified at that thought."[43] Fe's abrupt and complete transition from one who has always taken great pains to keep order in her life in every way possible to one who depends on others for her basic upkeep shows the extent to which her appearance is connected to her sense of control over herself. When the societal expectation that a woman should marry seems within her reach, she preoccupies herself with her looks; when this anticipation no longer seems available, Fe's self-image shatters along with the image she projects to those around her.

Not only does Fe give in to societal myths about "proper" gender roles, but she also holds fast to destructive neoliberal ideas about self and society. She fervently believes in the tenets of the American Dream: she desperately yearns to be a wife and mother, and she insists that if she just works hard enough, she can get ahead and "make it." Unfortunately, the damaging power of this individualist ethos that is perpetuated by dominant mythologies and advanced by institutional structures of control leads to her undoing at more than one point in her life. When the first part of her American Dream seems out of reach after Tom leaves her, Fe falls apart. She not only fails to pay attention to her appearance, but she neglects to care for her body as a whole. As she wails nonstop, she is granted the nickname La Gritona (the one who yells/hollers). With this nickname, Fe is likened to La Llorona, whose signature trait is her persistent howl. Associated with La Llorona in this way, Fe forms part of a legacy of spurned women deemed mad.

Due to her incessant cries, Fe "severely damage[s] her vocal chords," such that when she finally speaks, not all of her words come out. Just as her speech pattern is marked by ellipses after her constant hollers, "when she spoke now her voice was scratchy-sounding, similar to a faulty World War II radio transmitter." Possessing a voice that is likened to an inanimate object and no longer being able to convey complete sentences or ideas, nor to maintain the same crisp cadence when she speaks, Fe's body itself reveals just how broken she has become: she has lost her ability to express herself clearly. Not wanting to believe that she could be responsible for inflicting such destruction on herself, she attributes the damage to a sickness, "which she thought must have been terrible indeed since no one at home ever wanted to talk about it, so that eventually she herself had to give it a name." She settles on "adult measles."[44] Medicalizing herself in this way, while refusing to acknowledge the real reason why she kept herself isolated from the outside world during her heartbreak, Fe physicalizes what others would readily characterize as a type of mental breakdown. She renders the psychological physical, and the brokenness of her literal voice vividly elucidates just how much psychological pain can lead to corporeal damage.

Eventually, though, Fe moves on with her life, clinging to hopes that she can somehow still attain the American Dream that she so eagerly craves. And, for a fleeting period, it seems that this sought-after dream is within reach: Fe marries her cousin Casey; she switches jobs—from banker to assembly worker at a company called Acme International, a company that manufactures parts for war weapons and financially compensates its workers based on productivity; and she even becomes pregnant. Monetarily rewarded for her work ethic, in a marriage with a man who worships her, and with a nuclear family of her own forthcoming, Fe appears to be on her way to realizing the ever-elusive American Dream. As soon as this dream is about to become a reality, however, it promptly shatters.

Here is where Castillo's critique of institutionalized power (represented through Acme International), the U.S. government, and neoliberalism notably comes into play. In her analysis of *So Far from God*, Kamala Platt holds Fe at least partly responsible for her own demise because Fe does not question the work that she does, even though it is quite obvious that this work hurts her and others. Platt raises an important point about the ways personal and structural responsibility cannot be neatly disentangled, and, as she suggests, there are bitter ironies in Fe's devotion to the work that ultimately kills her and perhaps her sister Esperanza as well. But there is a significant difference between an individual—particularly one who lacks race, gender, and class privilege—who buys into neoliberal ideologies imposed from above and without and a company that capitalizes on such pervasive mythologies for the sake of building its military arsenal. There is an even bigger difference between an individual who notes that something is "off" about her workplace but does not know exactly what is going on and a company that knowingly imperils its workers—who most notably are working-class women of color. While I agree with Platt that Castillo is not ignoring the question of personal responsibility, there is a danger in placing blame on Fe for the harm that befalls her, especially as doing so downplays the tremendous power of the institutional forces that compel her to work at Acme International in the first place and that keep her there even after she starts having health problems.

Castillo bluntly states, "And it was that job that killed her." Presenting this information in a one-sentence paragraph, Castillo places accountability for Fe's death first and foremost on the workplace. Indeed, Castillo explicitly points out that before beginning to work at Acme International, Fe "had a clean bill of health at her pre-wedding gyn exam." After working at the factory for a period of time, though, Fe suffers a miscarriage. This loss marks the second time her American Dream slips away from her grasp. Fe does not give up, however, nor does she stop working, as doing so would mean letting go of the socially constructed aspirations that she has internalized as necessary for happiness. Yet her multiple "promotions" increase her contact with toxic chemicals, which she is never warned are deadly. Although she is given "special gloves and a cap," she is not even given a mask to protect herself from inhaling the noxious fumes to which she is exposed.[45] While those in positions of power at the company do what essentially amounts to nothing to protect Fe, they take great pains to safeguard themselves and others by isolating Fe downstairs, leaving her alone to work with one particularly toxic chemical, under the guise of ether. The chemical seeps into all parts of her body, causing irreparable damage.

Eventually Fe learns that she has cancer that has spread throughout her body. Castillo details Fe's grotesque bodily corrosion both before and after her cancer diagnosis, and she implicates Acme International in exacting such harm on Fe. Castillo draws attention to Fe's constant nausea, migraines, and indigestion, her miscarriage, the "red ring around her nose," "breath that smelled suspiciously of glue," the permanent chemical smell on her body, decimated fingernails, "cancerous moles," and insides that had been eaten "like acid." Not only do the chemicals to which Fe is exposed, and the cancer that she contracts, wreak havoc on her, so does the medical treatment she receives. Fe has "her whole body surgically scraped," scarred, and swollen to such an extent that she cannot walk. The doctors also accidentally insert a catheter inside her incorrectly, so that the chemotherapy she receives is misdirected to her brain, causing her to feel as if her head will explode and leading her to develop an infection.[46] Fe has no respite from harm, not even from the treatments designed to alleviate her symptoms. Even if the medical treatment Fe receives cannot save her, the fact that it exacts *further* damage on her speaks to a dangerously flawed health care system.[47]

Using the word *torture* to describe Fe's medical care (as Fe herself does), Castillo echoes her similar characterization of the harm Esperanza undergoes before her demise. Castillo not only draws parallels between the moments just prior to Fe's and Esperanza's deaths, but she also links medical torture with military torture, bitingly critiquing both structures of power in turn. The differences for the family members are that they see Fe die, whereas they learn of Esperanza's death thanks to Loca's supernatural visits with La Llorona. Likewise, they have Fe's corpse in their possession, while they never retrieve Esperanza's body. This said, the corporeal devastation Fe undergoes is so horrific that by the time she dies, her corpse is so torn apart that her family feels as if there is no choice but to cremate it. Unlike Loca, who is resurrected, and Esperanza, who returns ectoplasmically, "Fe just died"; and unlike Caridad, whose death potentially could be construed as a return to the earth and attainment of everlasting life, Fe's death can only be considered devastatingly tragic.[48] The finality of Fe's death and the prolonged suffering she endures prior to it make it so.

In her portrayal of the harm that Fe experiences, Castillo does not just depict a flawed medical system, but she provides a scathing critique of a company that makes its workers susceptible to becoming gravely ill without informing them of the dangers posed by their workplace. Indeed, Fe is not the only one whose life is put at risk at Acme International. Many of her female coworkers also experience health problems, including nausea and migraines. At least three of her coworkers additionally have had hysterectomies. Although "they all went to complain to the nurse at some point or another," the nurse dismisses their complaints, claiming that they are simply having "womanly" issues.[49] Showing how each of the women's concerns is trivialized and tossed aside, Castillo reveals both a specifically gendered pattern of harm and the feminization of illness. That the workers' complaints are dismissed as "womanly" speaks to the troubling historical medicalization of femininity. That those who readily are subject to illness are women illustrates how their bodies and lives are the ones rendered dispensable by those with institutionalized power. That so many of these women's reproductive health systems are jeopardized because of the toxins to which they are exposed highlights how the health care system (embodied through the nurse) fails to serve its patients adequately and arguably contributes to a form of population control. Considering Castillo's insinuation that Fe's coworkers are also predominantly working-class Mexican American and indigenous women, the dismissal of their suffering is not only gendered but also racialized, ethnicized, and classed. The individual harm Fe experiences accordingly is connected to the collective, intersectional harm her coworkers, fellow working-class women of color, endure.

Castillo highlights how the U.S. government is complicit in this harm, for Acme International contracts jobs with the Pentagon, helping brandish the weapons the military uses. And just as Acme International absolves itself of blame for the harm to which its workers are subjected, the federal government likewise places responsibility on the workers for any damage caused rather than holding the company accountable. Upon discovering that Fe has been letting the toxic chemical that she has been instructed to handle evaporate, the FBI and U.S. Attorney General's Office intervene. Instead of listening to Fe, the one who is dying because of her exposure to the chemical that she was ordered to let evaporate, the FBI and U.S. Attorney General's Office hold Fe responsible "since it was Fe alone who had used it."[50] In her portrayal of the company, the FBI, and the U.S. Attorney General's Office, Castillo bitingly criticizes the type of justice system that would allow such extreme neglect and denial of accountability to take place without consequence, and she beckons readers in turn to question what is considered justice in the first place.

Castillo draws attention to the ethical breach that takes place in Acme International's, the FBI's, and the U.S. Attorney General's Office's convenient refusal of responsibility for the role they play in Fe's acquisition of cancer on the basis of a mere technicality and in their utter lack of concern for her well-being: "Fe didn't understand none of it. Especially what she did not understand was how the Attorney General's Office could be so concerned about who was to blame for the illegal use of a chemical but it was not the least bit concerned about her who was dying in front of their eyes because of having been in contact with it."[51] Through Fe's observations, Castillo reveals what I might call a politics of absurdity, as she signals the Attorney General's Office's misplaced concern. Highlighting how this government office is focused on semantics rather than empathy or responsibility, and illustrating the hypocrisy and unfairness of this reaction, Castillo shows just how little the justice system in this country is actually concerned with justice in the ethical understanding of the term. For Castillo and the Tome community depicted in So Far from God, justice should not be incompatible with equity. That the U.S. government in the narrative positions these at odds with one another, though, inflicts yet another form of harm on Fe.

Upon learning that she has cancer, and facing a lawsuit for letting the chemical with which she had been working evaporate, Fe changes.

Attacked by both the disease plaguing her and the U.S. government, she begins to question the neoliberal tenets to which she previously ascribed. She undermines the logic and rhetoric of blame that the Attorney General's Office deploys; she determinedly tries to find out the name of the chemical the company had hired her to handle, despite the company's resistance to give her this information; and she stands up for herself, fighting for her right to access the data sheet containing such information. When she discovers that the chemical with which she had worked daily is "heavier than air," Fe asks, "If she had been supposedly letting it evaporate all those months she worked down there by herself . . . then where had it gone? . . . 'WHERE DID __ GO, PENDE__, SON-__-A- . . .' . . . 'IF NOT IN____ ME?'" Asking these questions and passionately asserting her broken voice, Fe reveals just how far she now strays from "the manicured, made-up bride of a few months before," who fervently clung to the American Dream and all that it stood for.[52]

Because of the profound physical and psychological changes Fe undergoes, it is difficult to read her as "accountable to her lifestyle," as Platt charges.[53] Even if Fe initially buys into the idea that working for Acme International is "very important work," as Platt points out, Fe eventually realizes that she has been duped into believing this myth.[54] By highlighting a changed and harmed Fe, Castillo primarily holds the institutional structures that perpetuate the illusion of the sought-after American Dream accountable for Fe's demise. In her portrayal of Fe's interactions with Acme International, Castillo emphasizes structural and corporate responsibility above all else, and she signals the inherent risks in relying on a neoliberal rhetoric of individual responsibility. Emphasizing the importance of collective responsibility in other parts of the narrative means that Castillo does not hold Fe exclusively "accountable to her lifestyle"; doing so would fall dangerously close to relying on the very same rhetoric deployed by Acme International and the U.S. Attorney General's Office, a rhetoric that conveniently absolves Acme International of its own accountability in the harm it causes.

Castillo presents her ecofeminist message through the questions Fe asks about where else the chemical could have gone, if not inside her. Apart from highlighting how the toxins at the factory endanger the health of the workers therein, Castillo illustrates how these same chemicals endanger the surrounding community: "The chemical [Fe] more than once dumped down the drain at the end of her day [prior to being ordered to let it evaporate] . . . went into the sewage system and worked its way to people's septic tanks, vegetable gardens, kitchen taps, and sun-made tea."[55] The phrase "sun-made" undoubtedly refers to the Sun-Maid raisins found in grocery stores throughout this country. Considering that *So Far from God* was published after both the grape boycott of the 1980s that decried the widespread use of pesticides on grapes and the creation of the Chicana visual artist Ester Hernández's scathing print *Sun Mad*, which depicts the damage caused by pesticides, Castillo's descriptor elucidates how her commentary about Acme International and the U.S. government and military is ecofeminist.[56] Just as Hernández plays on the name of the iconic raisins in her print to criticize the deadly use of pesticides to harvest grapes in this country, Castillo critiques the lack of institutional oversight that all too easily allows dangerous chemicals to seep into the food the Tome community members eat and the water they drink. Showing the widespread devastation created by the chemicals used in a company that manufactures weapon parts for the U.S. military, and locating this company in the predominantly Mexican American community of Tome, Castillo both implicates the U.S. government in a form of environmental genocide and also demonstrates how the individual harm that Fe experiences is connected to the collective harm exacted on her community.

The environmental critique that Castillo provides cannot be separated from her portrayal of racialized, ethnicized, classed, gendered, and sexualized harm. Because of the intersectionality of this depiction, it would be apt to label this critique U.S. Third World feminist. Because Castillo reveals the intersections of these multiple forms of harm, she also exposes the environmental racism practiced by Acme International (as a synecdoche for U.S. governmental and military power).[57] Acme International's positioning in the Tome community, the makeup of this community, the makeup of the workers in direct contact with the poisons, and the company's refusal to acknowledge any culpability for the environmental hazards it poses to its workers and the surrounding community together elucidate the company's environmentally racist practices. In her portrayal of the company responsible for Fe's death, yet absolved of any legal culpability for its environmental neglect, Castillo reveals the abuses of corporate, military, and governmental authority, and she compels readers to hold such institutional authority accountable for the environmentally racist destruction it wreaks.

## Geopolitical Genocide and Communal Cries

Throughout *So Far from God*, Castillo evokes the same sentiment as that offered by the epigraph to this chapter: "For subaltern actors it is *their* land and *their* bodies that are at risk."[58] Castillo emphasizes that *both* the lands and bodies of the subaltern Tome community members are at risk. Castillo's geopolitical, ecofeminist, and material feminist commentary is present in her portrait of land appropriation, the displacement of natives, and the mistreatment of the environment.

For the Tome community in the narrative, colonization—as a practice of settlement, appropriation of land, and displacement of natives—does not end in 1848 with the signing of the Treaty of Guadalupe-Hidalgo that ended the Mexican-American War. It continues in a de facto modus operandi even in the 1990s setting of the novel. Castillo presents the Mexican American community of Tome as the original owners of land therein and positions the *gringos* (as she calls them) as outsiders who seize this land. This appropriation of land follows from economic pressures that drive the native inhabitants from their homes, lands, and even nation. As a result, farming, once an integral part of the Tome community, has largely dissipated. While illustrating how the *gringos* dislocate the native residents, Castillo reveals that these outsiders do not even know how to harvest the land they are so eager to usurp; they overuse it "so that in some cases it was no good for raising crops or grazing livestock no more." Apart from misusing the land, the non-natives have questionable grazing practices. As one of the Mexican American residents complains, "All we have ever known is this life, living off our land, that just gets más smaller y smaller. . . . all I got left of my father's hard work—and his father's and his father's—is casi nada. . . . And now we have los gringos coming here and breeding peacocks. . . . Now, I ask you, what can you do with peacocks?"[59] Relying on stinging humor and absurdity, Castillo critiques the displacement of the Mexican American natives who have lived on the land and harvested it for generations, and she compels readers to question the misuse of land by those who have appropriated it.

The land is also contaminated by factories (like Acme International) and nuclear power plants that have taken over the area once known for its agricultural production. The effects of the boost in industrialization in Tome are deadly (evidenced in Fe's experiences with Acme International), as factory workers, plant workers, and community members are all exposed to toxic chemicals and radioactive waste. The community members, however, do not meekly let this geopolitical devastation happen without saying or doing anything. Instead, they band together in protest.

Toward the end of the novel, the community forms a procession that at once resembles a manifesto, a call to arms, and the Stations of the Cross because of the revolutionary and religious imagery deployed.

Using language remarkably similar to that found in *The Ladies' Gallery*, where Irene Vilar writes of environmental devastation in Puerto Rico thanks to U.S. industrialization and militarization, Castillo here paints a bleak portrait of environmental genocide. In this procession, the community members decry the environmental hazards that are destroying them and every living thing around them, voicing their fear of imminent extinction and comparing themselves to an endangered species fighting to survive. They express outrage over the pollutants dumped in their sewage systems that infiltrate the air they breathe as well as the canals where their children play and animals swim. They denounce the "uranium contamination" that causes their "babies [to develop] brain damage and cancer," and they rail against the noxious pesticides sprayed on the fields where they work and on the foods they ingest, leading "their babies [to die] in their bellies from the poisoning."[60] Castillo's emphasis on the harm done to the *children* underscores the particularly insidious effects of the industrialization of Tome. In passages evocative of those in Moraga's play *Heroes and Saints* that similarly expose the tragic, disabling, and fatal effects of pesticides on the lives of a Mexican American community, *So Far from God* depicts images of environmental decay and devastation alongside ones that detail the harm that affects the vulnerable and the innocent. As in *Heroes and Saints*, community members in *So Far from God* carry photographs of loved ones who have died due to exposure to environmental toxins, creating a visual and visceral display of the overwhelming deadly destruction caused by environmental racism and environmental devastation. Through these images, Castillo reveals how the mistreatment of the environment creates a mass genocide.

The procession scene in *So Far from God* juxtaposes these images with ones of profound poverty, war, disease, and crucifixion, pointing to parallels between killing civilians and destroying the environment. The union of seemingly disparate political commentaries in this section resonates with Castillo's similar juxtaposition of seemingly distinct issues in her essay collection *Massacre of the Dreamers*. In one essay therein, Castillo simultaneously addresses the exploitation of the labor of impoverished women of color, sterilization incentives for such women, pesticide use, and the contamination of lands and people, courtesy of widespread spraying practices. Presenting these issues together in her novel and essay compilation alike, Castillo demonstrates that "nothing is separate from anything else."[61] This vantage point speaks to the one articulated throughout *Intersections of Harm*: different forms of harm are integrally intertwined.

The procession sequence marks the culmination of the geopolitical commentary in *So Far from God*, but Castillo portrays community organization, protest, and social activism in other parts of the narrative as well, and she demonstrates that social activism can manifest itself in myriad ways. In Caridad's refusal to adhere to social dictates of womanhood, Loca's decision to cut the label from the jeans that she has inherited from Caridad to boycott the company that manufactures the jeans and mistreats its workers, Esperanza's *Raza* politics, and Fe's ultimate defense of her rights and stance against Acme International, Castillo illustrates how social activism can happen on an individual and everyday basis. In her depiction of Sofi and the Tome community members, Castillo shows how community organizing can be both effective and important.

Apart from coming together for the procession, the Tome community—led by Sofi, who decides to run for mayor of the unincorporated town of Tome—unites to form Los Ganados y Lana Cooperative, "modeled after the [real-world] one started by the group up north that had also saved its community from destitution."[62] Like the similarly named Ganados del Valle cooperative community that actually exists in northern New Mexico, the cooperative in *So Far from God* "empowers individuals and provides a renewed cultural and ethnic identity, but also seeks to improve their economic well-being in an environmentally sustainable fashion by building a series of integrated businesses based on sheep."[63] Establishing a business centered around wool weaving, the Tome community responds to the inefficient and harmful grazing practices deployed by those who have usurped their lands and the one outsider who has decided to raise peacocks there, just as the Ganados del Valle sheep-focused businesses position themselves in contradistinction to the environmentally unsound elk industry that has infringed upon the livelihood of the predominantly Mexican American population residing in northern New Mexico. The establishment of these sheep-centered cooperatives largely centers on allowing native resident communities to harvest the land in ways that best serve their needs, which includes treating the land with the utmost care.

But the cooperative to which Sofi and her fellow town members belong, like the one that actually exists in the northern part of the state, entails more than instituting sound grazing practices and more than establishing a self-propelled industry that can sustain its resident community. It consists of community improvement more broadly speaking. The cooperative in *So Far from God* creates opportunities through arrangements "with the local junior college" and through the development of trade skills that would allow "those who were interested [to] work for college credit and potentially earn an associate's degree"; these educational opportunities in turn increase the types of job opportunities available to members of the Tome community. The cooperative harvests and provides "hormone-free meat" and "inexpensive access to pesticide-free food." It founds a SWAT team to address drug use in the Tome schools. It addresses gendered divisions of labor, as "the mothers among them didn't worry so much about their babies and childcare because they could bring their 'jitos to work."[64] Ultimately it consists of the Tome community members coming together as a collective, despite lack of governmental assistance, to establish and maintain something that benefits them all in the immediate *and* long term.

Sofi's mayoral campaign fosters the spirit of communal activism behind Los Ganados y Lana Cooperative and leads to the establishment of the Carne Buena Meat Market, a food cooperative that provides hormone-free meat. Despite the ways in which Sofi and her daughters are marked as deviant because of their defiance of socially constructed norms, and despite the ways in which others initially regard Sofi's decision to run for mayor with disbelief (since no one has ever been mayor of the town, nor does Sofi supposedly know anything about politics), Sofi nevertheless is able to effect important change in her community and bring the members within it together for a shared cause. Although her husband, Domingo, at first attributes her declaration that she will run for mayor to a "psychological breakdown because of all the pressures she'd been under," Sofi does not let anyone's skepticism deter her from pursuing her passions. Because of her determination to effect social change for the betterment of her community, and because of her reliance on her personal knowledge and intuition, Sofi engages in a U.S. Third World feminist praxis that showcases how the personal *is* political and that reveals how the individual cannot be separated from the collective. As Sofi herself implores, while invoking Esperanza's social justice rhetoric about needing to "work to change the 'system,'" "the only way things are going to get better . . . is if *we*, all of us together, try to do something about it."[65] If readers take away just one message from Castillo's novel, this is it. Change can happen, but it requires collective mobilization to take place.

## A Call to Action

With this message, Castillo speaks to one of the central arguments of *Intersections of Harm*: hope can be found even amid pervasive and often deadly harm. As Castillo illustrates, hope springs from the development of a social consciousness, a recognition that the individual is connected to the collective, and a desire to work as part of a collective to create needed social change. Whereas *So Far from God* contains seemingly endless examples of material harm, Castillo does not leave readers with a sense of utter despair. Like Laura Pulido, who argues that the actual Ganados del Valle provides "a sense of ownership [for 'the women who previously saw themselves solely as housewives'] . . . , which, more than anything, means they have hope for the future," Castillo demonstrates that Los Ganados y Lana Cooperative and the Carne Buena Meat Market function as hopeful venues for (female) solidarity in the process of community improvement.[66] Although she portrays four young women who die by the novel's close, and although she highlights a community devastated by industrialization and environmental destruction, Castillo displays the power of communal activism.

In her analysis of *So Far from God*, Caminero-Santangelo charges that the final chapter, which centers on M.O.M.A.S. (Mothers of Martyrs and Saints), counters the political activism found throughout the rest of the narrative, as it is written in a tongue-in-cheek tone that pokes fun at the group's often ridiculous concerns. This chapter admittedly has a vastly different feel than the penultimate one, which describes the procession and which is explicitly written in a tone of political urgency. However, by juxtaposing these chapters, Castillo reveals the possibilities and limitations of collective formations, and she demonstrates that humor exists alongside tragedy.[67] In the exaggerated language, sarcasm, and humor of the last chapter, Castillo highlights absurd elements that can come with coalition building (especially that founded on pseudo-religious tenets). As Caminero-Santangelo likewise observes, in Castillo's farcical portrayal of M.O.M.A.S., she positions the group as less than an exemplar of coalition formation to be emulated. Instead, through her characterization of the group, Castillo critiques devotion without understanding. She also criticizes the historical gendered burdens faced by women through institutionalized religion. This critique cannot be disentangled from the feminist one that Castillo weaves throughout her narrative. With her closing sequence, she shows that the type of social activism that she positions as vitally important revolves around understanding and seeks to destabilize patriarchal systems of oppression. Although she concludes her novel with two chapters written in starkly distinct tones, the humorous tone deployed in the last chapter does not take away from the dire tone invoked in the penultimate one, nor does the parodic collective organization M.O.M.A.S. undo the earnest collective mobilization of either the procession or of Los Ganados y Lana Cooperative. Rather, the last two chapters together illustrate the centrality of ecofeminism, material feminism, and U.S. Third World feminism (and more specifically Xicanisma) to the type of collective activism for which Castillo calls, and they reveal the intersections of harm, hope, and humor.[68]

The humor Castillo deploys does not necessarily consist of the type of feel-good qualities readily associated with it, despite Sandra Cisneros's description of the book (on its back cover) as "Wacky, wild, y bien funny." As the literary scholar Susan Thananopavarn explains in "Conscientización of the Oppressed," the humor on which Castillo relies advances a highly politicized purpose. I would extend this to say that Castillo's humor functions in a Brechtian manner, calling upon readers to laugh and instantly wonder why they are laughing. The laughter immediately precedes a moment of critical social awareness in which readers realize the very seriousness of that which led them to laugh in the first place. After all, the rumor that concludes the narrative about whether women need to prove that they have wombs to be able to be members of M.O.M.A.S. initially is likely to cause laughter (because of its absurdity) and subsequently is likely to cause readers to question patriarchal and transphobic systems of oppression that would allow such a rumor to exist at all. Considering that Castillo uses humor in a way that triggers social consciousness, her conclusion of her narrative with a chapter replete with humor arguably leaves readers with the type of call to action explicitly articulated in her penultimate chapter.

This call to action resonates with the ethical imperative at the heart of Intersections of Harm. Concluding So Far from God with two chapters devoted to a community coming together, Castillo underscores the importance of collective mourning and organizing. She also shows how the individual tragedies that befall Sofi's four daughters cannot be, nor should be, forgotten by those who survive them. As elucidated in chapters 1 and 2 of Intersections of Harm, remembering is connected to hope and is key to social change.[69] In the context of So Far from God, part of this remembering consists of holding the forces responsible for the deaths of the sisters accountable for the devastation they have imposed. Like Frantz Fanon, who positions pathology in the environment, Castillo holds institutional structures accountable for the material harm and madness they perpetuate. Indeed, by the end of the novel, it is clear that the principal madness lies within the institutional structures that lead to sociopolitical and geopolitical oppression, dispossession, and material harm.

Castillo emphasizes the tremendous harm that Sofi's family and community experience as part of her call for social change. Since remembering the harm is integral to the process of effecting change, the book vividly depicts multiple examples of the devastating harm exacted on the Tome community. The figure of La Llorona, who haunts the narrative, serves as a regular reminder of the pain and suffering felt by the community. This figure's recuperation by Chicana feminist scholars like Anzaldúa, Moraga, and Castillo as a misunderstood woman who committed infanticide arguably to *protect* her children from the horrors they undoubtedly would have faced had they lived helps explain her centrality in a narrative that vehemently critiques patriarchal systems of oppression. That La Llorona is feared and denigrated in Mexican (American) lore because of her defiance and supposed madness situates her alongside each of *So Far from God*'s female protagonists. La Llorona's agonized and agonizing wails particularly resemble those of Fe during the period labeled "El Big Grito," as Fe is described as "lost" in "the internal caverns of her mind," seeing an "image of herself with her eyes bulging and her mouth wide open," and "hear[ing] from somewhere far, far away the spine-chilling cry of an agonized woman," an image I revisit in my analysis of *How the García Girls Lost Their Accents.*[70] Considering La Llorona's centrality in Castillo's narrative, considering that she is said to wander by bodies of water at night hollering for her lost children, and considering that each of the daughters in Castillo's novel dies, this distant "spine-chilling cry" could refer to the collective grief over Mexican Americans who have had their lives taken from them prematurely. Indeed, the image Castillo paints here parallels the images of the photographs carried by the Tome community members during the procession at the novel's end and the communal cries of woe and activism heard then. As the "spine-chilling cry" emanates from a nameless "agonized woman," it represents an individual and collective cry at once: from Fe herself, who cries over her loss and solitude; from La Llorona, who howls over her deceased children; and from any of the mothers or *comadres* in the text who wail for their lost children. It is a cry of indescribable anguish, but it is also a cry of remembrance and in turn a cry for change.

# 4 / Artistic Aberrance and Liminal Geographies in Cristina García's *Dreaming in Cuban*

*Art . . . is the ultimate revolution.*
—CRISTINA GARCÍA, *DREAMING IN CUBAN*

Cristina García's acclaimed first novel, *Dreaming in Cuban*, focuses on the roles that art and revolution play in the formation of its female protagonists: Celia, Felicia, Lourdes, and Pilar. Primarily set in postrevolutionary Cuba and New York City, *Dreaming in Cuban* depicts a family separated ideologically and geographically. Revolution forms the backdrop to the novel, both in terms of the Cuban Revolution and the female characters' rebelliousness. This rebellion is connected to the characters' defiance of normative gendered and creative expression. Creativity allows the main characters to seek to find a voice of their own, but it also casts them as aberrant in others' eyes.

Art *is* revolution in the narrative, as the youngest protagonist, Pilar, proclaims.[1] The characters who turn to art are labeled deviant by their family and communities and are subject to myriad forms of harm. Celia, the novel's matriarch and ardent Castro supporter, has multiple revolutionary and creative passions. She serves the Cuban Revolution, plays the piano, writes secret love letters to her former Spanish lover, Gustavo, enjoys poetry, and issues unorthodox, creative sentences as a civilian judge. These passions, however, mark her as psychologically unstable in the eyes of her family and community and lead to her temporary institutionalization in a mental hospital. Celia's daughter Felicia expresses her rebellion by defying Caribbean ideologies of pigmentocracy, allying herself with the Afro Cuban religion of *santería* (which she considers a type of poetry), and marrying a man of African descent. She also challenges dominant ideals of womanhood and purity in her sexuality: she is an escort, marries three times, contracts syphilis, and displays incestuous tendencies toward her son. Her syphilis causes her to go "mad" and hurt herself and others. Like her mother, Celia, and sister Felicia Lourdes experiences devastating harm. Her unflinching adherence to neoliberal ideas of self and society, rejection of leftist politics, and binary way of thinking stem from her suffering in revolutionary Cuba, when she undergoes a miscarriage and survives a rape by Cuban soldiers. In the United States, she devotes her attention to the baked goods she creates at her Yankee Doodle Bakery chain and the service she provides as an auxiliary policewoman. But her body continues to be the receptacle of harm, as Lourdes develops an eating disorder. Her daughter, Pilar, contests the black and white ideologies to which Lourdes ascribes. Pilar embraces ambiguity in her painting, music, and interest in punk subculture. Like her mother, she is sexually assaulted. That these protagonists exhibit a creative passion along with a spirit of rebelliousness and are placed in harm's way reveals the damage associated with geopolitical, gendered, sexualized, racialized, and artistic revolution and highlights the subjugation, oppression, and condemnation that fuel such defiance.

These characters' self-expression through art/revolution, however, demonstrates how creativity and rebellion are connected to harm *and* hope for change. The characters rebelliousness admittedly is met with resistance, revealing a cyclical pattern—paralleled in the novel's nonlinear, polyphonic structure—that places them as targets of the very structures of patriarchal oppression from which they seek to break free. Yet through their defiance, the female characters try to assert their voices and effect change. The hope in the novel's content arises from the protagonists' refusal to abide by oppressive norms, and the hope in the novel's structure springs from both its deviation from conventional narrative form and its blurring of genres. Throughout *Dreaming in Cuban*, García, like Irene Vilar, emphasizes the importance of *historia* telling, underscoring the ways story and history come together and cannot be neatly distinguished from one another. Through her merging of story with history, imagination, and truth and her equation of art with revolution, García reveals an important relation between creative expression and social change.

## Celia's Pathologized Passions

Celia's rebelliousness manifests itself through her creative, romantic, and political passions. These passions cause others to construct her as dangerous or mentally ill. Rather than read her mental imbalance as a given or as following from heartbreak, as Kimberle López suggests, I seek to complicate Celia's portrayal as "mad."[2] Focusing on Celia's representation as a Cuban artist whose passions are affiliated with blackness, I explore how her "insanity" is racialized and gendered and needs to be understood as something that is *constructed.*

Celia's husband, Jorge, places her in an insane asylum supposedly for her own good. However, García reveals Jorge's dubious motives in institutionalizing Celia. Although Celia herself concedes that she needed medical treatment because "she was dying of love for the Spaniard," García calls into question the conditions that dictate that Celia be institutionalized.[3] García notes that Jorge's jealousy underlies his decision to place Celia in a mental ward; she points out the central role that his mother and sister play in contributing to Celia's supposed psychological instability; and she provides a critical portrait of the practitioners who treat Celia. García therefore casts doubt on the pronouncement of Celia's psychic imbalance, troubling Celia's medicalization and highlighting the harm that accompanies its construction.

To understand García's complicated portrait of Celia's mental state, it is useful to contextualize the roles that Jorge, his mother (Berta), his sister (Ofelia), and Celia's doctors play in Celia's pathologization in relation to extant literary scholarship on the feminization of madness. Naming Jorge's mother and sister Berta and Ofelia, García gestures toward their literary namesakes: *Jane Eyre's* and *Wide Sargasso Sea's* Bertha and *Hamlet's* Ophelia, two of the most iconic literary "madwomen." By positioning Berta and Ofelia in postcolonial, prerevolutionary 1930s Cuba, though, García obscures the invocation. Berta and Ofelia's names and bodies become disjointed; they do not share their literary precursors' fates, as neither commits suicide nor is labeled insane. Rather, they contribute to *Celia's* psychological distress.

Despite her intertextual twist, García invokes some of the same discourses of femininity and "madness" utilized by Charlotte Brontë, Jean Rhys, and William Shakespeare. In particular, she draws on gendered associations between grooming and madness in her portrayal of Berta, Ofelia, and Celia. In her analysis of the novel, López explains how García's representations of female grooming correspond with Elaine Showalter's observations about the relation between extremes in grooming and female instability. López comments on Berta and Ofelia's view of Celia as "a harlot because she wears a flower in her hair," and she notes that Celia occasionally neglects her appearance altogether, marking her as "mad" according to socially constructed ideas of normalcy.[4] García's portrayal of grooming is also racialized. Unlike Celia, who voluntarily works in the sugarcane fields while "the sun browns her skin," Berta and Ofelia struggle with their self-image, "rubb[ing] whitening cream into their dark, freckled faces. Berta Arango left the paste on overnight to remove any trace of her mulatto blood."[5] Despite the disjunction between Berta's name and body, Berta's efforts to whiten herself accentuate her preoccupation with her skin color, evoking Rhys's foregrounding of Bertha's *créolité*. Noting that mother and daughter resort to drastic measures to adhere to racialized standards of beauty and illustrating how the two mistreat their daughter-in-law/sister-in-law, who does not readily adhere to these pervasive ideologies, García reveals that dominant racial ideologies are connected to gendered constructions of "madness." Highlighting the extremity of the pain to which Berta and Ofelia subject their bodies to appear lighter-skinned, García, like Loida Maritza Pérez, reveals the pervasive "Hispanic Caribbean tendency toward lactification" and compels us to question who among the three— Berta, Ofelia, or Celia—is "really" the "madwoman."[6] To make sense of their disparate attitudes about "proper" gender and race roles, Berta and Ofelia try to strip Celia of her sanity; they arguably succeed in doing so, at least insofar as Celia is subsequently interned in a mental hospital.

Years later, Jorge ectoplasmically confesses to his daughter Lourdes that he played a principal role in Celia's institutionalization and "breakdown." He even admits that he ordered the doctors to provide Celia with a treatment designed to render her "properly" docile: "I [Jorge] left her in an asylum. I told the doctors to make her forget. They used electricity. They fed her pills. . . . Her hands were always so still."[7] Jorge's preoccupation with his wife's amnesia and docility corresponds with the (mis)treatment of women elucidated by López, Showalter, and Michel Foucault—who highlight how the methods of "care" provided to women historically have revolved around rendering women docile—and situates Celia alongside such women. Rather than concern themselves with the best interests of their patients, Celia's doctors help maintain her supposed insanity, abiding by Jorge's orders as if he were their trained medical supervisor instead of treating Celia based on their own prognoses or diagnoses. Their "treatment," like that of the dentist portrayed by Gloria Anzaldúa in the epigraph to *Intersections of Harm*, demonstrates a patriarchal complicity whereby the female patient's voice is silenced.

Although Celia never blames her doctors for contributing to her diagnosed instability, her interaction with them implicates them in fraudulent practice. Apart from taking medical orders from Jorge, the doctors tell Celia that "nothing [is] wrong" when her body deteriorates to the point of being "a fragile pile of opaque bones, with yellowed nails and no monthly blood," when she once used to be a physically strong woman who was "a head taller than most men."[8] The doctors rely on conventional forms of medicine alone to determine Celia's condition. When these methods fail to explain why Celia is wasting away, the medical practitioners do nothing more to help her heal. Illustrating the discrepancy between the "caretakers'" pronouncement that "nothing [is] wrong" and Celia's visibly corroding body, García highlights the limitations of mainstream medicine and the doctors' adherence to gendered notions of health and illness that paradoxically position women's fragility as desirable.

The practitioners' skewed construction of women's health is further revealed in their reactions to Celia's lies. When Celia tells them, "My father raped me," and when she declares, "I eat rusted sunsets, scald children in my womb," the doctors "burn [her] skull with procedures. They tell [her she's] improving."[9] As she invents stories of unspeakable harm inflicted on or by her, her doctors continue to harm her with their medical procedures and link the treatment that impairs her mind with her improved mental health.[10] Celia's fabrication of violent tales in the mental hospital, meanwhile, shows how she, like Lolita in *The Ladies' Gallery*, "makes it crazy" presumably to survive her institutionalization.[11] Indeed, after acting as if she were "crazy" by lying about arguably gendered forms of injury (rape and scalded fetuses), after having her brain subjected to excruciating procedures, after undergoing a bodily deterioration, and after seemingly accepting her institutionalization (she does not overtly challenge it), Celia is told she is recuperating.

The doctors' questionable assessment of Celia is heightened by García's depiction of the mental hospital and the barren natural environment against which it is set. Just as Vilar elucidates the confining constructedness of the hospital where she is institutionalized, García draws attention to the constructedness of place and emphasizes the lack that characterizes the built and natural environment where Celia is kept. García deploys metallic imagery to describe the mental ward ("gold stars in the hallways" and a "tree with metallic leaves") and emphasizes how the natural environment parallels the negativity of the built one: "[Jorge] sits with me [Celia] on a wrought-iron bench. Nature is at right angles here. No bougainvillea. No heliconia. No flowering cactus burning myths in the desert." She elaborates, "Others surround us in the sun. Their words are muted as the winds they allow through the netting. It's a sweet-scented rot."[12] Illustrating the constructedness of the natural environment (through its *unnatural* right angles), repeating the word *no* to describe the desolate landscape, recounting the silence that accompanies the stifled voices of the institutionalized, and highlighting the permeating bittersweet stench, García underscores the lack and rancor that define the hospital.

Whereas García harshly characterizes the doctors and mental institution, she depicts Celia's neighbors in a more ambiguous manner. Celia's neighbors initially support her by relying on their own folk remedies when the mainstream medical system cannot explain her visibly ailing body. When they conclude that "she is determined to die," though, they give up trying to help her and shun her:

> Neighbors had kept their distance, believing she was destined
> for an early death and anyone she touched would be forced to
> accompany her. They were afraid of her disease as if it were fatal,
> like tuberculosis, but worse, much worse.
>
> What they feared even more, Celia realized later, was that
> passion might spare them entirely, that they'd die conventionally,
> smug and purposeless, having never savored its blackness.[13]

Unlike the doctors, the neighbors recognize that something is wrong with Celia because her body is wasting away. But the distance they later keep from her reveals their own anxieties. They attribute this distance to a fear of contagion of an unnamed, fatal disease.[14] As Celia points out, though, their principal fear is that they will never be able to feel the passion she has experienced. Likening Celia's passion to a disease, the community medicalizes both her emotions and her defiance of convention and treats this passion as something to be tamed.

Much as the Tome community in *So Far from God* constructs the female protagonists as "crazy" because of their out-of-the-ordinariness, the neighbors in *Dreaming in Cuban* pathologize Celia because of her deviation from communal norms. García illustrates how this deviation and these norms are similarly racialized. Although García cursorily describes Celia as phenotypically pale, she reveals how Celia's medicalization is racialized in her characterization of passion's "blackness."[15] The link between passion and blackness in this context is ironic, however, for the neighbors and Celia alike have complicated relationships with blackness. The neighbors exhibit a general uneasiness toward blackness, only eventually turning to *santería* to save Celia. Celia similarly expresses concern about her daughter Felicia's devotion to *santería* and friendship with Herminia (an Afro Cuban), even while she herself browns her skin in the sun. The neighbors' envy of Celia's blackened passion that they cast as taboo underscores the paradoxes surrounding their treatment of Celia and their complex race politics, a complexity that undercuts the imagined notion of a monolithic, privileged, and white *cubanidad*.

García's emphasis on ambiguity is further elucidated through her depiction of Celia's internalization of the labels of deviance imposed on her by her family, doctors, and community. Celia too pathologizes her heartbreak, explaining that "she was dying of love for the Spaniard."[16] Celia does not name the Spaniard here, suggesting that he may have more than one referent. He may refer to Gustavo, the Spanish lover Celia had prior to marrying Jorge. Celia's description of her passionate romance with Gustavo, coupled with Jorge's acknowledgment that his jealousy makes him "want to punish" Celia and "break her," positions Gustavo as the likely referent.[17] If this is so, then Celia's substitution of Gustavo's name with his nationality positions him as lover and colonizer, complicating Celia's own nationalism.[18] If Gustavo functions as Spanish colonialist, and if he is the Spaniard Celia references when she medicalizes herself, then we find a causal relationship between Celia's "love for the Spaniard" and her pathologization that is tied to the Spanish colonization of Cuba and Celia's arguable internalized oppression, as she claims to be "dying of love" for her country's colonizing power. Even her husband and doctors treat Celia as a colonized subject when they exert patriarchal control over her to render her docile. The harms that befall her thus are manifold: she experiences heartbreak; she is subject to an externally imposed oppression that is subsequently internalized; and she defines herself by her loyalty to the Cuban Revolution while she longs for a Spaniard and yearns to be in Spain.

Celia's preoccupation with Spain, chiefly Andalucía, extends beyond her love for Gustavo and carries over into her creative interests. She is inspired by the poetry of Andalusian writer Federico García Lorca, and she enjoys playing French composer Claude Debussy's piece "La Soirée dans Grenade" on the piano. She even fancies herself a flamenco dancer when her granddaughter Pilar asks her how she would like to be painted. That Celia is so drawn to Spain and envisions herself there troubles her identification as a Cuban nationalist and reveals her ambiguous, interstitial positioning as a character caught among (geo)political, familial, romantic, and creative allegiances.

Apart from alluding to Gustavo, the Spaniard for whom Celia is "dying of love" could also refer to Lorca given her interest in his ballad poems and considering the language of seduction García uses to characterize Celia's relationship with Lorca and his poems. The tenor of Lorca's voice, amid a backdrop of sorrow, entrances Celia. Celia is also fascinated by Andalucía's Moorish makeup and the black timbre of the *duende*, a dwarfish figure as well as a concept, "power," and "struggle" associated with the attainment of artistry.[19] Envied and dismissed by her neighbors for savoring passion's blackness, here Celia is drawn to a place and sound characterized by blackness: "The black sounds of the *duende* shivered in the air with mystery and anguish and death. Death was alluring, seductive, and Celia longed to die in the thrill of it over and over again."[20] This attraction shows Celia's complex and conflicting desires, ones that can be likened to the ambiguity undergirding the idea of *duende* itself, especially since *duende* can be achieved only at the brink between life and death.[21]

The enticing morbidity associated with Lorca's poems and the *cante jondo* (flamenco) that inspires them can be connected to the Debussy piece that captivates Celia and that plays a central role in her rebelliousness and institutionalization. In much the same way that attending Lorca's reading lets Celia imagine herself in Spain, playing "La Soirée dans Grenade" on the piano transports her across space to Andalucía and symbolically allows her to revisit her passion for Gustavo and Lorca. Arguably because of the multilayered defiance behind this fantasized reunion—as it could be considered to contribute to her traitorous desires (in her allegiances to a man who is not her husband *and* her nation's former colonial power)— Celia's husband and doctors forbid her from playing Debussy's songs. Although they encourage her to play the piano in her "recovery," they allege that Debussy's music contributes to her psychic restlessness. Celia, however, does not let their attempts to control her repertoire prevent her from playing this music. She simply waits for Jorge to go away on business to do so, expressing a surreptitious rebelliousness that allows her to escape (even if just temporarily) the patriarchal oppression she experiences at her husband's and doctors' hands.

Celia's allegiance to the Revolution offers another example of her rebellion. Her defiance presents itself most overtly in her role as a judge in Castro's Cuba. Turning civilians into "productive revolutionaries," she doles out punishments that encourage them to pursue creative endeavors or reconsider the gendered division of labor.[22] Most notably, she sentences an adulterous husband to work in a nursery to realize the demands on the women staff there. With such rulings, Celia works within yet beyond the confines of the Revolution to articulate her own gendered and artistic resistance.

Celia also rebels against Jorge by secretly writing love letters to Gustavo, handing them to Pilar later in life. Hiding her Debussy and letters alike, Celia keeps these aspects of her artistic identity—the pianist and the poet—private, as both represent the forbidden. García herself concedes that the letters are "the most lyrical parts of the novel."[23] They blend letter writing, poetry, and music and serve as diary-like entries that grant readers insight into Celia's personal reflections. The letters therefore illustrate how Celia's defiance emanates from the intersections of multiple forms of creative expression.

Apart from the letters, the only other place in *Dreaming in Cuban* when we hear Celia's extended first-person narration is in the chronologically concluding section of the novel. This section, along with the narrative's final page that presents the last of Celia's letters written over twenty years earlier, is where García most explicitly weaves together Celia's artistic outlets: letter writing, poetry, and song. Celia's unmediated voice finally has the possibility of coming into being in the narrative's chronological close, without the mediation of a musical instrument, writing utensil, or judge's gavel. Here the *duende* beckons Celia toward the sea, "to sing for the black sea that awaits [her] voice."[24] The *duende*'s summon takes on a multilayered significance. For one, it evokes the *duende*'s sounds from Lorca's reading years earlier that Celia then found morbidly alluring. The *duende*'s call at the novel's end thus functions as a type of distorted echo. Whereas the *duende*'s gender is never overtly mentioned during the Lorca reading, at the narrative's close, the *duende* explicitly is gendered female, invoking some comparison—with a difference—between this figure and Homer's Sirens, who likewise lure others with a song of seduction. Although the Sirens entice male characters, here the *duende* ensnares a female character. While the Sirens' song is considered to lead those it attracts to their death, the effects of the *duende*'s sounds are ambiguous, as the *duende* is affiliated with both the production of song and the allure of death. Just as Celia is drawn to the *duende*'s song, the *duende* invites Celia to produce a song alongside her. The portrait of the *duende* that García provides complicates the narrative's final sequence and evokes a correlation among artistry, femininity, and liminal subjectivity. This connection, which draws upon a Third World feminist subjectivity in its emphasis on ambiguity and interstitiality, is elucidated through the contradictory associations accompanying the concept of *duende* and through the similarly conflicting images provided in García's last pages.

Celia's call to song reveals a bittersweet irony: her unmediated voice can exist only in the space between life and death. What are the implications of achieving artistry and finding an unmediated voice while submerged? Does this sequence portray the archetypal literary madwoman who, upon hearing voices spurring her onward and possibly discovering her own voice in a world unwilling to listen to it, drowns to death? Celia's underwater liminality and articulation of voice herald Anabelle's suicide upon uttering her first and only sound in *Geographies of Home* and position Celia within a trajectory of literary "madwoman" with similar "endings": Alfred Lord Tennyson's Lady of Shalott, Kate Chopin's Edna Pontellier, and William Shakespeare's Ophelia. The very picture of a Celia urged to sing, with loosely floating hair while the "water rises quickly around her," evokes these predecessors' and successor's final images.[25] Like Edna, Ophelia, and the Lady of Shalott, who are characterized as "mad, alienated artist[s]," Celia is found in the water after being called forth to "sing her [first and arguably] last song."[26] The connection among "madness," artistry, and song is notably gendered in all of these cases. The characters' "madness" does not necessarily render them powerless, though. The creative writer Rosario Ferré, for instance, challenges traditional interpretations of Ophelia as powerless, describing Ophelia's death scene as a peaceful renunciation necessary for the achievement of artistry.[27] Ferré's reading of Ophelia closely resembles Lorca's description of *duende*. If Ophelia's death scene is not about tragedy but about artistic attainment, then, by analogy, Celia's final underwater scene can be understood beyond the framework of suicide or tragedy and alternatively viewed as related to the discovery of *duende*.

Positioning Celia within this trajectory of literary "madwomen" and destabilizing a reading of Celia's final underwater scene as a suicide mission, García, like Pérez, situates Celia alongside her Anglocentric literary predecessors with a difference. This difference relates to context, time, and setting; it also pertains to Celia's racialization, which stems from her name, the blackness of her passions, her fascination with Granada, the *duende*'s black sounds, and "the black sea that awaits [her] voice."[28] Her name contributes to her racialization, signaling how her musicality is scripted onto herself: it can refer both to the patron saint of music and the famed Afro Cuban singer Celia Cruz, alluding to Cuba's Spanish, Christian colonizers and Cuba's colonized African population, respectively. The extensive intertextuality-with-a-difference upon which García relies demonstrates how the multilayered harm that Celia experiences is not simply individualized. This does not mean that Celia does not undergo harm at an individual level; it does mean that this harm corresponds with broader patterns of gendered and racialized subjugation.

Among her intertextual invocations, García subtly references *the* paradigmatic emblem of female hysteria: Dora, arguably the most famous of Sigmund Freud's patients. García obliquely alludes to Dora in her repeated attention to Celia's drop pearl earrings, the same piece of jewelry mentioned in the first dream Dora recounts to Freud. In Dora's case, Freud dismisses her words and brands her hysterical. By deploying the same language to describe this piece of jewelry that is so aligned with Celia's persona as that used in Philip Rieff's edition of *Dora*, García situates Celia alongside Dora and affiliates her with female hysteria. Yet unlike Freud, who discounts the emphasis Dora places on the earrings, García underscores their centrality, bookending her narrative with a focus on the pearls. García recognizes the importance of these earrings to her matriarch's sense of self, and she troubles the gendering of hysteria to which Freud ascribes.

When Celia enters the water after hearing the *duende*'s cries, she releases these earrings (that Gustavo gave her and that she has removed only nine times to clean) to the sea. Given that the earrings are a constant reminder of Gustavo, Celia's decision to let them go could signify her ultimate break with Gustavo and freedom to be her own liberated self. Parting with these earrings that she has worn throughout her life, though, could also be considered a gesture of hopelessness. Metonymically the earrings are a central part of the woman she has become because they emblematize her desires and aspirations. The word choice García employs here—"absence," "surrender," and "extinguishing"—certainly evokes a loss of self.[29] If the earrings symbolically represent Celia, then their extinguishing implies hers.

But García includes one page—the last of Celia's letters—after the narrative's chronological conclusion that complicates the novel's close. In this letter, Celia references the onset of the Cuban Revolution, her birthday, and that of Pilar. Celia conjoins these events to emphasize just how much her identity is grounded in her leftist politics and to highlight that revolutionary death is connected to rebirth. Juxtaposing Celia's underwater song/battle with that signaled by the letter, García stresses the cycle of birth and death, a cycle emphasized by the focus on Celia, the sea, and the Revolution in the novel's beginning and end. This is why, when Celia is called upon to sing at the novel's chronological close, she imagines herself as a "soldier on a mission."[30] Her "last stand" forms part of an anti-imperialist narrative that critiques U.S. involvement in Cuba and that opens with her lookout as a Cuban coast guard scoping the shore for "*gusano* traitors."[31] If Celia personifies revolutionary Cuba, as the literary critic Andrea O'Reilly Herrera posits, then the individual struggles that Celia undergoes and the pathologization she experiences revolve around her *cubanidad*, one that is complicated by its ambiguous racialized and gendered focus. García's complicated positioning of her novel's matriarch locates *Dreaming in Cuban* within a Third World feminist framework. Indeed, García underscores the "connection between the private and the political," central to Third World feminism, through "Celia's private letters which interweave actual historical events with her own personal commentary."[32]

In her final letter, Celia declares that she will no longer write to Gustavo, as she does not need to record any more information about her life because Pilar "will remember everything."[33] Celia points to the connection that she and her granddaughter share by virtue of having the same birthday and communicating with each other through dreams. In the bond and legacy that Pilar inherits from her grandmother, García suggests that knowledge and history can be passed down matrilineally across generations without the need for information to be chronicled in written form. Apart from the final sequence, when the *duende* beckons Celia to sing, Celia's voice can be heard in the otherworldly space she and Pilar occupy and in the memories she transmits to Pilar via their shared dreams. In this respect, Celia's unmediated voice has the possibility of emerging either underwater or through the mediation of her granddaughter's memory and imagination. Although this facilitates the transmission of voice while perpetuating its erasure, it also reveals the interconnectedness of voice and subjectivity, showing how an individual's voice is tied to that of her predecessors and successors.

## Felicia's Fire

Like Celia, Felicia is a defiant female character who finds solace in art, is temporarily institutionalized, and is the recipient of gendered, physical, and psychological harm. Whereas García calls into question Celia's mental instability, she portrays Felicia's mental illness in quite a straightforward manner, highlighting how Felicia's behaviors can be attributed to the syphilis she contracts from her adulterous and abusive first husband, Hugo. While Celia's attitude toward blackness is ambivalent, Felicia openly embraces blackness, identifies with the Afro Cuban religious tenets of *santería*, and dismisses the ideology of pigmentocracy. Like Celia, Felicia exhibits defiance by countering dominant associations of femininity with docility, purity, and virginity; unlike Celia, Felicia explicitly denounces racialized norms.

Felicia's creative interests begin when she is a child. Poetry brings mother and daughter together, as Celia recites poems to Felicia during sleepless nights. Felicia subsequently adopts the poetic language her mother shares with her to express herself. As an adult, Felicia again turns to poetry, namely the metaphorical poetry she finds in *santería* and its ceremonies.[34] As her closest friend, Herminia, explains, for Felicia, these ceremonies "were a kind of poetry that connected her to larger worlds. . . . Our rituals healed her, made her believe again." In her childhood and adulthood, then, poetry gives Felicia a sense of intimacy with others. Yet, as with Yolanda in *How the García Girls Lost Their Accents*, who is largely pathologized because of her poetic mode of expression, poetry keeps others from understanding Felicia—"people told her she didn't make any sense at all" when she would "borrow freely from the poems she'd heard" as a child—and it causes others to brand Felicia delusional. Likewise, neither community nor family members can relate to Felicia's devotion to the poetic *santería* ceremonies. Felicia's figurative language, reliance on imagination, and resistance to gendered, sexualized, and racialized norms mark her as aberrant in the eyes of her community and family, particularly in the eyes of her daughters, who pathologize her—as they repeatedly comment on the "meaningless," "alphabet" words Felicia strings together—and in the eyes of Celia, who cannot comprehend Felicia's enmeshment in "the clandestine rites of the African magic" of *santería*.[35]

Felicia's yearning for human connection, emblematized by her fascination with poetry and *santería*, can also be detected in her relationships with men, including her lovers and son. Her longing for attention begins at a young age and finds expression in her sexualization and pattern of devastation. Like Irene in *The Ladies' Gallery* and *Impossible Motherhood*, Felicia realizes that she can use her body to garner others' interest in her. In her teenage years, she therefore takes a job as an escort; as an adult, she marries three times, with each marriage ending in ruin. Even the close relationship she has with her son is damaged. The connection that Felicia finds in all of her relationships with men therefore can last only so long before it becomes strained or is destroyed.

The longest sexual relationship she has is the abusive one with her first husband, Hugo. The first time García describes Hugo in detail she mentions the sadomasochistic way he treats Felicia and the sadomasochistic way Felicia responds. Like Pérez, who details the cycles of abuse in which Rebecca finds herself in *Geographies of Home*, in *Dreaming in Cuban*, García illustrates verbal, physical, and psychological abuse, sexualized violence, the threat of deathly harm, and the cyclicality of brutality (as both Hugo and Felicia hurt one another). Hugo comes in and out of Felicia's life. The two things on which Felicia can count with respect to him are that he regularly leaves her and that when he comes back he is sure to hurt her. This is evident from the moment García introduces Hugo, when she mentions his multiple return visits to Felicia and their children, the blinding "blow to [Felicia's] eyes," and the time he comes back "to sire Ivanito and leave his syphilis behind."[36] Even in this cursory initial description, García notes the destruction Hugo leaves behind, inserting a gendered critique of the multilayered harm Felicia undergoes. The psychological and physical damage Felicia experiences and then inflicts on herself and others emanates from a specifically male-imposed harm exacted on her.

This harm possesses a distinctive racial history. García describes Hugo as a "descendant of slaves," and she endows him with animal attributes, notably his giraffe-like gait.[37] In this depiction, García highlights Felicia's pull toward her country's African diaspora, but she risks succumbing to stereotypes about black men as "out-of-control," "hypersexual" "brute beast[s]."[38] Even her depiction of Felicia as a hypersexualized, deviant, and defiant character, who affiliates herself with blackness, likens Felicia to the stereotypical image of the black jezebel and the "'tropical' prostitute."[39] This characterization, in turn, racializes Felicia and situates her outside the confines of "true womanhood." Her portrayal resembles that signaled by the African Americanist Hazel Carby, who explains that "the figurations of black women [have] existed in an antithetical relationship with the values embodied in the cult of true womanhood, an absence of the qualities of piety and purity being a crucial signifier. Black womanhood was polarized against white womanhood in the structure of the metaphoric system of female sexuality, particularly through the association of black women with overt sexuality and taboo sexual practices." Felicia's hypersexual positioning and sadomasochism position her within the ready figuration of black womanhood outlined by Carby; her defiance of race and gender norms likewise places her outside of the "cult of true womanhood," as defiance signals nonconformity to gender norms.[40] That both Hugo and Felicia have syphilis further risks adhering to medicalized myths of syphilis as an "'essentially' . . . Caribbean [and racialized] disease."[41] The gender commentary that García provides here is therefore complicated by the overly sexualized racial politics within it.

Such criticism is further confounded by the role Felicia, like Marina in *Geographies of Home*, plays as the recipient and perpetrator of harm. Felicia fights back against her first husband, actively hurting and pleasuring him and avenging herself by setting him on fire. García contextualizes this arson by emphasizing how Felicia's body is medicalized (pregnant, nauseous, and "infected with syphilis and the diseases Hugo brought back from Morocco and other women") and by situating Felicia in the feminized domestic space of the kitchen. In this gendered space, Felicia attains a sense of "clarity" and releases a flaming rag onto her husband's face.[42]

Felicia's retribution resembles Marina's turn to arson in *Geographies of Home* and likens Felicia to *Jane Eyre's* and *Wide Sargasso Sea's* Bertha Mason (born Antoinette Cosway) and her namesake in *Dreaming in Cuban*, Felicia Gutierrez (a patient who befriends Celia in the mental hospital).[43] Although García includes the character of Berta in her narrative, Felicia most closely resembles Bertha. The language García uses to describe the moment when Felicia sets Hugo on fire resonates with that which Brontë and Rhys use to characterize Bertha and the fire she starts. Both Felicia and Bertha attempt to set their husbands on fire (Felicia actually does); Felicia's laughter offsets Hugo's screams, as Bertha's "demoniac laugh" haunts the Thornfield estate where she is confined; and while Felicia holds "a fiery ball," Bertha's eyes are depicted as "red balls." Just as "delicate flames consumed the rag" in *Dreaming in Cuban*, the "tongues of flame darted round [Mr. Rochester's] bed" in *Jane Eyre*; and Felicia stands over her husband as the flames consume him just like Bertha "stand[s], waving her arms, above the battlements" before jumping to her death.[44] Portraying Felicia in a manner that so closely resembles Bertha allows García to show how the madness that marks this character emanates from literary traditions that pathologize specifically racialized women. After all, Bertha (at least Brontë's Bertha) is depicted as the mad creole antagonist to the white Anglo protagonist Jane; as such, she is imprisoned in an attic allegedly to protect her and others from her animalized violence. Felicia is similarly dismissed by her family and community as a racialized madwoman, and she too is confined (in a makeshift guerrilla camp) because of her violent actions. By trying to set their husbands on fire, Felicia and Bertha attempt to escape the abuse they suffer at their husbands' hands, even if this escape only serves to "prove" their madness.[45]

Felicia's arson and destructive rampage are foreshadowed by her namesake's actions. Jorge worries about naming his daughter Felicia because he fears he is dooming her to share Felicia Gutierrez's fate. Sure enough, while Felicia douses her husband with a fiery rag and dies at a young age, her namesake dies prematurely in a fire in the mental hospital where she is kept. Her namesake also sets her husband on fire, killing him in the process. Fire follows Felicia. Even her second husband, Ernesto, dies by fire. Although Felicia does not set this fire, she is haunted by it, causing her to search for answers to Ernesto's death. In a frenzied grief, aggravated by her worsening syphilis, she convinces herself that a town resident, Graciela, is responsible for Ernesto's untimely demise. Seeking retribution, Felicia invites Graciela to the beauty shop where she works and slathers a noxious mixture on Graciela's hair designed to "eat her vicious brain like acid."[46] The placement of revenge in a beauty shop locates Felicia in a feminized site, speaks to the gendered pathologization of grooming discussed by Showalter, and arguably positions the scene in dialogue with the Mexican playwright Rosario Castellanos's *El eterno femenino*, a feminist play set in a beauty salon that challenges the historical (mis)treatment of (in)famous Mexican women. Indeed, Felicia uses this traditionally feminized space to subvert the gendered propriety associated with it and assert her gender-nonconforming vengeance.

After retaliating against Graciela, Felicia experiences a blackout that lasts for months. When she begins to regain a semblance of awareness, she discovers that she has remarried a man named Otto. Reassembling the pieces of her life, she abruptly murders Otto. García does not provide the reader with much detail about this, other than to reveal that as Otto grows aroused while he and Felicia are on a roller coaster, Felicia "closes her eyes" and pushes him off the ride.[47] Despite marrying three times, Felicia cannot sustain a lasting romantic relationship with a man: destruction always gets in the way. Yet she is constantly described in relation to men, as the eroticized object of their violence, fantasies, or admiration.

Even her relationship with her son, Ivanito, is depicted as excessively intimate. Felicia shares a happiness with Ivanito that her daughters, Luz and Milagro, cannot understand. She dances a little too close to him, sees his face while having sex with Otto, sleeps by him, and dresses him well beyond infancy, leading to accusations that she is an "unfit mother" who has "irreparably damaged" her son. The harm to which Felicia subjects Ivanito and herself extends to near infanticide and suicide. As with Otto's murder, García mentions this incident in passing but notes Felicia's sense of resignation: "Felicia remains quiet. She has no energy left for defiance."[48] Illustrating how Felicia's temporary *lack* of defiance leads her to try to end her and her son's lives, García troubles the ready pathologization of female defiance. It is when Felicia is quiet and succumbs to the type of female docility that the medical system in the narrative paints as healthy that she inflicts the utmost harm upon herself and her child.

Unlike her mother, who is institutionalized in a hospital, Felicia is sent to a makeshift guerrilla camp to address her impaired mental health. Like her mother, though, she is confined during her "treatment." Like the institutionalization of "socially undesirable persons" in seventeenth- and eighteenth-century European madhouses, Felicia is placed in "a unit of malcontents, a troop of social misfits" who are there to be molded into Castro revolutionaries.[49] García demonstrates how serving the Revolution supposedly functions as a cure for the "malcontents," both revealing the conflation of the mentally ill with the criminal elaborated by Thomas Szasz and Foucault and depicted by Vilar in *The Ladies' Gallery* and also substituting the place that the hospital previously occupied with that of the militarized camp. Emphasizing how those who are held at the camp are considered rebellious because they do not conform to the ideals and regulations of Castro's Cuba and highlighting the irony in forcibly sending rebels to serve the Revolution because of their rebelliousness, García undermines the rationale for Felicia and the other "patients'" internment. García paints the place itself as a prison-like, Foucauldian boot camp that revolves around an "imperative of labor" and demands that the "misfits" work the land, such that labor and militarization stand in for therapy.[50] García thus reveals how the camp where Felicia is sent, like the mental hospital where her mother is temporarily kept, does not cater to the needs of its patients. Showing how not all those at the camp are patients in the strict sense of the term, and that those confined there are described as guerrillas, García reveals just how little care is given to care.

Felicia remains skeptical about the camp's practices. Her interaction with the medical practitioners, like that of Celia when she was institutionalized, is strained at best. The psychiatrist Felicia sees makes her feel like "a willful child," and the doctors treat her accusatorily rather than working with her to help her heal. She also questions the doctors' mission: to redirect her and her fellow guerrillas toward a revolution she mistrusts. Her suspicion of her doctors extends to her fellow "inmates," causing her to stay silent, as she does not know how her words may be used against her. Her decision not to speak indicates her refusal to participate in her medicalization and militarization. Unlike Celia, who arguably "makes it crazy" to survive her institutionalization, Felicia remains silent and disengages from her medicalization altogether. Since she does not voice her ideas while confined, Felicia feels like she needs "something to do with her hands" and begins to smoke.[51] In this act, she mirrors Celia's preoccupation with exercising her hands (playing the piano was Celia's outlet), and she echoes her namesake's death by burning cigarette. At the camp, Felicia also dreams and reflects on her life. Taking advantage of her night duty to think about the gods of night to whom slaves had prayed or to recall the poetry Celia once recited to her, Felicia relies on creativity to survive her internment. That her recollections consist of both her best friend, Herminia, sharing stories about slaves' religious beliefs and her mother reading her poetry shows how African diasporic religiosity and poetry are linked for Felicia. Situating these particular reflections at night, García draws on the creation and "escapism" that is "often associated with night," revealing how Felicia's memories metaphorically release her from her confinement.[52]

Felicia does not see *santería* as escape, however; she considers it her calling. As a child, she stands by Herminia, even though others label Herminia a *bruja*. As an adult, Felicia attends every *santería* ceremony held by Herminia and her father, finding the rituals healing and fulfilling. Eventually, she decides to become a *santera*, but something goes awry: "Her eyes dried out like an old woman's and her fingers curled like claws until she could hardly pick up her spoon. Even her hair, which had been black as a crow's, grew colorless in scruffy patches on her skull. Whenever she spoke, her lips blurred to a dull line in her face. . . . Felicia's eyesight dimmed until she could only perceive shadows, and the right side of her head swelled with mushroomy lumps. . . . Felicia continued to grow worse."[53] Unlike the radiance exhibited by most newly minted *santeras*, Felicia undergoes a debilitating bodily deterioration. *Santería* on the surface thus appears to betray Felicia despite her allegiance to it.

Yet it is unclear whether *santería* is actually responsible for Felicia's bodily decay. After all, her syphilis has grown quite advanced by this point, Felicia insists on being buried as a *santera*, and her body ultimately returns to its formerly healthy state after undergoing a *santería* purification burial ritual. García describes the remarkable corporeal transformation that follows from this ritual, noting how "the terrible lumps on Felicia's head had disappeared, and her skin was as smooth as the pink lining of a conch. Her eyes, too, had regained their original green."[54] Highlighting how *santería* is responsible for Felicia's physical restoration upon her death and illustrating Felicia's unwavering faith in *santería* until her death, García undermines the notion that *santería* is the force *par excellence* behind Felicia's demise.

Indeed, earlier in the narrative, García attributes Felicia's physical and psychological corrosion to her syphilis. Just as her physical features grow dry and colorless prior to her death, earlier in the narrative, her "skin appears enameled in pinks like the wallpaper of Old Havana Inns."[55] Comparing Felicia's skin to old wallpaper and describing Felicia as delusional, García arguably likens Felicia to the protagonist in Charlotte Perkins Stetson Gilman's "The Yellow Wallpaper," who similarly exhibits a delirium that is only intensified when enclosed in a room with "a smouldering unclean yellow" wallpaper.[56] With this likeness, along with that which links Felicia to Bertha, García situates Felicia within literary traditions that pathologize women. Where García's portrait differs from that of her precursors is in her intersectional attention to race and gender, even though the attention she pays to race risks falling into stereotypes of blackness. Not only is Felicia arguably likened to a jezebel who contracts syphilis from a hypersexualized and animalized man of African descent, but she also is stained by an uncleanliness, as a "damp filth" accompanies the decline in her physical and psychological well-being.[57] Although this uncleanliness resembles that associated with Gilman's protagonist, it also feeds into racist discourses linking blackness to filth.[58]

Upon contracting syphilis, Felicia suffers memory loss and, like the protagonist in "The Yellow Wallpaper," develops delusions that alter her auditory and visual senses. Felicia hears things others can't hear. The shapes of objects grow distorted for her. Colors intensify. She makes constant connections among ideas such that it becomes difficult for her to sleep, arguably exacerbating the delusions she experiences.[59] And she becomes unable to voice her thoughts, as they "erase themselves before she can speak. Something is wrong with her tongue. It forms broken trails of words, words sealed and resistant as stones. She summons a stone and clings to it, a drowning woman."[60] Felicia's difficulty expressing herself, considering her outspoken character, and futile attempt to cling to the stone-like words that make her feel like she is drowning show just how much her syphilis has affected her. Even the image of something being "wrong with her tongue" resonates with the similar image deployed by Anzaldúa about the patient who struggles to control her tongue. The tongue symbolically bridges the physical and psychological damage Felicia undergoes because of her syphilis.

Apart from relying on imagery akin to that used by Anzaldúa, placing Felicia within predominantly Anglocentric traditions of literary madwomen, and highlighting how Felicia has a similar fate as her namesake, García demonstrates how Felicia is tied to her mother. Mother and daughter both are pathologized, share a psychic connection, and work the land. Body, mind, and place unite the two. When Celia returns home from working the land in the name of the Revolution, she finds that Felicia's health has worsened. In this section, García points to "the scarred terrain" of Celia's palms and the Cuban landscape alike.[61] Positioning Felicia's worsened condition just after Celia's return home from having tilled the fields and just before the description of Celia's damaged hands, García ties Felicia's deteriorating health both to the scarred land and Celia's marked body, as Celia's palms themselves are a harmed geography.

The sea also metaphysically links Felicia and Celia, foreshadowing Felicia's death and Celia's final sequence. Celia has a recurring dream that consists of a young girl going out to sea, "float[ing] underwater with wide-open eyes" as "the seas rush over her," and that concludes with a mango tree "shrivel[ing] and d[ying]."[62] Although the underwater imagery in the dream is analogous to that found at the end of *Dreaming in Cuban*, unlike the moment when the *duende*'s voice invites Celia to the sea, here the girl ignores the voices arguably warning her *against* going out to sea. The dream's image of the dying tree prefigures Felicia's death and can be juxtaposed against the rooted gardenia tree at the novel's chronological close.

Celia has another ominous dream in which she hears voices "call[ing] to her in ragged words stitched together from many languages, like dissonant scraps of quilt," with syllables "drifting into an icy blur of white."[63] This dream is placed after the Lorca reading that Celia attends, where she is drawn to the *duende*'s morose sounds. Upon awaking from the dream, Celia senses that Felicia's life is in immediate danger; in the next section where Felicia appears, Felicia is interned in the guerrilla camp after having almost killed herself and her son. The order in which these events are presented suggests that Lorca's reading, Celia's dream, and Felicia's near suicide and infanticide are connected. That Celia panics about her daughter's well-being and feels compelled to find Felicia as soon as she awakens from her dream, even while sensing that any effort to save Felicia is futile, illustrates how Celia's dream foreshadows Felicia's imminent death. Moreover, both Celia's and Felicia's closing sequences are linked by the underwater imagery of Celia's recurrent dream and the image of the *duende*. Through these similarities, García highlights how the harm that befalls Felicia needs to be understood in relation to that which her mother experiences.

Felicia's dreams further connect mother and daughter. Felicia's dreams consist of mourning for strangers: "for lost children, for the prostitutes in

India, for the women raped in Havana," and for those readily forgotten in the course of history. Grief bridges mother's and daughter's dreams, and this shared grief illustrates how the individual harm that Felicia undergoes is linked to that felt by her mother and by a broader and primarily female collective. This grief isn't necessarily immobilizing, though. Like Celia, Felicia "adapted to her grief with imagination."[64] Grief, suffering, and imagination pervade this narrative. Imagination and dreams are adaptive mechanisms through which mother and daughter alike can deal with their pain and connect to others.

## With a Whisk in Her Hand: Lourdes's Madeleines

Like Celia and Felicia, Lourdes experiences devastating patriarchal harm and relies on creativity to move forward with her life. The harm Lourdes undergoes shapes her political views and impacts how she treats herself and her loved ones. Suffering a miscarriage and surviving a rape cause Lourdes to flee Cuba and seek refuge in New York City. Like Rebecca in *Geographies of Home* and Fe at the start of *So Far from God*, Lourdes fervently believes in the American Dream. She opens her own bakery chain that she names Yankee Doodle to display her proud and public allegiance to her adoptive country. Food not only serves as the vehicle through which Lourdes pursues her capitalist enterprises, but it functions in other ways central to the formation of her character. Food sustains Lourdes. Through food, Lourdes both exerts control and arguably loses control over her body. Through food, she also supports herself and her family financially and expresses herself artistically, as her baked goods are ones she crafts with her own hands. This act is revolutionary: it signifies Lourdes's rebellion against her mother, Castro's Cuba, and the Cuban soldier who raped her.

Lourdes redefines herself in the United States through food, and she subverts *and* succumbs to gender norms by baking. The entrepreneurial success she enjoys, as she is able to open a second bakery shop, is indicative of her business savvy, a quality that demonstrates how Lourdes has the capacity to break conventional gender roles that relegate women to the domestic sphere and define business acumen as a male trait.[65] This is not Lourdes's sole expression of gendered defiance. Even after marrying into a wealthy family, she rejects a life of female domesticity and immediately sets out to work on the family ranch. This work ethic stays with her when she moves to New York. Apart from running two bakeries there, she is the first auxiliary policewoman in her precinct. Patrolling the streets, she again situates herself in the traditionally masculine public sphere. She gains a sense of power with this positionality; this perceived power, contextualized against the backdrop of her rape, arguably allows Lourdes to usurp the status of authority figure and make this role hers. What unites these manifestations of rebelliousness is Lourdes's gender-bending positionality: she, like her mother, places herself in public arenas, and she creates work opportunities where she is in charge.

Considering her spirited gendered defiance, Lourdes's decision to create a bakery chain is ironic since bakeries straddle the public and private spheres, situating Lourdes in an in-between gendered space. Lourdes's bakeries represent her ability to enter into the public domain that is readily coded masculine. As soon as she positions herself in this public sphere, though, she is relegated (or relegates herself) back into the private sphere of the kitchen, a space all too readily feminized, to make her business the success that it is. Even her (pre)occupation with food and fluctuation between obsessing over her body or neglecting it reveals how ambiguous her gendered positionality is.

As López suggests, Lourdes's eating disorder can be understood with respect to Showalter's analysis of the medicalization of women. Lourdes's alternating excessive attention to, or disregard for, her body image speaks to the historically feminized pathologization tied to extremes in grooming that Showalter discusses.[66] Viewing Lourdes as an archetypal "madwoman" allows us to see how the thread of female madness runs through the representations of the novel's protagonists even while García troubles this pathologization by implicating patriarchal oppression in the pathologization of all four characters. For Lourdes, patriarchal harm underpins her complicated relationship with her body.

Gaining and losing over one hundred pounds, Lourdes reconfigures herself at her own volition:

> Lourdes Puente welcomes the purity, the hollowness of her
> stomach. It's been a month since she stopped eating, and already
> she's lost thirty-four pounds. She envisions the muscled walls
> of her stomach shrinking, contracting, slickly clean from the
> absence of food and the gallons of springwater she drinks.
> She feels transparent, as if the hard lines of her hulking form
> were disintegrating. . . . Lourdes has lost 118 pounds. Her
> metamorphosis is complete. She will eat today for the first time
> in months. The aroma of food is appealing again, but Lourdes is
> afraid of its temptations. . . . There is a purity within her, a careful
> enzymatic balance she does not wish to disturb.[67]

Lourdes's willed bodily transformation evokes Susan Bordo's writings about anorexia that theorize the eating disorder in terms of a desire for bodily control, even if such control paradoxically harms the body.[68] Lourdes here notes the "enzymatic balance" within her body that she wishes to keep intact upon deciding to eat food again. Her attention to her body suggests that her purging and binging do not so much represent a loss of bodily control as they indicate a self-conscious effort to control her body. This yearning to control her physical appearance follows from Lourdes's miscarriage and rape, both of which she entwines and links to Cuban male soldiers. The sensations of hollowness, transparency, and purity she welcomes when she does not eat can be understood as her desire to cleanse herself of the harm she has experienced. When Lourdes does eat, she does "not battle her cravings; rather, she submit[s] to them like a somnambulist to a dream."[69] The cravings to which she voluntarily succumbs and about which she dreams can be considered to fill the void left by the loss of her second child and the assault on her person. Given that the belly acts as the signified site of loss and potential rebirth, Lourdes's fixation on her changing body shows just how much the trauma of her miscarriage and rape stay with her well past the moments when they transpire.

García first mentions Lourdes's miscarriage and rape immediately after noting Lourdes's insistence that she live in a place substantially cold enough arguably to distance herself physically, climatologically, and emotionally from Cuba. In the next scene that appears in the book—but that transpires two months earlier in Cuba—Lourdes loses her second child after falling off a horse. She returns home, only to find soldiers there. She yells at them to leave, and they retreat. Once they do, her body lets her know that she has suffered a miscarriage. Rather than explicitly name Lourdes's loss here, García concentrates on Lourdes's bodily pain, depicting the fragmentation she senses as a clot moves through her breasts, belly, and thighs toward her feet.[70] The soldiers' attempt to exert their force (pointing their weapons at Lourdes's husband, Rufino) in the midst of Lourdes's miscarriage reveals that home is not the place of refuge Lourdes needs, and it contextualizes why Lourdes subsequently resists the revolutionary politics of Castro's Cuba that the soldiers embody.

Soon after Lourdes's miscarriage, the same soldiers who had been in her home that fateful day return to dispossess her of her house, claiming it the property of Castro's government. When Lourdes again demands that the soldiers leave, one of them rapes her, while the other assists. Lourdes fights back, charging against one soldier and directly meeting the gaze of the other, as she then spits in his face. But her refusal to accept the soldiers' imposition of power only intensifies their attempts to exert power over her. Indeed, the only words we hear either soldier utter in this scene are about Lourdes's defiance, as one asks, "So the woman of this house is a fighter?"[71] While one soldier holds Lourdes, the other rapes her after tying her riding pants around her mouth. Showing how the soldier stifles Lourdes's ability to scream, or even speak, with Lourdes's *riding* pants, García links Lourdes's rape to her miscarriage after being thrown off a horse.

Both events affect Lourdes's body and psyche. As with Marina in *Geographies of Home*, who copes with the physical and psychological aftereffects of rape, Lourdes's rape in *Dreaming in Cuban* literally and figuratively scars her. Apart from battering her with his rifle, Lourdes's rapist etches a "primeval scraping. Crimson hieroglyphics" onto her belly. After Lourdes enters the bathroom once the soldiers have left, she tries to rub her stained body clean "with detergents meant for the walls and the tile floors," and she examines her reflection in the mirror to read the markings imprinted on her.[72] The illegibility of these carvings emphasizes the inexplicability of the harm she has just endured in a manner evocative of Elaine Scarry's contention that physical pain cannot be expressed, and it hauntingly etches Lourdes's unspeakable, unreadable trauma onto her body, such that she cannot ever leave her assault in the past. Lourdes's scars permanently script her emotional pain onto her body, revealing the actual interconnectedness of body and mind, effectively countering Scarry's dissociation of body from mind. The placing of these "hieroglyphics" on Lourdes's *belly* acts as a constant reminder of her rape and miscarriage.

García uses sensory language to describe Lourdes's miscarriage and rape. Blood imagery links both events. García also repeats the word *smell* in the rape scene, illustrating how this sense lets Lourdes see into her assailant's past and future in a manner evocative of the transportive qualities of the French novelist Marcel Proust's proverbial madeleine. In Lourdes's case, unlike that of Proust's narrator, the events she remembers and envisions do not belong to her. Nevertheless, her olfactory sense allows her to move back and forth in time in much the same way that the taste of the madeleine does for Proust's narrator. The connection between smell and memory in this sequence corresponds with the flashbacks inserted throughout *Dreaming in Cuban* and the novel's nonlinear style, and it also presages Lourdes's intense attachment to and rejection of food later in the narrative.

Haunted by her miscarriage and rape, Lourdes repeatedly imagines what her son would have been like had he lived. In her New York neighborhood, she sees a young boy, the son of a former employee of hers to whom she refers as the Navarro boy, who is the same age her son would have been. She positions this boy as foil to her unborn son, convinced that her son would not have been the delinquent she considers this boy to be. The dream she sustains of her child is strikingly similar to the final depiction of the Navarro boy: the two are underwater images of vanishing. In both sequences, Lourdes is a bystander to loss. Whereas she cannot help her son during her miscarriage or in her imagined underwater vision of him, her ability to rescue the Navarro boy is ambiguous. While her unborn child "disappears before she can rescue him," the Navarro boy's death is cryptic. The boy jumps into the Hudson River, and Lourdes follows, but "the river smells of death." García continues: "Only one more fact is important. Lourdes lived and the Navarro boy died."[73] The uncertainty of Lourdes's role in this death reflects her ambiguous attitude toward the boy, as he serves as a painful reminder of her son's preempted existence.

Water is the immediate catalyst for Lourdes's remembrance of what she has lost. As she gazes into a reflecting pool, she thinks about her miscarriage: "Mesmerized by the greenish water . . . a wound inside her reopens. She remembers what the doctors in Cuba had told her. That the baby inside her had died. That they'd have to inject her with a saline solution to expel her baby's remains. That she would have no more children." This memory prompts her to "see the face of her unborn child" and to seek to save him from the waters that envelop him.[74] For Lourdes, as for Celia, water therefore functions as a source of comfort and pain, connecting and separating loved ones.

Although the pool into which Lourdes stares acts as the portal that takes her back in time, it is not the sole trigger for her recollection of her miscarriage. The collective sequence of events leading to this reflection could be considered to cause it. Indeed, Lourdes begins that day by reading the newspapers, looking for articles about disasters. Among the stories she finds, she notices one about a mother who has lost her children in a fire, and she "grieves for these victims as if they were her beloved relatives. Each calamity makes Lourdes feel her own sorrow, keeps her own pain fresh."[75] After breakfast, she accompanies her daughter to an art museum. On their way there, Lourdes makes multiple stops to eat. Inside the art museum, she stops to gaze at the reflecting pool. These events together help contextualize her turn to her haunted past. Seeking out horrific news stories, intimately relating to those who have suffered, and "keep[ing] her own pain fresh," she ties her individual pain and sorrow to those experienced by a broader collective, and she courts her own suffering ostensibly because that is her only way of holding on to what she has lost. Showing how Lourdes eats voraciously after emerging from a lengthy fast, García links food—or at least the extremes that accompany fasting and binging—with an association with the past. Locating Lourdes's recollection of her miscarriage in an art museum, García emphasizes the ability of art to transport its viewers across time and place. The combination of the daily happenings illustrates the void that Lourdes cannot fill after losing her son. These events take her back in time to her miscarriage and then out of time, to a fabricated vision of her son, revealing her desperately futile attempt to change the past and fill the emptiness she feels inside.

The references to Lourdes's rape do not function as a series of flashbacks in the way that the recollections of her miscarriage do, but this does not indicate that the rape has had less of an impact on her. The rape helps contextualize why she settles down in New York, prides herself on her entrepreneurial success, and gains and loses so much weight. There are two moments when Lourdes explicitly remembers her rape. The first is prior to her return to Cuba when she is speaking with her father's spirit by the Brooklyn Bridge, as he tries to convince her to go to Cuba and reach out to Celia in the wake of Felicia's death. Just as Lourdes's gaze into the reflection pool prompts her memory of her miscarriage, her location by the river here takes her back to her sexual assault. Upon maintaining that returning to Cuba is "impossible," she recalls her rape, fragmenting her assailant's person and remembering the sensations of smell and touch that she experienced during her violation: "'You don't understand,' Lourdes cries and searches the breeze above her. She smells the brilliantined hair, feels the scraping blade, the web of scars it left on her stomach." When her father ectoplasmically admits that he, unlike Celia, knows about her rape, Lourdes struggles to breathe. This is the only moment when we hear Lourdes talk about her rape. Even in this conversation, however, she does not put words to her trauma. Her father's spirit does this for her by saying, "I know about the soldier." Showing how Lourdes acknowledges her rape only to her father's ghost, and that she does so following his admission of knowledge about the assault, García reveals the unspeakability of the harm Lourdes undergoes. That Lourdes imagines herself singing "in a high, pure voice" upon having this conversation with her father's spirit, though, suggests that the admission of her rape allows her to envision herself coming to voice and that talking about the assault is a way of coming to terms with it to move on with her life.[76] The image of Lourdes singing in a religious setting ("high mass") suggests that confessing that the rape happened is part of the process that will finally allow her to face the place that she associates with this trauma.[77]

The only other time Lourdes recalls her rape is after she has returned to Cuba for Felicia's funeral. During her visit, she fixates on the decay she observes around her and constantly criticizes what Castro's Revolution has done to the island. As she travels from place to place, memories flood her thoughts, as the sites trigger recollections of her past. Once she reaches the villa where she and Rufino married and lived, she remembers her rape, miscarriage, and "a story she read once about Guam, about how brown snakes were introduced by Americans. The snakes strangled the native birds one by one. They ate the eggs from the nests until the jungle had no voice."[78] Reflecting on this story after traveling through (what she considers) a crumbled Cuba and upon remembering her own traumatic experiences, Lourdes links her individual suffering to the harm inflicted on her birth country and the natural world at large, devastation brought about by a disruption of the natural world order.[79] The story she recalls about the disastrous consequences of bringing American snakes to the jungle in Guam highlights the damage inflicted by the introduction of a foreign species onto native soil, serving as a type of ecopolitical and sociopolitical commentary about the damaging effects of U.S. imperialism in the Pacific Rim. The image of the eggs eaten before they hatch, meanwhile, links the destruction of the birds to the tragic loss of Lourdes's son before he, like the birds, could be born. Likewise, the snakes can be compared to the soldiers whom Lourdes ties to her miscarriage and rape. Like the snakes that rob the jungle of its voice, the soldiers—introduced to Cuba as a result of the Revolution that seeks to change Cuba—note Lourdes's outspokenness and silence her by raping her.

In this scene, Lourdes first remembers her miscarriage, then the story, and then her rape. This order suggests that the story acts as a bridge linking both types of individual harm Lourdes experiences and locating individual, collective, ecopolitical, and sociopolitical harm alongside one another. Indeed, immediately after remembering the story about the extinction of the native birds, Lourdes relays her worst fears: "that her rape, her baby's death were absorbed quietly by the earth, that they are ultimately no more meaningful than falling leaves on an autumn day.

She hungers for a violence of nature, terrible and permanent, to record the evil. Nothing less would satisfy her."[80] Her yearning for "a violence of nature" to unearth the harm she has undergone, a harm that otherwise has been subsumed by the earth, implicates the natural world in her suffering, but it also locates the natural world as potentially giving this suffering meaning. Remembering and recording the "evil" she has faced are integral to giving voice to what otherwise would be swallowed and forgotten.

The memories Lourdes has upon returning to her former home affect her emotionally and physically, causing her to move unsteadily in their wake and preventing her from being able to speak when asked if she can be helped. She wishes she were a dog that could "dig for her bones" and that could "claim them from the black-hooded earth, the scraping blade."[81] Yearning to be animalized to reclaim part of herself that has been buried, and positioning the earth as a grim reaper that utilizes the same type of instrument as that used on her during her rape, Lourdes reveals both the destructive power of the natural world order and the importance of disinterring what has been buried. In her case, she has buried memories of her past traumas. Coming back to Cuba and returning to the place where she experienced more than one form of devastating harm mark the steps she can take to "dig for her bones" and reclaim them from "the black-hooded earth."

## Pilar's Pierced Liberty

A painter, musician, student, and admirer of punk subculture, Pilar forms part of the youngest generation of female characters in *Dreaming in Cuban* to display creative passions, express rebelliousness, and experience sexualized harm. A member of the 1.5 generation, Pilar is drawn to her birth country, shares an uncanny connection with her grandmother, criticizes her mother's capitalist mentality and dichotomous outlook, and sees the American Dream as a myth, while considering New York home. She is the character who most evidently occupies an interstitial positionality. Identifying as a Cuban American who has been shaped by the aftereffects of the Cuban Revolution, Pilar recognizes that Cuba forms a critical component of who she is, even while ultimately realizing that she "belongs" in New York "not *instead* of . . . but *more* than Cuba."[82] Pilar's recognition of her complicated positioning and her embrace of ambiguity can be considered acts of rebellion against Lourdes's belief system. Beyond an expression of defiance against her mother, though, Pilar's interstitial perspective represents the vision of the future of the del Pino family with which García leaves readers. Since Pilar is left to inherit her family's memories and *historias*, she straddles her family's conflicting ideologies. She also inherits her matrilineal family's artistic tendencies and susceptibility to harm. She is the carrier of the past and the harm tied to it, but she is also the harbinger of the future and the hope that accompanies it.

As a child, Pilar begins to take painting classes, but her mother does not support such pursuits. Lourdes's opposition to her daughter's artistic vocation corresponds with their contentious relationship and dissonant convictions. Even when Pilar wins a scholarship to art school, Lourdes refuses to let her take this opportunity. Claiming "that artists are a bad element," Lourdes allows negative generalizations about artists to prevent her from understanding the importance of painting to her daughter. Apart from criminalizing artists, Lourdes exclusively sees the "morbidity" in Pilar's paintings.[83] Pilar, however, pursues her artistic interests, not allowing anything to dissuade her from expressing herself.

Pilar paints to protest social injustice and comment on the neoliberal dystopia she sees around her. Since her paintings consist of a left-leaning social critique, she is suspicious when Lourdes commissions her to create a "'pro-American'" mural to celebrate their adoptive country and the grand opening of Lourdes's second bakery. Although Pilar accepts, she insists on painting the piece on her own terms. She takes the emblematic figure of U.S. patriotism, the Statue of Liberty, as her subject. Rather than celebrate the freedom and democratic principles associated with this icon, though, she questions whether these tenets hold true. She takes a "pro-American" symbol but twists it to critique the American Dream, placing the statue against an "irradiated, nuked out" background with pulsating stick figures that resemble "thorny scars that look like barbed wire."[84] This background reveals an irony: the Statue of Liberty is surrounded by an electrified, harmful, and confining atmosphere, one that highlights how Liberty herself is in a state of disarray. The barbed wire–like scars/stick figures around Liberty counter the message at the base of the actual statue that invites the "huddled masses" to U.S. shores; instead, the image of barbed wire connotes a strict division between insiders and outsiders and is linked to animalization, militarization, and criminalization. The stick figures themselves reveal an American Dream gone frighteningly awry.

Pilar also depicts a muddled nationalism here. Instead of holding the tablet bearing the inscription of the date of the Declaration of Independence, her statue's right hand "reach[es] over to cover her left breast, as if she's reciting the National Anthem or some other slogan." Pilar thus removes the marker of independence linked to Liberty, and she describes the National Anthem as a slogan like any other, undermining its weight by likening it to a capitalist catchphrase. Even if the hand gesture suggests a recitation of the National Anthem, the positioning of the left hand troubles any patriotism Pilar might be portraying, as Pilar paints "Liberty's torch slightly beyond her [left hand's] grasp." With this portrait, Pilar shows that liberty, symbolized by the torch, is just out of reach and, as separate from the whole, no longer serves as a synecdoche for what it has been designed to represent. Such disjuncture is only exacerbated by the "punk rallying cry" that Pilar adds to the base of the statue: "I'M A MESS."[85] These words function as a form of graffiti, branding the statue; their capitalization emphasizes the extent to which Liberty is identified with chaos and is anything but the emblem of the ideal nation it is designed to represent. Instead, Pilar suggests that the alleged freedoms associated with the neoliberal, "democratic" principles tied to Liberty turn Liberty into a mess.

This mess is punctuated by the final touch Pilar adds to her painting: "a safety pin through Liberty's nose." Considering that in punk subculture the safety pin preceded the nose ring as a symbol of defiance, the inclusion of this image departs from conventional renderings of the statue, and it positions Liberty within punk subculture. Pilar thus displays manifold rebellions. For one, this image prefigures that used by the punk rock band the Sex Pistols in their God Save the Queen cover. Pilar herself later acknowledges the similarly sought-after reaction of shock and anarchy elicited by both her and the band, even though she subsequently realizes that even this act of punk rebellion eventually gets commodified. Her portrayal of the safety pin as nose piercing could also be considered a subtle attack against Lourdes. Earlier in the narrative, García describes Lourdes's anger at being gifted a book by Pilar that she believes contains communist propaganda. Lourdes drops the book into a tub of water, removes it, and "fasten[s] a note to the cover with a safety pin. 'Why don't you move to Russia if you think it's so great!'"[86] Deploying the same object that her mother uses to criticize her gift, and piercing this object through the ultimate symbol of Americanness, Pilar utilizes her mother's tactics and ideologies against her. Moreover, by using a symbol of female domesticity to pierce Liberty, Pilar offers a gendered critique of this country's treatment of women. In all of these ways, Pilar's painting epitomizes her spirit of rebellion and displays her view of the American Dream as anything but the utopia it promises to be.

Surprisingly, Lourdes defends both the painting and her daughter when customers attack the piece. Pilar is moved by her mother's defense of her artwork, and this moment temporarily unites mother and daughter in a manner unparalleled in the text. It unites them in terms of the love Pilar feels toward, and senses from, her mother, and it brings them together by revealing that their beliefs are not as different as either would make them out to be. Lourdes later admits to Jorge's spirit that she "hadn't approved of Pilar's painting," but she explains that "she wouldn't tolerate people telling her what to do on her own property." Jorge's ghost replies, "That's how it began in Cuba," adding, "You must stop the cancer at your front door."[87] Pilar arrives at a similar conclusion regarding free expression. When discussing her artwork with her grandmother, Pilar asks whether she could have artistic liberty in Cuba. Celia responds, "Within the revolution, everything; against the revolution, nothing," leading Pilar to wonder what Castro would think of her rebellious paintings: "Art, I'd tell him, is the ultimate revolution."[88] Despite Lourdes's staunch capitalist beliefs and Pilar's capitalist critique, mother and daughter unite in their belief in First Amendment liberties and in their opposition to any system that would suppress these. Both Pilar's painting of the statue and Lourdes's defense of it illustrate the two characters' defense of the tenets of freedom the statue signifies. Free expression temporarily brings mother and daughter together.

This allegiance is ironic considering Lourdes's general dismissal of Pilar's artistry. Lourdes attributes an extreme morbidity to her daughter's artwork, one that feeds into her pathologization of Pilar. This pathologization is made manifest when Pilar sees a psychiatrist named Dr. Vincent Price. In their session, Dr. Price asks Pilar to tell him "about [her] urge to mutilate the human form," to which Pilar does not know how to respond. Instead, she reflects on her strained relationship with her mother and her yearning to be in Cuba with her grandmother. She also is convinced that her mother and doctor must have spoken about her and her art behind her back. She wonders why her psychiatrist and mother alike conflate the violence in her paintings with a troubled psyche, thinking, "A paintbrush is better than a gun so why doesn't everybody just leave me alone? Painting is its own language, I wanted to tell him. Translations just confuse it."[89] With such a portrayal, García illustrates how Pilar's mother and psychiatrist both rely on popular (mis)conceptions of mental illness as affiliated with creativity and pathologize Pilar as a result of these ideas, and she undermines the validity of Lourdes's and the psychiatrist's construction of Pilar as psychologically disturbed.

García's characterization of Pilar's alleged mental imbalance troubles the idea that Pilar, like Celia, is unstable: García highlights how Pilar and her psychiatrist speak across one another, and she reveals a complicity between Lourdes and the psychiatrist that positions Pilar as an outsider in her own therapy sessions. Showing how Pilar's art is the focus of the conversation she has with her psychiatrist and a primary area of concern in the presumed conversation between Pilar's mother and doctor, García reveals how Lourdes and Dr. Price treat Pilar's art as *the* tangible manifestation of Pilar's supposed psychic distress. Lourdes and Dr. Price fail to understand that assuming a causation between the violent subject matter in Pilar's art and her presumably disturbed psyche displays a flawed logic: the subject matter of a creative piece does not necessarily correlate with the state of mind undergirding its creation. As Pilar herself explains, her artwork cannot be summarily translated or explained; reading it literally is an act of misreading. Her reaction to her psychiatrist's imperative that she discuss her "urge to mutilate the human form" reveals her perception of her art as multilayered and shows how her art lets her express her desires, feelings of unbelonging, and rebellion *productively.* Pilar's use of art to express her pain thus speaks to Suzanne Bost's contention that pain can be productive and to Anzaldúa's description of her creative process as vampiric and yet renascent, countering Dr. Price's view of Pilar's painting as stemming from destructive impulses.[90]

Despite Lourdes's and Dr. Price's efforts to stifle Pilar's expression by directing her away from the type of art she is compelled to produce, Pilar continues to paint. Her painting allows her to criticize neoliberalism, the objectification of women, and the suppression of women's voices. She expresses outrage over women's ready positioning as nude models to serve as objects of male artists' gaze; she instead calls for an overdue recognition of women's achievements. Just by virtue of painting, Pilar engages in a type of gendered rebellion by putting herself in the subject position of artist. She recognizes that she is not the only one to do so, that she is among "all the women artists throughout history who managed to paint despite the odds against them," who are readily regarded as "anomal[ies]" and "product[s] of a freak nature," or unlike her, are viewed as successful as "a direct result of [their] association with a male painter or mentor."[91] By locating Pilar alongside these women, García demonstrates how Pilar's pathologization forms part of a trajectory whereby women artists are cast as aberrants who reside in men's shadows.

García accordingly illustrates how Pilar's individual experiences need to be understood in relation to a broader collective, and she challenges how (and what) history is recorded, remembered, and understood. Even Pilar's insistence that "painting is its own language," her telepathic communication with her grandmother, and her assertion that the bulk of what she has learned has come at her own initiative or from what Celia has taught her indicate that history need not be transmitted exclusively through writing. Other forms of *historia* telling are just as valid and important to reveal *historias* that otherwise have been marginalized or omitted from textbooks. The connection between history and *historia* is central to the type of recovery project in which García is engaging, as she demonstrates that story is not altogether distinct from history and need not be falsely constructed as such. Pilar's assertions that imagination exists in place of history, that "we're all tied to the past by flukes," and that alternative modes of *historia* merit validation form part of her gendered and artistic rebellion.[92] The revolution for which she calls does not consist of governmental upheaval, but it demands a reconceptualization of what counts as *historia*. Pilar positions art as something that itself is a type of *historia* and as such has the capacity to effect social change.

Music is a muse, inspiring Pilar's artistry and vision. Not only does Pilar highlight how music, like art, is its own type of language, but she also notes that music assaults and confronts its listeners.[93] The sense of rebellion elicited by the music she hears can be likened to the morbidity Dr. Price and Lourdes attribute to her painting. Just as with her artwork, though, the feeling of violation generated by the music inspires Pilar, allowing for artistic creation.

There is a bitter irony in Pilar's love for the "artistic assault" generated by the music to which she listens, though, as she herself is later sexually assaulted while carrying a Beny Moré record album. One of the boys who attacks Pilar throws her record aside, and Pilar imagines hearing music, "imagine[s] picking up the record, feeling each groove," arguably to cope with the assault as it transpires. While the boys violate her, she "hear[s] the five-note pounding of Lou Reed's 'Street Hassle'" as she tries to reassure herself that her attackers are mere children.[94] Her reliance on her imagination to sense herself touching her record and hearing "Street Hassle" demonstrates that music is her solace just as it is for Celia. Pilar and Celia alike see music as a mode of rebellion and escape.

Indeed, the imagery used to describe Pilar's assault resonates with that found in both Celia's walk into the sea at the novel's end and Lourdes's rape. García emphasizes voice(lessness) in Pilar's assault and Celia's closing scene, noting the stifling of voice in the former and the fostering of voice in the latter. While the boys suppress Pilar's voice by placing a knife on her throat as they violate her, Pilar describes the cello that plays in her head during her attack as having a "low, dying voice." Celia, by contrast, is urged to sing at the narrative's end. On the surface, this difference seems to suggest that Pilar's assault functions as a type of death scene, whereas Celia's entry into the sea is one of awakening. García complicates this reading, though, in part by inserting the image of fireflies in both sections. She likens Pilar's attackers' eyes to fireflies, just as she describes Celia imagining the pearl earrings that she has released to the sea as similar to a firefly, tying the boys' eyes to Celia's earrings. With this link, and with her description of the fireflies as "erased of memory" and "extinguishing," García suggests that the fireflies signify loss.[95] In neither scene, though, do the fireflies explicitly refer to Pilar or Celia; instead, they are tied to characters who harm them in some way. Yet the women characters are the ones who experience loss: Pilar loses a part of herself in her violation, and Celia loses earrings connected to her subjecthood. García troubles a reading of Pilar's assault as a type of death scene by highlighting how Pilar responds to her attack. The violation Pilar undergoes prompts her to paint and determine that she will go to Cuba. The assault therefore does not render her permanently voiceless; rather, it triggers her long-sought-after return to her birthplace.

Pilar's assault also mirrors that of Lourdes, and García deploys analogous imagery in both scenes. García depicts flies in her portrayal of Celia's call to sea, Pilar's assault, and Lourdes's rape. When Lourdes sees her rapist's future, she envisions "flies blacken[ing] his eyes." Not only does this vision arguably foretell her assailant's future, but it foreshadows her daughter's attack by boys with eyes like flies. The assailants in both attacks use knives, and they prevent the women from crying out in protest. Lourdes's rapist muffles her mouth, while Pilar's attackers place a knife with a scar-like edge on her throat, an image evocative of the scars left on Lourdes's belly after her rapist scrapes her with a knife.[96] García also uses sensory language to narrate both assaults, relying on smell in the former and sound in the latter. Lourdes and Pilar even have comparable immediate reactions to their attacks: Lourdes scours her body in the bathroom, and Pilar bathes for nine days. The similarities between the scenes highlight the repetition and reproduction of gendered harm.

The comparisons among Pilar's and Lourdes's assaults and Celia's underwater surrender of her pearls emphasize how the individual violation Pilar experiences is connected to her mother's rape and her grandmother's underwater liminality. As the inheritor of memories, Pilar carries her matrilineal family's *historias* with her, and she, like her mother, grandmother, and aunt, relies on creativity to express herself and survive the harm that befalls her. Although Pilar, like her maternal predecessors, is silenced via her pathologization, she does not let her "wild" tongue be tamed. Art allows her to articulate her rebellion and critique the forces that try to prevent her from being heard.

## Embracing *Duende*

All the protagonists in *Dreaming in Cuban* are drawn to art; they all are constructed as deviant and to varying degrees are pathologized; and they all experience devastating harm. None, though, is utterly immobilized by the labels of aberrance thrust her way or the many types of harm she undergoes. Instead, the harm leads all of the characters to express themselves artistically/rebelliously, in a manner evocative of the movement that Bost claims to follow from pain.[97] Their creative expression, however, marks them as transgressive, situating them within a cycle whereby art/revolution paradoxically contributes to the harm cast their way and helps them both cope with this harm and defy the forces that hurt them. Locating her characters within this cycle, García reveals how they are neither completely silenced, as Marta Caminero-Santangelo might argue, nor completely agentic, as Bost might claim. They are silenced and agentic at once, inhabiting an interstitial space.

This space is replete with the ambiguity and contradictions that characterize Third World feminist writing and that undergird the concept of *duende*. Given that *Dreaming in Cuban* primarily takes place in the aftermath of the Cuban Revolution, García's emphasis on liminality is not surprising. This emphasis speaks to García's own Cuban American identification as schizophrenic, not in a clinical sense, but in terms of the multiplicity associated with the label and her diasporic subjectivity.[98] García's use of the word *schizophrenia* to describe this subjectivity can be extended to her treatment of madness in the novel, as she problematizes her characters' ready pathologization.

In her portrayal of Pilar, the character who most overtly embraces ambiguity, as representative of her family's future, and in her open-ended close to the novel, García underscores the importance of developing "a tolerance for ambiguity" and embracing multiplicity.[99] Part of this embrace consists of recognizing the integral relation between art and revolution and among imagination, dreams, history, and story. Arguably one of the most cited lines of the novel is "And there's only my imagination where our history should be." As Pilar comes to the realization that imagination stands in for history and that the histories she would like to know are those that are often suppressed, unwritten, or unspoken, she reveals the violence that corresponds with stifled or censored expression, and she emphasizes the significance of adopting a hybrid perspective that would recognize *historias* beyond those provided in textbooks.[100] Despite/because of the violence and struggle that accompanies a hybrid perspective, García highlights how a hybrid positionality can allow for the emergence of artistry.[101] Artistry, emblazoned in the figure of the *duende*, exists in conditions of unrest, suppression, and violation; it arises at the intersection of deviance and defiance; and it inhabits a liminal space between harm and hope.

# 5 / Clamped Mouths and Muted Cries: Stifled Expression in Julia Alvarez's *How the García Girls Lost Their Accents*

*Word is power.*
—JULIA ALVAREZ, IN MARTA CAMINERO-SANTANGELO, "'THE TERRITORY OF THE STORYTELLER': AN INTERVIEW WITH JULIA ALVAREZ"

The title of Julia Alvarez's first and semi-autobiographical novel, *How the García Girls Lost Their Accents,* makes clear that language is central to the narrative. *The book,* set in the Dominican Republic and the United States during and after Trujillo's dictatorship, explores the relation among language, voice, and subjectivity. The novel is written in reverse chronological order, primarily in a third-person narrative voice. It centers on the lives of the García sisters—Sofía, Carla, Sandi, and Yolanda—and to a lesser degree, their parents, Laura and Carlos, chronicling the characters' rocky adjustment to the United States and the downward race and class mobility they experience upon moving to this country. This is not a narrative about a fulfilled American Dream, nor is it one about assimilation, despite reviews claiming such; it is a narrative about unbelonging and muffled expression.[1] Language is power in the text; without it, or without recognition of it, the characters are "nobody."[2]

By "language," I am not referring only to the words with which the characters communicate or are prevented from communicating; I am also exploring how language has "the power to define." While conceding that there exists a difference between language and voice—recognizing that a study of language might ask, "Who says what to whom . . . ?," whereas one of voice might ask, "Who says?"—my analysis examines language in relation to voice.[3] These questions cannot be neatly disso-ciated from one another in the context of Alvarez's novel, as who has the power to say is directly tied to what is and isn't being said or heard. The relation between language and voice is manifest in the "accents" that the girls have supposedly lost and in the abundant imagery of clamped mouths and muted cries.

Language in Alvarez's text consists of more than verbal expression. It entails bodily and artistic (visual and literary) expression as well. It is the articulation of a "theory in the flesh." As Gloria Anzaldúa would say, language is entwined with ethnicity, race, gender, and sexuality and evokes pride and shame. What does it mean, then, for Alvarez's female protagonists to experience what Anzaldúa might label a form of linguistic terrorism, and how do these characters respond to the attempts to squelch their expression? Anzaldúa describes linguistic terrorism in relation to Chicanas from the borderlands who have been shamed, "told that [their] language is wrong."⁴ The concept of linguistic terrorism could be applied to the characters in *How the García Girls Lost Their Accents* who are attacked because of the ways they express themselves and who inhabit psychological, cultural, and gendered borderlands. The linguistic terrorism to which Alvarez's protagonists are subjected locates them in a similarly interstitial space as that portrayed in Anzaldúa's *Borderlands*. How each character confronts the attempts to stifle her expression differs. The attacks against Sofía's sexuality lead her to sexualize herself further. Carla and Sandi, by contrast, react in silent horror to the violations they experience. Yolanda, ostensibly the author's double, internalizes the linguistic terrorism directed her way while simultaneously resisting it. Through these portrayals, Alvarez highlights the power of language to inflict devastating harm on her protagonists as they come of age.

The structure of the narrative parallels the linguistic motifs presented therein. The inconsistency of the narrative voice and the primary use of the third-person narration both undo the idea of a unified narrative voice that typifies many works of fiction and also arguably deprive the protagonists of their own voices through which to present their tales. At the same time, the multiple narrative voices illustrate how the individual struggles the García girls undergo are connected to the collective struggles of their family and even their extended community. The intermittent insertion of the first-person singular and plural narration similarly emphasizes the relation between the individual and collective while also revealing the occasional possibility of self-expression at the structural level. The hybridity and complexity of narrative voice(s) in Alvarez's text underscore how "Who says?" is tied to *what* is said.

Just as important as what is said is what isn't. If "word is power," as Alvarez claims, does that mean that a silenced speaker is powerless? To help answer this question, let us re-turn to the epigraph that opens

*Intersections of Harm.* This passage portrays a male dentist seeking to control his female patient's allegedly wild tongue. As noted in my introduction, Anzaldúa uses the anecdote of the dentist and patient to present the concept of linguistic terrorism and to illustrate how the dentist's attempts to "tame" his patient's tongue mark his violent imposition of patriarchal and arguably racial power over her.[5] Just as Anzaldúa depicts the tongue as both a physical body part that is being controlled and a figurative language that is being stifled, Alvarez similarly uses images of tongues, clamped mouths, and muted cries to highlight the damage wreaked on her characters' bodies, language, and sense of self. Likewise, just as the patient in *Borderlands* actively resists the smothering efforts to control her body and language, the García girls notably struggle to make themselves heard.

## Sofía's Second Sex

Sofía is the "maverick youngest" of the García girls.[6] Her rebelliousness presents itself in her manipulation of gender norms. Although all of the protagonists are described in relation to their changing bodies, Sofía is the one who most clearly expresses herself through her body either to defy or to adhere to gender norms. The harm she experiences stems from the suppression of both her gender bending and her gender conformity, and it is primarily exacted by her own family members onto her.

Sofía is first presented to readers when she is a grown woman, during a birthday celebration that she has organized for her father, Carlos. Alvarez here emphasizes the friction between daughter and father, which she links to Sofía's refusal to abide by gendered Catholic and Dominican dictates that she remain a virgin until marriage. Indeed, while growing up, Sofía is the sister "with 'non-stop boyfriends.'"[7] During her college years, she drops out of school to travel to Colombia with her boyfriend to consummate their relationship. But the two quickly break up. Just a few days later, Sofía meets a man named Otto, whom she takes as a lover, with whom she subsequently exchanges love letters, and whom she asks to marry her. From these descriptions, Alvarez demonstrates how Sofía, like Caridad in *So Far from God,* bends gender norms expected of her: she surrounds herself with men, goes to great lengths to have sex, has more than one sex partner prior to marrying, maintains a secret correspondence with Otto, and proposes to *him*.

Upon discovering his daughter's love letters, Carlos is incensed. He charges her with "misbehavior," labels her a "loose" woman, and accuses her of "dragging [his] good name through the dirt."[8] In this reaction, he reveals his belief in the types of pervasive, binary patriarchal ideologies that relegate women to the status of virgin or whore, ideologies that Sofía battles and stubbornly rejects. Suggesting that Sofía's actions affect his reputation, Carlos treats Sofía as a piece of property: he refuses to see her as a woman in her own right, one who consists of more than her family name. With his indictment of Sofía, Carlos imposes a form of linguistic terrorism on her. Although he does not silence her in the strict sense of the term, he imposes his language on her by defining her as sexually irresponsible (marking himself as right and her as wrong), tries to constrain her alleged waywardness, and cuts off communication with her by banishing her. He therefore suppresses her language and voice by refusing to listen to her.

Even after Sofía and Otto marry and have two children, the relationship between father and daughter remains strained. Evidence of this tension can be found when Carlos fails to appreciate Sofía's efforts to make a success of his aforementioned birthday party. Instead, he congratulates her husband on the choice of band, and during a game when he is to surmise who is kissing him, he guesses the names of all the women in his family except Sofía. Upon realizing that her father is rendering her invisible and giving her the proverbial silent treatment, Sofía angrily inserts herself in the festivities. Using the very "misbehavior" that causes Carlos to shun her to make her presence known, she relies on her sexualization to assert her voice. Unlike the simple pecks her sisters give their father, Sofía uses her *tongue* as her trademark, giving Carlos "a wet, open-mouthed kiss in his ear," running "her tongue in the whorls of his ear and nibbl[ing] the tip."[9] Rather than feel embarrassed for her "inappropriate" kiss, she shames her father, inverting where the shame lies. Instead of experiencing the indignity her father claims she should feel for her "loose" ways, she indignantly uses the labels of looseness thrown her way to her advantage to ensure that she will be heard. Sofía does not assert herself through words here; she does not rely on her figurative tongue to express herself. Like Anzaldúa's patient who uses her literal tongue to resist the dentist's oral invasion, Sofía similarly fights her father's efforts to control her through her manipulation of her physical tongue, sliding it into her father's ear to guarantee that he finally listen to her and end his harmful stifling of her voice. Her decision to insert her tongue in her father's ear, the body part tied to listening, reflects her determination to make herself heard.

Although Sofía asserts herself here, she is unable to do the same while growing up. While she exhibits signs of the rebellious adult she eventually will become, as an adolescent, she struggles to own her voice. When a teenage Sofía and her sisters are warned to "examine [their] consciences," Sofía concedes, "The problem isn't I can't find anything to worry about but that I find so much." When Laura confronts the girls about a bag of marijuana that she has found, Sofía admits that the bag is hers and hers alone. As her punishment, she stays in the Dominican Republic for one year. When her family members return to the island, they are surprised to discover a seemingly changed Sofía. Instead of seeing an outwardly defiant sister, they find one who, on the surface, appears to conform to gender expectations. Rather than reunite with the Sofía they knew, "who always made a point of not wearing makeup or fixing herself up," the Garcías meet one preoccupied with her looks, who "looks like the *after* person in one of those *before-after* make-overs in magazines." Sofía's close attention to her grooming here and her claim to be "seeing someone nice" reveal how the island has supposedly "tamed" her formerly nonconforming self, as she now seems to adhere to gendered conventions about how women should behave.[10]

Yet Alvarez complicates her portrait of Sofía's relation to gender norms in this section. Despite superficially succumbing to gendered dictates of grooming and dating, Sofía knowingly and proudly rebels against these by dating Manuel Gustavo, a secret cousin. In her relationship with him, however, she does not speak her mind; Alvarez insinuates that Sofía's preoccupation with her looks follows from her efforts to try to placate Manuel Gustavo. Sofía lets him "tell her what she can and cannot do" and read, allows him to pressure her sexually, and "grows withdrawn and watchful" around him.[11] Her submissive behavior counters her prior and subsequent outspokenness. In this case, Manuel Gustavo silences Sofía by prioritizing his ideas and wants over hers; her sisters silence her by letting their parents know that Sofía has been meeting privately with her cousin; and Sofía silences herself by quietly acquiescing to Manuel Gustavo's demands and tossing her thoughts and wants to the margins.

As an adolescent and as an adult, Sofía accordingly experiences a suppression of her voice. Whereas she internalizes this as a teenager, she battles it as an adult. Ironically, her internalization of and resistance to her suppression manifest themselves in comparable ways: via a sexualized display of her body. By wearing the labels of looseness thrust her way and asserting herself as a grown woman, Sofía refuses to be silenced, proudly projecting her voice by owning her sexuality. Her inability to reconcile with her father while expressing herself, however, reveals that she continues to be subjected to gendered harm.

## The Trespasses That Haunt Carla

Carla, like Sofía, is silenced. Unlike the muzzling that Sofía undergoes at the hands of family members, though, the muffling of Carla's voice comes from peers and strangers. The chapter "Trespassing" elucidates the linguistic terrorism Carla experiences and the feelings of shame and unbelonging that accompany her stifled expression. The chapter chronicles twelve-year-old Carla's difficult acclimation to life in the United States. It details her homesickness for the Dominican Republic, a yearning only exacerbated by the taunting Carla experiences from schoolmates and the unwelcome changes Carla notices in her pubescent body. And it narrates her horror at witnessing a grown man gratify himself in front of her, only to have to recount the incident to policemen whose "very masculinity offended and threatened."[12] Each of these instances harms Carla and renders her speechless.

"Trespassing" positions place at its center. Place here is not so much a fixed, geographical site as a state of mind: it operates in the manner described by Henri Lefebvre as "indistinguishable from mental [and social] space."[13] Alvarez begins the chapter with an attention to physical place but quickly reveals the intersections among physical, social, and psychological space. She mentions the Garcías' move to Long Island to give the girls more space than they had in their crowded New York City apartment, and she notes Carla's perception of her family's new yard. Looking at the trees therein that "were no taller than little [Sofía]," Carla nostalgically recalls the "lush grasses and thick-limbed, vine-ladened trees around the compound back home," the natural environment where she and her cousin Lucinda would share their knowledge "about how babies were made."[14] The contrast Carla draws between the two islands reveals not only a difference between the sparse, developed Long Island environment and the overgrown Dominican one but also between the sentiments she attaches to each. Although Long Island is where she currently resides, the Dominican Republic is the place she still calls home, evoking bell hooks's theorization of home as shifting, multiple, dispersed, and sometimes alienating, outlined in chapter 2 of *Intersections of Harm*.[15] Just as Loida Maritza Pérez and Irene Vilar illustrate how home is not always commensurate with abode, Alvarez presents Carla's feelings of dislocation in the United States and rootedness in the Dominican Republic to elucidate that home is not necessarily about the domicile where one resides. By linking Carla's remembrance of the natural world surrounding her family's Dominican compound with Carla's memories of her conversations with

Lucinda, Alvarez also posits a relation between Carla's sense of home and her sex education, a connection that is particularly prescient considering the feelings of exile and the "real world" sex education forced upon Carla soon after this flashback.

Examining the landscape of her new neighborhood, Carla notices the "grasses and real trees and real bushes" growing at the end of the block in undeveloped farmland. Her view of the greenery at the neighborhood's edge as "real" contrasts with what she considers to be the artificial, overly trimmed greenery in the developed portion of her new neighborhood and instead resembles the lush landscape of her former residence in the Dominican Republic. As Carla looks at the section where her new neighborhood ends, a sign catches her attention. It reads, "PRIVATE, NO TRESPASSING."[16] Given her Catholic upbringing and lack of fluency in English, she does not realize that the sign is warning her to keep out of the property; she is familiar with only one definition of trespassing: the religious one dissuading her from sinning. Upon learning that words can have multiple meanings in English and that the sign is telling her to "keep out," Carla experiences a feeling of unbelonging. The physical place that surrounds her, coupled with her linguistic misunderstanding, reminds her just how much she feels out of place *socially and psychologically* in the United States.

The idea of trespassing runs throughout the chapter, as Carla repeatedly is made to feel like an outsider in her family's adoptive country. The boys at her school constantly stress that this is not her birth country and that this is not a hospitable environment for someone born elsewhere. They harm her physically, psychologically, and linguistically, hurling stones and epithets at her. Their insults are directed at her racialized and gendered body and at her language. The boys demand, "Go back to where you came from, you dirty spic!"; tease, "No titties. . . . Monkey legs!"; and "mimic her. 'Plees eh-stop.'"[17] These taunts make Carla feel ashamed of her racialized ethnic identity, seemingly unlovable changing body, and "accented" English that differentiates her spoken language from that of her classmates.[18] Even after she switches schools and is no longer bullied, the boys' words continue to haunt her, "trespass[ing] in her dreams and in her waking moments."[19] Showing how the boys' insults stay with Carla well past the moment when they are thrust her way, Alvarez reveals the injurious power of words and illustrates Anzaldúa's claims about the damaging, long-lasting effects of linguistic terrorism. By likening the psychological harm the boys inflict on Carla to a form of trespassing, Alvarez demonstrates how language can encroach on others in a manner comparable to entering someone's territory without permission. In both cases, there exists an invasion of place, whether this place be land, psyche, or "the geography closest in—the body."[20]

Likewise, Carla's encounter with a sex offender functions as a type of trespassing on her, as the man, like the boys, invades her sense of place by exposing himself to her. On her way home from the school where she is bullied, Carla is followed by a man in a car. He stops her, Carla thinks, to ask for directions. Instead, the man, naked from the waist down, urges Carla to enter his car, only to masturbate before her. Astonished, Carla's "mouth hung open. Not one word, English or Spanish, occurred to her."[21] As with the boys' taunts, the sex offender's exposure to Carla renders her vulnerable. In both instances, Alvarez emphasizes the centrality of language and the damaging silencing effect of the violations to which Carla has been subjected.

When Carla tells her mother about the incident, her mother worriedly informs the police, who come to the García household. As with her encounters with the boys at school and the sex offender that render her mute, Carla's conversation with the police similarly makes her feel small, uneasy, fearful, and speechless. Part of her apprehension can be attributed to the ingrained suspicion of authority that she grew up having because of the terror that Rafael Leónidas Trujillo's secret police instilled in the Dominican population and because of her father's own anti-Trujillo activities. But the discomfort Carla feels at this moment extends beyond a residual, haunting fear of police under a dictatorial regime and is particular to her feelings of unbelonging in the United States. Alvarez elucidates this through her use of intensifiers: "They were so big, so strong, so male, so American."[22] The repetition of the modifier so illustrates that Carla sees the policemen through a lens of excess and sees herself in stark opposition to them, such that the adjectives that correspond with the modifiers arguably reveal more about Carla's self-perception than her view of the policemen. If the policemen are "so big, so strong, so male, so American," then it follows that Carla feels so small, so weak, so female, so un-American by contrast.

When the police ask Carla about the suspect and incident, Carla has difficulty finding the words to describe what she witnessed. Her inability to answer many of their questions has to do, in part, with her lack of knowledge about makes of cars, a knowledge that she attributes to maleness and Americanness, as the boys who bully her regularly converse about car types. The confusion she experiences upon being interviewed by the police, though, also has to do with both their anatomical questions and the language in which she is asked to describe what she has witnessed. Because she was brought to the United States as a preteen, has not been in this country for very long, and attends a Catholic school, she hasn't had the sex education in either Spanish or English that would provide her with the needed vocabulary to explain what she has seen. Her incomplete vocabulary here feeds into her insecurities about her own changing body, just as it highlights the silencing she feels by the sex offender and policemen. For these reasons, when she is trying to find the words to describe the sex offender's bald head "but could not remember the word for bald," she immediately associates the man's hairlessness with her own legs that are beginning to grow hairs and thinks of how "her body was already betraying her."[23] Betrayal links Carla's encounter with the man and her view of her body. While the man has betrayed her confidence by inappropriately displaying his bodily pleasure before her, Carla considers her own body to betray her by similarly forcing her to grow up before she feels ready to do so.

Carla's lack of vocabulary with which to narrate what she has seen not only makes her keenly aware of the intersections among body, gender, and race politics, but it also underscores the central role that language plays within and among these politics. If "ethnic identity is twin skin to linguistic identity," as Anzaldúa maintains, and if gender identity is entwined with ethnic/linguistic identity, then the silencing Carla feels while being made to replay the masturbation scene consists of more than a taming of her tongue: it entails a suppression of her voice and, correspondingly, her subjectivity.[24] The intersection of these identities helps explain why her encounter with the police exacerbates her linguistic and psychological distress and leads her to reflect on previous moments when she has felt Othered. Her conversation with the police and frustration with their inability to recognize her linguistic and emotional difficulties conveying what has happened to her causes her to liken the one policeman who is matter-of-factly asking her questions to the boys who tease her: "Carla was forced to confront the cop's face. It was indeed an adult version of the sickly white faces of the boys in the playground. This is what they would look like once they grew up."[25] With this comparison, Carla shows how she associates the harm she undergoes in the playground with that she experiences while struggling to communicate with the white male cops. Alvarez herself has described Carla's frustration and insecurity in this scene as tied to a silencing that comes from Carla's powerlessness: "[Carla] is disgusted and terrified," but, as Alvarez underscores, "[Carla] has no power, she has no words, she can't describe it, she is silenced."[26]

The link that Alvarez posits between silence and powerlessness resonates with Anzaldúa's articulation of linguistic terrorism and Richard Ruiz's connection between voice and subjectivity in his research on language-minority students. Ruiz notes, "When *voice* is suppressed, it is not heard—it does not exist."[27] If voice corresponds with subjectivity, and if voice unheard does not exist, then neither does subjectivity. This idea of nonexistence can be observed in Carla, who is repeatedly unheard and rendered powerless, first by the bullies, then by the sex offender, and finally by the policemen. Already out of place in a land far away from the one she considers home, she is further displaced by her encounters with boys and men who make her feel like an outsider who does not belong. Carla most evidently experiences her unbelonging through language: through the confusing multiple meanings words carry, the harmful and unfamiliar words directed at her, and the words she cannot find to express herself.

## Sandi's Void

Like Carla, Sandra (primarily referred to as Sandi) struggles to feel a sense of belonging. Although Alvarez characterizes Sandi as prototypically beautiful (given her Nordic physical features), this beauty does nothing to fill the void that Sandi feels from childhood to adulthood. Like Pilar in *Dreaming in Cuban*, Sandi is a gifted visual artist. Unlike Pilar, Sandi's ability to draw and paint is cut painfully short, finding expression only in her childhood. When she and her family move to the United States, Sandi is left with a gaping hole inside her. As a recent and young immigrant to the United States, she feels like an outsider; as an adult, she has a mental breakdown, causing her to be institutionalized. The emptiness she carries with her from childhood to adulthood can be contextualized against the backdrop of her preempted artistry. When Sandi loses her artistry—ceasing to be able to express herself freely—she arguably loses her voice.

The last chapter that Alvarez devotes to Sandi chronicles Sandi's artistic talents as a child living in the Dominican Republic. Her artistic skills single her out among her three sisters and thirteen cousins. Not only do her abilities have mystical qualities, they are a form of language through which Sandi expresses herself. When she is reprimanded for drawing cats on her family's house and is told to remove her artwork, the house is subsequently inundated with rodents. Believing in the restorative potential of Sandi's artistry, the family nursemaid, Milagros, asks Sandi to burn one of her drawings to help cure Milagros's ailing son; by the next day, the boy has recovered. With these portrayals, Alvarez reveals the power of Sandi's art, an aptitude reminiscent of what Anzaldúa describes as the shamanic state. Although Anzaldúa primarily associates the shamanic state with writing, the qualities that she ascribes to this state resonate with those that Sandi possesses as a visual artist. The shamanic state, according to Anzaldúa, consists of the ability of art to transform and cure; likewise, Sandi's drawings have transformative as well as healing qualities.[28] The drawings thus function in a manner akin to shamanistic writing, serving as Sandi's mode of self-expression, or voice.

The power of Sandi's artwork is so awe-inspiring that her immediate and extended family decides to send all four García girls and thirteen cousins to art classes to nurture their creativity. But the art teacher, Doña Charito, insists that her students engage in calisthenic exercises, check that the paintbrushes are properly aligned, and correctly hold the brushes. A bored Sandi, eager to paint, does not heed her teacher's orders. Her need to express herself visually is too great to suppress; with feline artistic impulses that "paw" and "claw at" her, she is compelled to draw cats.[29]

Her artistic defiance and self-expression cause Doña Charito to isolate her, such that Sandi's articulation of her creative voice puts her in harm's way. As a curious Sandi wanders the grounds, seeking revenge against her teacher, she overhears a man (Doña Charito's "crazy" husband, Don José) shouting from a shed.[30] Peering through the window, she sees the sculpted beginnings of a nativity scene, noticing partially built statues of animals along with one of a woman. But this is not the holy scene she might expect. Just as Carla years later sees a grown man pleasure himself before her, bare from the waist down with a lasso around his penis, Sandi here witnesses a man, wearing only a halter and chain, sexually satisfy himself on an unfinished statue of the Virgin Mary. Like Carla, whose "mouth hung open" in silent shock, Sandi is similarly astounded: her "mouth opened in a voice-less scream."[31] Both sisters react in horrified silence to the violations upon which they unwittingly trespass, and both scenes underscore the centrality of voice, or lack thereof, to reveal the powerlessness felt by Carla and Sandi alike.

Images of mouths and cries abound in the wake of the scene upon which Sandi stumbles. Prior to opening her mouth in a muted scream, Sandi "crie[s] out to warn the woman beneath [Don José]." Viewing the statue as a woman whom she feels compelled to warn, Sandi personifies it and fears it is in some sort of danger, even though Sandi cries out after observing Don José's seemingly tender touch on the statue's face. This scene is replete with contradictions. Sandi conjoins the tenderness she believes she sees in Don José with the harm she senses the statue will experience when Don José prepares to pleasure himself with his creation against her/its supposed will. Although the cry that Sandi releases at this point is heard, it does not reach its intended target. Instead, a startled Don José turns Sandi's way. Petrified, she throws herself to the ground to avoid his reach. She cries out a second time. This time, though, when she is attempting to scream to protect *herself* instead of the statue, she initially cannot merge sound with howl. Her fear silences her, just as it does Carla when she encounters the sex offender. This silence likens Sandi to the lifeless statue that cannot cry out to protect herself/itself against Don José. When Sandi is finally able to find the voice with which to accompany her screams, it is too late. Not only has she unwillingly trespassed on a scene that terrifies her, but her fall has broken her arm, causing "her hand [to] los[e] its art." This moment is one of doubled trespassing, as Sandi both intrudes on Don José's private creation, and arguable attempted sexual assault, and also *is intruded on* as a result of her traumatizing exposure to this scene. The doubled trespassing here thus leads to irreparable loss and devastating harm. Having lost her art, Sandi loses a central part of her subjectivity. After her fall, she is "a changed child." Although her bone eventually heals, "almost perfectly," the adverb *almost* suggests that her bone, like her artistic talent and sense of self, will never be the same.[32]

Despite the harm she experiences because of her physical injury, "lost . . . art," and doubled trespassing, Sandi claims to undergo "one moment of triumph during that year of art lessons." This "moment of triumph" is curious. It comes during the unveiling at midnight mass of the nativity scene that Don José has sculpted. At this point, Sandi is especially drawn to the formerly faceless statue of the Virgin Mary that she previously tried to warn against Don José's advances; now, however, "My eyes were drawn to the face of the Virgin. . . . I put my hand to my own face to make sure it was mine. My cheek had the curve of her cheek; my brows arched like her brows; my eyes had been as wide as hers, staring up at the little man as he knocked on the window of his work-shed."[33] Julie Barak and Ellen McCracken interpret this scene as one of reclamation. Barak maintains, "Don José's art reclaims [Sandi's] body," and McCracken argues that art, specifically the sculpture of the Virgin Mary, helps Sandi find self-worth.[34] Barak and McCracken alike signal the power of art in allowing Sandi to experience triumph.

While it is possible to read Sandi's immortalization in the Virgin Mary statue and Sandi's self-characterization as triumphant as reclamations of her physical and psychological self, it is difficult to view this scene as one of strict reclamation, or joy for that matter. The term *triumph* to describe the sensation Sandi experiences is ironic at best. Whereas Sandi connects art to self-worth, the art that is linked to her self-worth is that which *she* creates, not necessarily that which is created to immortalize her. Rather than reclaim her body or subjectivity, the reflection of Sandi's facial features in the statue renders these features immobile and inanimate. By seeing her own face mirrored in that of the statue that has been (nearly) desecrated by its "mad artist" male creator, she likens herself to a potentially violated, inanimate, *silent,* female object unable to defend herself/itself against the sexual advances of a "madman." What is more, the facial resemblance the statue bears to Sandi indicates that Don José has rendered the witness to his creation and sexual exploitation akin to the subject of his artwork and disturbed sexual fantasies. In this way, the likening of the sculpture's face to that of Sandi, while immortalizing Sandi, objectifies her. Considering Sandi's sense of incompleteness and preoccupation with her appearance throughout the rest of the novel, the midnight mass scene therefore reads less like one of reclamation and more like one of misguided triumph or loss.

Understanding this scene through the lens of loss helps explain Sandi's subsequent struggles. When she and her family move to the United States, she feels, and is made to feel, like an outsider who is trespassing on someone else's territory. The downstairs adult neighbor, "La Bruja," animalizes the García girls, describing them as loud, "wild burros," and she treats them as invaders, resorting to the same racial slurs the schoolchildren direct toward the girls: "Spics! Go back to where you came from!"[35] This mistreatment instills a sense of unbelonging in Sandi, emphasizing that her home, like that of Carla, is not in her adoptive country. Despite Sandi's initial defiance of her neighbor (Sandi deliberately stomps on the floor to assert her presence and fight back against La Bruja), the neighbor's hateful epithets stay with Sandi, aggravating any misgivings she might have about her place in the United States.

Sandi's anxieties about belonging are connected to her preoccupation with her body image and her concern over others' perceptions of her. It is impossible to dissociate the treatment she receives from her view of herself. Just as Vilar and Pérez highlight how external perception affects internal perception, Alvarez similarly draws attention to the power of the gaze when she again places Sandi in the role of witness. As an onlooker, Sandi forms part of the action *at the same time* that she is apart from it. In this role, she observes her surroundings and takes note of her and her family's sense of place. She looks around the Spanish restaurant where she and her family are eating with the Fannings, a white couple from the United States whom the Garcías met in the Dominican Republic, and she arrives at a mixed realization: "All the other guests were white and spoke in low, unexcited voices. Americans, for sure. They could have eaten anywhere"; however, Sandi thinks, "They had come to a *Spanish* place for dinner. La Bruja was wrong. Spanish was something other people paid to be around."[36] On the one hand, Sandi notices that she and her family stand out against the rest of the restaurant guests. If the other guests are white, quiet, and American, then she and her family are brown (or at least nonwhite), loud, and un-American by contrast. She and her family thus are marked as outsiders. As Spanish speakers, though, the Garcías simultaneously have an insider status in the restaurant where guests choose to eat. Although Sandi conflates a shared language with a shared culture here, substituting her ethnic identity with her linguistic one, her observation that Spanish is a desired commodity reveals that she discovers a sense of self-worth through a language of economic worth and that she relies on notions of value to counter La Bruja's claims that she and her family do not belong in this country.

Throughout this scene, Sandi pays particular attention to ideas of place as tied to the intersection of geographical sites, positionality, and power. She notes that her family, who previously held a position of race and class privilege in the Dominican Republic, now finds itself on lower rungs of the racial and socioeconomic ladder. Because of their light skin and wealth, the Garcías experienced advantages while living in the Dominican Republic. Once in the United States, however, they no longer have these same advantages. Jorge Duany attributes this type of shift in positionality to different ideas about the meaning of race in Latin America and the Caribbean and in the United States; quoting Frank Moya Pons, he describes this adjustment as a "traumatic racial experience."[37] The Garcías undergo such an adjustment and, to varying degrees, are traumatized by their new racialization and marginalization in the United States. Even if they are phenotypically pale, they nevertheless are racialized by virtue of their *latinidad*, as elucidated in Sandi's observation that her family is different from the white guests in the restaurant.

This racialization is coupled with a downward class mobility. Whereas on the island the Garcías host the Fannings, in the United States, the

Fannings invite the Garcías to dinner, as the Garcías can no longer afford the luxuries they previously enjoyed. Sandi realizes how rare it is for her and her family to take a taxi to the restaurant where they meet the Fannings; in the restaurant, she notes how much her parents worry about the price of the dinner to which they are being treated. She notices her father's discomfort around Mrs. Fanning specifically, and women from the United States in general, and she sees how this unease causes him to "look down at his feet," prompts him to "round his shoulders," and leads him to become "stiffly well-mannered, like a servant." These are the gestures that Alvarez ties to the Garcías' former servants in the Dominican Republic. Sandi's father's adoption of these same poses here, where he averts the gaze of the white woman before him, reveals the extent of the downward mobility and accompanying internalized sense of inferiority that the Garcías experience in the United States. As a wealthy white woman from this country, Mrs. Fanning's race and class privilege in this instance trumps Carlos's gender privilege and puts her in a position of power over him. For this reason, when a drunk Mrs. Fanning inappropriately "brushe[s] her lips on his," Carlos feels unable to voice his shame or assert her wrongdoing since the Fannings are the Garcías' "one chance in this country."[38] The Garcías' newly dependent positionality accordingly silences Carlos.

Sandi initially reacts to the untoward scene she has just witnessed in the same way as her father: she looks down. Only once she enters the restroom does she look up, not toward Mrs. Fanning, but at her own reflection in the mirror: "Looking at herself in the mirror, she was surprised to find a pretty girl looking back at her. It was a girl who could pass as American, with soft blue eyes and fair skin. . . . Her face was delicate like a ballerina's. It struck her impersonally as if it were a judgment someone else was delivering, someone American and important, like Dr. Fanning: she was pretty."[39] Sandi's self-gaze at this point, after having again trespassed on an unwanted scene with a skewed power dynamic, reveals her need to affirm her subjecthood. As with Irene in *The Ladies' Gallery*, Sandi seeks self-recognition by staring in the mirror. Seeing herself there functions in a manner akin to that when a younger Sandi sees her likeness in the face of the Virgin Mary statue. The mirrored moments confirm her subjectivity, but they do so only after Sandi has witnessed some type of violation. This combination links the affirmation of subjectivity to the type of psychological displacement signaled by Jaques Lacan and Antonio Viego, whereby self-affirmation follows from psychic displacement.

This time, Sandi is struck by the figure she sees before her, a figure connected to, and yet disconnected from, herself. Rather than use the third-person pronoun to characterize Sandi's view of herself, Alvarez, in Lacanian fashion, highlights a divide between Sandi and her mirrored reflection. Alvarez describes the image Sandi sees in the mirror as a girl, such that Sandi sees herself, or more precisely, her reflection, as a disparate entity. The girl startles Sandi because of her unexpected beauty—a beauty that significantly is tied to her light complexion—that could make her visible to someone "important, like Dr. Fanning" and that could allow her to "pass as American." This portrayal resonates with that found in *Geographies of Home*: Alvarez and Pérez alike demonstrate how pervasive myths equating beauty with fair skin are subsequently internalized in their characters' psyches. The correlation Sandi draws among beauty, phenotype, and passing suggests that she believes that beauty (a.k.a. fair skin) has the ability to approximate Americanness. The semi-equation she draws here echoes that offered by Frantz Fanon, who highlights how humanity is socially constructed as white. Fanon's desire to "make [himself] white" is tied to his desire to be treated humanely; but this desire is unattainable.[40] Similarly, for Sandi, beauty does not carry quite enough power to lead to full-fledged Americanness; it can only *pass* as such. Yet Sandi's perceived beauty brings with it the power of recognition and potential belonging: "Being pretty, she would not have to go back to where she came from. Pretty spoke both languages. Pretty belonged in this country to spite La Bruja."[41] Being pretty and being able to "pass as American" gives Sandi the promise of the sense of place that comes with belonging. With this promise, she gains a self-confidence that lets her move away from the marginalized position she previously felt she occupied. With this psychological shift, she concludes that Mrs. Fanning's inappropriate behavior makes *Mrs. Fanning* indebted to her. At the end of the dinner, as at the beginning, Sandi again relies on economic notions of value to assert her own worth. By the end of the evening, though, she has swapped places with Mrs. Fanning. Instead of seeing herself and her family as the ones who owe the Fannings for having made it possible for them to migrate to the United States, a newly assertive Sandi considers Mrs. Fanning to owe her, positioning Mrs. Fanning in the role of debtor and Sandi in the role of collector.

This sense of worth is fleeting, however, as Sandi continues to feel an inner void. This perceived hollowness arguably prefigures her nervous breakdown as an adult. Rather than present Sandi's breakdown through Sandi's eyes, or in a chapter exclusively centered on Sandi, Alvarez mentions Sandi's psychological issues in a chapter devoted to the stories Sandi's mother, Laura, tells about each of her daughters. Unlike the stories of Sandi's sisters that are narrated with pride, Laura begrudgingly shares the story of Sandi's psychiatric hospitalization. Although Laura very well could still tell other stories about Sandi, she chooses not to do so, as she would like to forget any part of the past that could be tied to Sandi's imbalance. The psychological harm that Sandi endures therefore instills both a willed amnesia in Laura and a suppression of Laura's creative expression through her stifled stories.

The last story Laura shares about Sandi is one she has to tell to Sandi's psychiatrist. Convinced that her daughter has gone "crazy," despite the doctor's diagnosis that Sandi has suffered a nervous breakdown but is "not clinically crazy," Laura relays her primary concerns about Sandi's appearance and intellectual pursuits.[42] She frets over Sandi's excessive weight loss and fixation on her body image. Laura also does not understand why Sandi cannot appreciate her beauty, especially because Sandi has inherited the physical features that Sandi herself once realized would be considered pretty in the eyes of "important," American others.

Unlike the scene when a young Sandi is startled by the pretty girl gazing back at her in the mirror and subsequently recognizes both her beauty and the possibility of belonging such beauty could bring her, as an adult, Sandi's self-perception changes. Not only does she yearn "to look like those twiggy models," but she "want[s] to be darker complected like her sisters."[43] Her desires here reflect a simultaneous internalization and rejection of beauty myths. While Sandi ascribes to gendered ideas of female beauty as connected to thinness, she destabilizes racialized constructions of beauty as tied to whiteness, as she yearns to look *less* white. Her adherence to, and rejection of, dominant beauty myths cannot be separated from her perpetual feelings of unbelonging. While her extreme dieting reveals the destructive power pervasive beauty myths hold, it could be construed as her attempt to assert control over her body in a manner that resembles Lourdes's fasting and binging purges in *Dreaming in Cuban* and that evokes Susan Bordo's contention that anorexia can function both as an assertion and a loss of control. Describing "anorexia as a species of unconscious feminist protest," Bordo elaborates: "The anorectic is engaged in a 'hunger strike,' as [Susie] Orbach calls it, stressing that this is a political discourse, in which the action of food refusal and dramatic transformation of body size 'expresses with [the] body what [the anorectic] is unable to tell us with words'— her indictment of a culture that disdains and suppresses female hunger, makes women ashamed of their appetites and needs, and demands that women constantly work on the transformation of their body."[44] Sandi's own type of "hunger strike" (like that of Lourdes) then can be read as her newfound mode of self-expression, one that has replaced her previous method of communicating through visual art, such that her body, like her art, functions as her language. As Bordo points out, this corporeal form of self-expression is explicitly gendered. In Sandi's case, it is also racialized. If Sandi never looks or feels quite American, then being darker-skinned might allow her to identify—and be identified—as Dominican American, Dominican (instead of American), or Latina and might grant her a shared sense of place at least within her family unit.

According to her mother, Sandi's dissatisfaction with her appearance and desire to be "darker complected" is not unconnected to her literary pursuits and belief that she eventually will turn into a monkey. Laura positions Sandi's passion for reading alongside Sandi's eating disorder, framing Sandi's appetite for reading as a substitution for her appetite for food. Describing Sandi's love for reading as extreme and tied to her "craziness," Laura juxtaposes and pathologizes Sandi's physical and intellectual behaviors. Laura pinpoints Sandi's hunger to read as the catalyst for Sandi's psychic distress instead of recognizing the complicated set of factors that contribute to her disarray. Whereas Laura supports her daughter's creativity as a child, she fears the form this creativity takes when Sandi is an adult. When Sandi replaces her childhood preoccupation with visual art with an adult fascination with literary expression, when she is the reader as opposed to the artist, and when she appears to be engulfed by art (as literature) rather than set free by art (as visual expression), Laura treats Sandi's relationship to art as unhealthy. Laura treats literature as the cause of Sandi's mental instability, in much the same way that Lourdes of *Dreaming in Cuban* treats her daughter Pilar's paintings as the source of her alleged imbalance. In the process, and in her refusal to share a favorite story about Sandi once she has been institutionalized, Laura endows stories with a frighteningly destructive power, such that stories themselves can perpetuate pathology.

Laura claims that the books Sandi reads and wishes to read make Sandi believe in reverse evolution and conclude that she will turn into a monkey, even though the writers whom Laura, Carlos, and Sandi's doctor list—Freud, Darwin, Nietzsche, Erikson, Dante, Homer, Cervantes, Calderón de la Barca—do not clearly focus on humans' eventual animalization.[45] Although all of these writers are male, and although they all, to varying degrees, are preoccupied with the human psyche and human development, Laura does not focus on these aspects. Instead, she concentrates on Sandi's conviction that she eventually will turn into an animal, convinced that the writers' words must have implanted this idea in Sandi's brain. Rather than try to understand what feeds into this certainty and examine how the environment surrounding Sandi might well contribute to this belief, Laura places full power in the written word.

Alvarez, however, draws attention to the environment, highlighting how Sandi's past arguably presents itself on hospital grounds. A depersonalized Sandi (by virtue of being described again as "the girl" rather than by her given name) walks on the lawn and panics after seeing "a man coming at her with a roaring animal on a leash."[46] The imagery in this scene recalls that which Alvarez utilizes to describe Don José in the scene that transpires years earlier. Here the leash holds the fearsome animal, just as a halter holds a frightening Don José during Sandi's childhood. In both cases, Sandi eventually screams. The image of an object holding back a man or a beast that instills terror in Sandi links the narrative sequences and reveals how the nativity scene upon which Sandi trespasses as a child stays with her well into adulthood. The similarity in the imagery also suggests that Sandi's trespassing and loss of art as a child are connected to the breakdown she experiences as an adult.

Sandi's fixation on regression (in terms of her preoccupation with the past and her belief in reverse evolution) worries her Catholic parents, who do not believe in evolution, let alone reverse evolution. This motif of regression also parallels the reverse structure of the novel.[47] Through the book's structure, Alvarez disrupts a conventional linear narration and highlights how a reverse chronological order can still drive a narrative forward, just as it can allow for an alternative understanding of the present. By tracing the characters' origins, the narrative itself arguably engages in a type of psychodynamic enterprise to unearth the childhood traumas that have made the characters the adults they are. Given this, Sandi's insistence that evolution is moving backward could be perceived as a way of helping her make sense of her present, just as it could be viewed as an eventual internalization of the animalized and racialized labels that have been thrust on her and her sisters.

It is important to contextualize Sandi's nervous breakdown and assertion that she is becoming a monkey against her continual struggle to find a place she can call home. The connection between animalization and unbelonging, after all, is not a new concept. In the novel, Sandi and her sisters are animalized by La Bruja and made to feel like unwelcome outsiders by La Bruja and their classmates alike. Alvarez not only references monkeys during Sandi's institutionalization; she also does so in the chapter detailing an adolescent Sofía's stay in the Dominican Republic and relationship with Manuel Gustavo. Once Laura discovers that Sofía has been meeting secretly with Manuel Gustavo, she sends Sofía back to the United States, and the four sisters are told that they no longer will be able to enjoy their summers in the Dominican Republic. Their reaction is one of sudden homesickness that is likened to a psychology experiment: "We are free at last, but here, just at the moment the gate swings open, and we can fly the coop, Tía Carmen's love revives our old homesickness. It's like this monkey experiment Carla read about in her clinical psych class. These baby monkeys were kept in a cage so long, they wouldn't come out when the doors were finally left open. Instead, they stayed inside and poked their arms through the bars for their food, just out of reach."[48] The juxtaposition of freedom, homesickness, captivity, and animalization here resonates with an adult Sandi's mental instability, hospitalization, and certainty that she is becoming a monkey. Like the monkeys who are the subjects of a clinical psychology experiment, Sandi is a type of clinical subject by virtue of being institutionalized in a mental hospital. Like the monkeys who do not know how to respond to their newfound freedom after having been held captive for so long and who therefore remain in the only home they have known (their cage), Sandi exhibits a constant and confusing yearning for home, having been uprooted from the habitat where she was born and having never quite felt like she belonged in the environment where her family relocated.

In the course of their conversation with Sandi's psychiatrist, though, neither Sandi's parents nor her psychiatrist mentions the role that displacement might well play in Sandi's psychic distress, let alone consider how Sandi's determination that "soon she wouldn't be human" ties into particularly racialized discourses of unbelonging.[49] Indeed, the animalization and dehumanization Sandi believes she soon will face speak to Fanon's writings about blackness and the plethora of racist stereotypes affiliating blacks with monkeys, and they arguably reference Henry Louis Gates Jr.'s *The Signifying Monkey*. The language Alvarez deploys here to depict a Sandi who has struggled with feelings of self-worth and who is now sure she will become an animal echoes that found in *Black Skin, White Masks*, when Fanon describes being made to feel like a "parasite" and "brute beast" that is "rob[bed] of all worth," colonized, and dehumanized.[50] Sandi's belief in her eventual dehumanization, along with her desire to be darker-skinned like her sisters, likens her to the colonized Malagasy described by Fanon and reveals the psychological damage that ensues from colonizing systems. Although Sandi is light-skinned and does not live under colonial rule, she is characterized as perpetually out of place. Despite her fair skin, she is animalized and racialized because of her *latinidad*.

If we interpret Sandi's repeated assertion that she will become a monkey as invoking Gates's Signifyin(g) Monkey, then we can see how her proclamation could signal both resignation and potential subversion. Her resignation can be understood through the internalized bestialization and racialization she displays by adopting the same racist language others place on her to describe herself. At the same time, if the monkey that Sandi is becoming is not just any monkey, but the trickster figure of the Signifyin(g) Monkey, or some sort of derivative thereof, then her imagined transformation is potentially defiant.[51] As Gates points out, the Signifyin(g) Monkey "who dwells at the margins of discourse" is central to the formation of discourse, as he (or, in Sandi's case, *she*) has the ability to interpret, translate, and mold language, working within it to revise— and hence transform—it: "The Monkey is a hero of black myth, a sign of the triumph of wit and reason, his language of Signifyin(g) standing as the linguistic sign of the ultimate triumph of self-consciously formal language use."[52] The linguistic play the heroic Monkey wields affords him (or, in Sandi's case, her) a significant power and *triumph*, something for which Sandi strives throughout the narrative. Although she may be speaking in a language that her family and psychiatrist cannot fully comprehend when she maintains that evolution is reversing course, her determination that she will become a monkey could be construed as her desire to manipulate the power of the word rather than have this power thrust on her from without. In a book that centers on the idea that "word is power" and that links ethnic identity to linguistic identity, Sandi's positionality as a potential descendant of the Signifyin(g) Monkey takes her out of the role of powerless Other and alternatively locates her as heroine.

## A Pathologized Poet, a Violeted Yolanda

Although Sandi explicitly likens herself to a monkey, Yolanda is the one who possesses traits similar to those of the Signifyin(g) Monkey described by Gates. A poet and writer, Yolanda expresses herself through, and finds herself in, language. Inspired by Scheherazade of *One Thousand and One Nights,* she associates storytelling with salvation, gendered expression, and defiance. Yet just as Laura and Carlos pathologize Sandi partly because of her "excessive" reading, Yolanda's loved ones pathologize her because of her preoccupation with language. This pathologization functions as a form of linguistic terrorism whereby Yolanda's loved ones cast her as mentally unstable because of the way she both identifies and expresses herself linguistically.

Yolanda's complicated relationship with language, experiences with linguistic terrorism, and gendered and psychological struggles can partially be understood through her many names. She has several variations of her given name as well as nicknames that are altogether distinct from it, whether they be abridged or Anglicized versions thereof or punned plays on such permutations: "Yolanda, nicknamed *Yo* in Spanish, misunderstood *Joe* in English, doubled and pronounced like the toy, *Yoyo*—or when forced to select from a rack of personalized key chains, *Joey*." Josephine, Yosita, Violet, and Squirrel are additional names her family and husband use to call her.[53] The abundance of names by which others refer to Yolanda splits her and underscores the numerous ways she is interpellated. The names themselves, divided between Spanish and English, highlight Yolanda's positioning between two languages and cultures. The affectionate, and arguably diminutive, appositive Yoyo that is applied to her emblematizes this interstitiality. In English, a yo-yo is a toy associated with a constant up and down movement (as opposed to a locatedness in one fixed place); in Spanish, *yoyo* is the doubling of the first-person singular pronoun *yo,* and its ending in the vowel *o* genders the word male. The perpetual motion associated with the nickname Yoyo corresponds with Yolanda's sense of unbelonging throughout the narrative and constant search for a place she can call home. The masculinization of the name Yoyo speaks to Yolanda's gender-bending positionality: as a child, she is a tomboy; as an adult, she devotes herself to writing and teaching, much like the gender-defiant single aunt she admires who spends her time reading. Yet the feminization of her given name, Yolanda, by virtue of ending with the vowel *a,* highlights how Yolanda straddles an in-between gendered space across her names. Meanwhile, the doubling of the Spanish *I* both punctuates Yolanda's hybridity and illustrates an irony: the one character in the novel to have the first-person singular pronoun (or the squared version thereof) function as her name is also the only one to have so many nicknames.

This irony is heightened in that the one character to be called by the first-person singular pronoun not only is split into two conjoined *yo*'s, but feels divided into more than two selves. When Yolanda leaves her monolingual Anglo husband, John, she leaves him a note that elucidates this pluralistic identification: *"I'm going to my folks till my head-slash-heart clear.* She revised the note: *I'm needing some space, some time, until my head-slash-heart-slash soul*—No, no, no, she didn't want to divide herself any-more, three persons in one Yo."* The slashes split Yolanda and reveal how she has so absorbed the multiplicity of names placed on her that she divides herself in turn, becoming a hybrid self. She eventually signs her note to John with "his name for her, *Joe*" instead of "her real name," one that "no longer sounded like her own."[54] No longer identifying with her "real name" and wrestling with how to sign her note, Yolanda grapples with defining herself when this self-identification is at odds with the identification placed on her. That she can easily fill a page with her husband's *single* name, by contrast, underscores her difference from him, her struggles to name herself, and her nominal plurality. Her institutionalization soon after she leaves John further highlights the effects of her nominal multiplicity on her psyche.

Apart from being called by variations on her name, Yolanda is called by entirely different monikers, most notably Squirrel and Violet. John gives her these pet names, supposedly as terms of endearment. However, the moments when he uses these suggest that they are not simply markers of affection but reflect tension and a struggle for control between husband and wife, such that the terms are loaded with psychological violence. By calling Yolanda *Squirrel*, John animalizes and belittles his wife. When he refers to Yolanda as Violet, he deliberately plays on her medicalization, "nam[ing] her Violet after *shrinking* violet when she had started seeing" her psychiatrist.[55] Although he hides behind a cloak of humor with his pun, he defines Yolanda according to her pathologization, while Yolanda's reaction to being called Violet emphasizes just how charged the term is. Indeed, Yolanda proclaims, "Stop violeting me! I hate it when you do that."[56] She turns the common noun (that John has converted into a proper one) into an active verb to underscore how the word's interpellation has formational power. In Yolanda's exclamatory sentence, she positions herself as the object of the verb *violeting* and reveals the word's homophonic likeness to *violating.* The ready slippage between *violeting* and *violating* underscores how John's act of calling Yolanda *Violet* itself is a violation. Her response to his word choice suggests that he is overstepping the bounds of her comfort zone by pathologizing her and imposing his name for her onto her against her will.

This is not the only way John violets/violates Yolanda or imposes his branch of linguistic terrorism on her. Throughout Alvarez's depiction of Yolanda's interactions with John, she highlights how language acts

as a barrier between husband and wife, and she emphasizes the disparate ways both characters relate to language and use it to assert themselves. Despite the superficially innocuous way the two treat language,
it is clear that "word is power." For John, language is something he
can wield to exert his patriarchal control over his wife. For the writer/
poet Yolanda, language *is* her identity. When the two engage in what
may initially come across as an innocent name game, they reveal how
the game they are playing is anything but innocent. The game itself
consists of one seemingly simple rule: John and Yolanda must find
words that rhyme with their names. What makes the game loaded is
that the process of naming is always laden with signification; in John
and Yolanda's case, this process only underscores the skewed power
differential between them.

Indeed, the two approach the game differently. Yolanda relies on
her creativity. She manipulates language by code-switching and using
puns to make the most of the game, and she urges John to do the same.
John, however, takes the game literally, claiming that nothing rhymes
with *Yolanda*. Although Yolanda uses the intonations of her voice to try
to coax John into taking the game less literally, he is less than compli-
ant. Whereas he initially appears to acquiesce to her suggestion that he
use one of her nicknames to play the game, John only invokes his pet
name for her: Squirrel. When Yolanda asks to be called anything but
this animalized name and instead asks to be called the sky, John ignores
the ingenuity of the request. Dismissing Yolanda's desire to be called the
sky and maintaining that she is in violation of the rules of the game,
he privileges his monolingual knowledge base over her bilingual one,
and he adopts a domineering stance, usurping control over the game.
Even though Yolanda points out, "I . . . rhymes with the *sky*" and "*Yo*
rhymes with *cielo* in Spanish," John snubs her clever bilingual word play.
Not only does he silence her by refusing to acknowledge what she has to
say, but he silences her with his body, asserting control over her through
a combination of verbal and physical language: "John pulled her up by
the shoulders. . . . He swept his hand across the earth as if he owned it
all. . . . His hand came from behind her; it owned her shoulder. . . . He
turned her around to face him. . . . John wagged his finger at her. . . . He
placed his mouth over her mouth and ohhed her lips open." At another
moment, he "printed J-o-h-n on her right breast . . . as if he were branding her his."[57] The sentence structure in these sequences alone tells a
story of domination. John, or one of his body parts, is situated as the
subject performing an action in each of these sentences. When Yolanda,

or one of her body parts, is mentioned, she/it is relegated to an object position. Even the verb choices—*pulled, swept, came, owned, turned, wagged, placed, ohhed, branding*—reflect John's imposition of force and illustrate his sense of territoriality, such that Yolanda, like the earth, is his perceived possession. These positionalities operate at the formalistic level (in terms of grammatical function) and the conceptual level (in terms of the figurative roles John and Yolanda, and their synecdochical body parts, assume).

John asserts racialized, gendered, and sexualized control here, highlighted by the repeated image of a stifled tongue. Placing linguistic restrictions on the game and dismissing Yolanda's bilingual puns, John engages in an insidiously and implicitly racist discursive practice. But he does not acknowledge his ignorance or bigotry. Instead, the more he treats Yolanda as something he owns, the more he grows aroused, and the more she becomes repelled. While "his eyes softened with desire," prompting him to "place his mouth over her mouth and oh her lips open," Yolanda realizes that her "words fell into the dark, mute cavern of John's mouth," causing her to "run, like the mad, into the safety of her first tongue, where the proudly monolingual John could not catch her, even if he tried."[58] The juxtaposition of John's and Yolanda's vastly disparate reactions to their interaction here underscores the different positions of power they each hold. For John, treating Yolanda as his property, literally and figuratively stoppering her tongue, and imposing his proud monolingualism onto her instills feelings of desire in him. A tremendous violence undergirds this desire, though, one that prompts Yolanda to run as far away from him as possible, toward the "safety of her first tongue." The push-and-pull imagery here suggests that John is trespassing on Yolanda and that this violeting/violating behavior is tied to Yolanda's mad-like retreat, showing how John's arguably colonizing attempts to force himself and his linguistic limitations on his wife precipitate her mad-like run away from him. Alvarez thus implicates the imposition of force in the creation of pathology, locating pathology outside of a strictly intrapsychic framework and revealing the role a hostile environment plays in its perpetuation.[59] She is not invoking a clear causality here, however. She does not describe Yolanda as mad following John's violeting/violation of her; instead, she depicts her as "*like* the mad." The use of the simile suggests that Yolanda is not in fact mad, prompting readers to question the grounds for her later psychiatric hospitalization. In this scene, Yolanda's pathologization is gendered, sexualized, and racialized and follows from the struggle for control. The end of this scene, with Yolanda retreating to Spanish, reflects her efforts to take some control back for herself in the face of John's attempts to strip control from her. Turning to Spanish, she fights back against her husband's staunch monolingualism; ending the game with her words, she asserts her voice, knowledge, and power as she renders *him* mute.

This is not the sole moment when either character tries to wield language as a weapon, when Alvarez portrays friction between spouses, when John violets/violates Yolanda, or when Yolanda resists John's forceful ways. During a quarrel the two have that revolves around the distinct ways they understand and use language, John again resorts to sexualized linguistic terrorism to end the fight. The argument overtly sparks from Yolanda's discovery of a list that John has made detailing her pros and cons, but it could be argued that, at least to some degree, it arises from John's rational approach to the world that stands in stark contrast to Yolanda's creative one. The very layout of John's lists illustrates his dualistic mentality. Yolanda, however, positions herself and words as separate from this type of "Real World," binary consciousness that Anzaldúa would claim lies at "the root of all violence."[60] Unlike John, Yolanda possesses an interstitial consciousness. John's reliance on dichotomies to grapple with any confusion he might be feeling not only diverges from Yolanda's emphasis on multiplicity and imagination, but it also relegates her alternative way of thinking to the realm of the irrational and the pathological. Indeed, upon finding the list, Yolanda urges John to "stop violeting [her]," highlighting a connection between John's binary consciousness and his pathologization and violation of her.

To appease Yolanda and end their fight, John resorts to what he might label physical intimacy and what I would term sexual force. The moment Yolanda asks John to stop "violeting" her, he does just the opposite, manipulating his voice and imposing himself onto her. He initially reaches for her "more as a test of her temper than a touch of desire," but he continues to touch her against her wishes, using his body in a manner that is anything but intimate. Although he performs tenderness—softening his voice and using endearing terms like "sweetie"—and although the two supposedly push and pull each other "in play" (he pulls, while she pushes), the "play" is violent from its inception. Throughout their interaction, the one word that is repeated time and again is *no*:

> He pulled her forward. She opened her mouth to yell, *No, no!* He pried his tongue between her lips, pushing her words back in her throat.

She swallowed them: *No, no.*
They beat against her stomach: *No, no.* They pecked at her ribs:
*No, no.*
"No!" she cried.
"It's just a kiss, Joe. A kiss, for Christ's sake!" John shook her.
"Control yourself."
"Nooooooo!" she screamed, pushing him off everything she
knew.
He let her go.

John interprets no to mean yes based on the "sweet" way Yolanda initially
says it and based on the way "the word open[s] her mouth, soft and ripe
and ready for him to bite into it."[61] Upon hearing the word no, John is
aroused, fixating on Yolanda's mouth, viewing her mouth as something
that is there for him to savor, and deluding himself into believing that
Yolanda uses the word to mean its converse. This convoluted mentality
corresponds with the type of perverse rhetoric that perpetuates violence
against women. By refusing to take Yolanda at her word, John attempts
to strip her words of their signification, effectively silencing her audible
voice. Even when he appears to hear her cries, in that he ultimately
acknowledges her resistance to his sexual advances, he justifies his actions
by claiming that he is "just" trying to kiss her. Instead of recognizing
his out-of-control aggression, he dismisses her cries, implies that she is
overreacting to the situation, and labels her out of control.

The language that Alvarez uses to describe this interaction notably
resembles that used by Anzaldúa when detailing the female patient's
visit to the male dentist. While John "prie[s] his tongue between
[Yolanda's] lips, pushing her words back in her throat," the dentist
in *Borderlands* tries to clamp his patient's tongue.[62] Just as Yolanda
attempts to ward off John's advances by tightening her lips and press-
ing her teeth together to form a makeshift "fortress," the patient in
*Borderlands* similarly uses her tongue to "push out the wads of cotton, . . . drills, . . . needles" to protect herself from the dentist's oral
invasion.[63] Like John, who charges Yolanda with being out of control, the dentist claims that he needs to control his patient's "wild
tongue."[64] And both John and the dentist grow visibly frustrated with
the resistance they meet. Considering that Anzaldúa uses the dentist-
patient anecdote to introduce the concept of linguistic terrorism and
to highlight the gendered, sexualized, and racialized forms linguistic
terrorism takes, Alvarez's strikingly similar imagery underscores the

multifaceted violence at the heart of this spousal scene and illustrates the insidious manner in which linguistic terrorism operates within it.

Instead of acknowledging his unstable, territorial behavior, John treats Yolanda as unbalanced. When he pathologizes her, claiming that she needs to seek psychiatric attention, she responds by suggesting that both of them seek help. In her efforts to placate him, while also implicating him in their relationship woes, Yolanda, like Lolita in *The Ladies' Gallery*, "makes it crazy," as Sue Estroff might say. "With other identities and roles cut off to her," Yolanda takes on the label of craziness that John thrusts on her; by including him in this same categorization, though, she demonstrates the type of "passive defiance" that accompanies the performance of "making it crazy."[65] She acts passive by performing the role of madwoman into which John casts her, but she is defiant in simultaneously casting him in the role of madman. Realizing that she is no crazier than he, Yolanda recognizes the arbitrariness of the labels of instability placed on her, as they just as easily could refer to her husband. This recognition fuels her defiance.

At the same time, by using John's language to try to plead her case, denying herself her own language, and increasingly mistrusting her husband, Yolanda appears to illustrate Audre Lorde's point that "the master's tools will never dismantle the master's house."[66] After all, in the process of taking on John's language, Yolanda eventually realizes that she and he are speaking in entirely different metaphorical tongues. This difference is made manifest when John brings her flowers and speaks in a language that is incomprehensible to her. Although she can hear the sounds that make up his words, she cannot find meaning in them. She simulates understanding, however, "mimicking" his "babble."[67] Alvarez's repetition of the word *babble* here and use of the term *mimicked* likely nods to Homi Bhabha's chapter "Of Mimicry and Man" in *The Location of Culture*, a text that adopts the same terminology and that focuses on the transgressive potential of mimicry.[68] Bhabha's analysis of the subversive potential of mimicry is at odds with Lorde's contention that invoking the language of the oppressor ultimately cannot topple systems of oppression. For Yolanda, mimicry does not allow her to subvert John's language, but neither does she use it to do so in this instance. The mimicry upon which she relies here represents her last attempt to work through her marital problems. Rather than bridge the gap between her and her husband, however, it reveals the inescapable divide separating them, so that all that is left is silence.[69] When Yolanda's parents later try to understand what has caused their daughter's marriage to fall apart, Yolanda declares, "We just didn't speak the same language."[70]

The explanation Yolanda provides not only reveals the impossibility of mimicry to reconcile differences, but it also emphasizes the profound linguistic-cultural-gendered divide between the spouses and the destructive power of John's aggression.

Struggling to understand John's language and find her own language and sense of self, Yolanda leaves John and is hospitalized in a mental ward. Elena Machado Sáez and Raphael Dalleo describe Yolanda's institutionalization as "a primarily verbal problem" and a "failed attempt at authorship," particularly problematic for a character who is a writer.[71] Karen Christian similarly takes Yolanda's "madness" as a given, arguing that "Yolanda is so traumatized by the schism that the competing languages produce in her psyche that she does indeed go mad, requiring hospitalization for a nervous breakdown. Although she recovers, she is destined to be defined by the split sense of self that is her legacy as a bilingual/bicultural individual."[72] Although Alvarez underscores the relation between Yolanda's language and hospitalization, to read this hospitalization as following from Yolanda's failure or her bilingual/bicultural split risks reinscribing and essentializing her medicalization, extricating John from any accountability for his mistreatment of Yolanda, "normalizing" "rational" and dichotomous thought, and pathologizing an interstitial consciousness.

Yolanda's parents do just this. They worry about Yolanda's mental health, much as they worry about Sandi's psychological state. Just as they attribute Sandi's love for reading to her alleged "craziness," they fret over Yolanda's preoccupation with language, alarmed that Yolanda

> talked too much . . . talked in comparisons, she spoke in riddles.
> She ranted. . . . She quoted famous lines of poetry and the
> opening sentences of the classics. How could anyone remember so
> much? . . . She was carried away with the sound of her voice.[73]

Their rationale again affiliates creativity with madness. Their pathologization of the figurative language Yolanda deploys resonates with Anzaldúa's description of the dismissal of those who possess an imaginative and interstitial consciousness and with Anzaldúa's association of writing with instability. Laura and Carlos's concerns over their daughter's mental well-being also echo John's pathologization of Yolanda because she, unlike him, does not have a dualistic consciousness. Instead, Yolanda inhabits the type of ambiguous space to which Anzaldúa refers as the borderlands. Meanwhile, it is difficult to dissociate dominant gender ideologies from Laura and Carlos's worries about Yolanda's constant talking and supposed fixation on "the sound of her voice." As Anzaldúa elaborates, language is gendered, and "to talk too much," to be considered *hocicona* or *habladora* (a woman who has "a big mouth") is to defy gendered (and cultural) expectations that affiliate "proper" femininity with silence.[74] Although Anzaldúa is referring to Chicana/o cultures here, the gender ideologies that she elucidates present themselves in *How the García Girls Lost Their Accents* through Laura and Carlos's pathologization of Yolanda because Yolanda, like the *hociconas* and *habladoras* about whom Anzaldúa writes, "talked too much." Yolanda's parents' worries about their daughter's preoccupation with language are particularly ironic in Laura's case, especially since she passes down her gift for invention to Yolanda and encourages Yolanda's writing when she is a teenager. Alvarez's emphasis on the matrilineal inheritance of creative expression, understood in the context of Alice Walker's assertion that stories are passed down from mothers to daughters and that the stories daughters write are those of their mothers, highlights just how much Yolanda's pathologization is gendered and positions Yolanda's individual pathologization within that of a larger female collective.[75]

Yolanda's parents and doctor alike determine that Yolanda be institutionalized "for her own good." However, Alvarez compels readers to question whether Yolanda's hospitalization is in her best interests, as she, like Vilar and Cristina García, provides a complicated portrait of institutionalization. On the one hand, Alvarez depicts a facility that appears inviting. It has "round-the-clock care; nice grounds; arts and crafts classes; tennis courts; a friendly, unintimidating staff, no one in a uniform."[76] The doctor too is described as "nice." The environment thus comes across as warm but exclusive, the type of place only members of a certain socioeconomic class could afford.

Yet Alvarez subtly offsets the built environment, and the friendly doctor and staff within it, against a backdrop of harm. On the surface, the idea of "round-the-clock care" may seem ideal in that Yolanda could receive help whenever necessary. But it is difficult to separate this notion of constant care from either the panoptical systems of "care" outlined by Michel Foucault in his study of eighteenth-century asylums, when patients were criminalized and kept under perpetual surveillance, or the habitual scrutiny under which the Garcías lived in the Dominican Republic. Likewise, while the street clothes worn by the medical staff allegedly render them nonthreatening to the patients, they also create a form of camouflage and deception by concealing the visible differentiation between patients and staff that feeds into the panoptical model and conjures forth images of guerrilla warfare emblematic of Trujillo's regime. Even the repetition of the phrase *for your own good* that is used to justify Yolanda's institutionalization encourages readers to question whether Yolanda's hospitalization really is "for her own good." This statement recalls a similar one uttered by Anzaldúa when she writes of cultures "shackl[ing] us in the name of protection," as she highlights an unsettling link between constraint and protection that fosters what she terms an "intimate terrorism" and that undermines the very concept of protection as something that is in anyone's best interests.[77] In the context of Alvarez's novel, the phrase *for your own good* echoes similar slogans disseminated during Trujillo's reign. Alvarez describes how the *guardia's* "routine searches" of Dominican homes under Trujillo's rule were carried out "for [citizens'] own protection," and she writes that the "slogan at station identification" stated, "God and Trujillo are taking care of you."[78] The similar wording and parallel concepts in the scenes depicting the horrors suffered under Trujillo's dictatorship and the one describing Yolanda's psychiatric hospitalization gesture toward a deeply disturbing association between geopolitical repression and mental health care, challenging us to think about what really constitutes "care" and how the rhetoric of care can camouflage insidious harm.

If care equals linguistic and creative suppression—and given John's, Laura's, Carlos's, and Yolanda's doctor's concerns about Yolanda's "excessive" talking and figurative speech, it is safe to say that Yolanda's care consists of stifling her voice—then care becomes something altogether different than what it should be. It is entirely unclear how silencing Yolanda's mode of expression is "for her own good," especially considering that Yolanda's immersion in and fascination with language are what allow her to find her sense of self-worth and belonging. Language is integrally connected to survival for Yolanda, in much the same way that Walker describes poetry writing as salvation from despair.[79] As a child, Yolanda is captivated by the story of Scheherazade and her sister, realizing the power of storytelling to trick and save. Alvarez's description of Scheherazade and her sister as tricksters likens these two female characters to Gates's Signifyin(g) Monkey and highlights how storytelling is connected to gendered and racialized survival. Yolanda relies on this type of intersectional survival when she is a teenager who feels out of place in the United States: "She needed to settle somewhere, and since the natives were unfriendly, and the country inhospitable, she took root in the language." Language is the one *place* that endows her with a sense of belonging. Even when the language she uses isn't her own, even when she feels like she finally has found her voice while plagiarizing Walt Whitman's words ("finally sound[ing] like herself in English!"), and even when her father imposes his own brand of linguistic terrorism on her by tearing up her plagiarized speech, Yolanda does not put aside her creative aspirations. Even in college, when she feels like an "intruder upon the sanctuary of English majors" who is struggling to carve out her own space within this sanctuary, Yolanda still enmeshes herself in English.[80] Her linguistic discovery is accompanied by a sexual one, linking her writing to her body. When her college boyfriend, Rudy, tries to coerce her into having sex with him, she refuses because of the coarse language he uses to persuade her. When Rudy introduces her to his parents, Yolanda again is attuned to the words he chooses and realizes that she is no more than the exoticized object of his fantasies. Through these interactions with Rudy, Yolanda realizes how language shapes her own sexual, gendered, racial, and embodied subjectivity. In all of these examples, Alvarez posits an integral connection among language, subjectivity, worth, and belonging. If Yolanda creates her home in language, then to silence her is to displace her from herself and her home.

## Open Mouths

Alvarez links linguistic suppression with displacement and alienation, just as she ties expression with a yearning to belong. This hunger to belong should not be confused with a desire to assimilate, as the former does not necessarily correlate with the latter. Reading *How the García Girls Lost Their Accents* as an assimilationist narrative fails to recognize the sense of unbelonging that pervades the text, an unbelonging that Alvarez brings to the fore from the opening of her book with a chapter titled "Antojos" (nostalgic cravings). Alvarez brings her novel full circle by beginning her last chapter at the narrative's chronological start and ending that chapter by catapulting the narrative across time, such that the book simultaneously concludes at its beginning and end. The parallel imagery of open mouths that closes the first and last chapters ties together the story, just as it emphasizes the centrality of voice to the tale.

In the first chapter that marks the narrative's overt chronological conclusion, Alvarez depicts an adult Yolanda's return to the Dominican Republic in search of a place where she can feel at home. Although she desperately wants to call her birth island home, her stay on the island reveals how out of place she feels there and how others too mark her as an outsider. This is evidenced twice. The first time is when Yolanda wants to go in search of guavas on her own, even though to do so positions her as a foreigner; the second is when two Dominican men approach her on the road. In this second instance, the men seek to help Yolanda, whose car has a flat tire, but Yolanda fears she is in danger, causing "her tongue [to] feel as if it has been stuffed in her mouth like a rag to keep her quiet." Only when the men ask her if she is *americana* does she feel more at ease: "The admission itself loosens her tongue."[81] Deploying the image of a tongue that has been stuffed or let loose, Alvarez again posits a relation among language, belonging, and sense of safety (or lack thereof). Showing how Yolanda's tongue only loosens upon realizing that, as an *americana*, she can speak in English, Alvarez situates Yolanda in an interstitial space. Identifying as *americana*, Yolanda is both Dominican and American at once; the Spanish-language identifier locates her in this in-between space.

Alvarez emphasizes this interstitiality by ending the chapter with a focus on a woman in a Palmolive ad that Alvarez has described earlier in the chapter when Yolanda stops at a cantina. In the first mention of the ad, Alvarez describes "[a] creamy, blond woman luxuriat[ing] under a refreshing shower, her head thrown back in seeming ecstasy, her mouth opened in a wordless cry"; at the chapter's end, "the Palmolive woman's skin gleams a rich white; her head is still thrown back, her mouth still opened as if she is calling someone over a great distance."[82] The double mention of this ad underscores its importance. It not only emphasizes a looming U.S. capitalist presence in the Dominican Republic, but it highlights how racialized, sexualized, and gendered ideologies, as related to hygiene, come together for the purposes of consumption. Although the woman in the ad has her mouth open, her cry is wordless. The repetition of the adverb *still* at the chapter's end suggests that Yolanda has expected something in the ad to change, but notes how it nonetheless remains the same. The distance to which the woman calls illustrates the difficulty of having her figurative voice heard. The ad serves as a commentary on gendered linguistic suppression and marks the centrality of this concept in the novel.

Not only does Alvarez portray abundant images of mouths wide open in wordless cries throughout her text—albeit cries of horror as opposed to ones of ecstasy—but she also ends the book with an image of an open mouth. At the novel's close, though, the open mouth does not belong to a woman but to "a black furred thing lurking in the corners of my life, her magenta mouth opening, wailing over some violation that lies at the center of my art." This "thing" could refer to the mother of Schwarz, the kitten that a young Yolanda takes from its mother and then releases out of guilt. After all, when Yolanda lets Schwarz go, she is haunted for years by the mother cat that "let out soft, moaning meows" and that "wail[ed] until dawn."[83] The similarity in the language used to describe Schwarz's mother and the "thing"—notably the repetition of their wails—suggests that the "thing" quite possibly is Schwarz's mother. If this is the case, then the final image with which Alvarez leaves readers is akin to a Llorona-like portrait, as Schwarz's mother wails at night for her lost kitten in much the same way that La Llorona of Mexican (American) folklore wails for her lost children at night, and as both Schwarz's mother and La Llorona are depicted as haunting figures. Ending her novel with a Llorona-like image, Alvarez situates her novel among recent writings by Chicanas who have invoked this same figure to reconfigure her misunderstood tale. Just as Ana Castillo includes a protagonist, Fe, who is forever marked by her persistent and "pathological" cries in *So Far from God*, Alvarez repeatedly deploys the analogous image of a female's wails to underscore the devastating gendered harm at the center of her narrative.

The "thing" at the end of Alvarez's text does not necessarily (exclusively) refer to Schwarz's mother, though. The ambiguity of the word *thing* to describe the hollering creature is heightened by the ambiguity of the narrative voice in the novel's last paragraph. Although the bulk of the final chapter is presented from the perspective of Yolanda, on the penultimate page, Alvarez creates a slippage where it is not clear whether the "I" is Yolanda, a separate narrator, Alvarez herself, or all three.[84] That Yolanda's nickname *Yo* means "I" renders this sequence all the more slippery. Meanwhile, Alvarez's use of the second-person pronoun *you* in this section, juxtaposed against the first-person singular pronoun, potentially directly addresses the reader of *How the García Girls Lost Their Accents*: "You understand I am collapsing all time now so that it fits in what's left in the hollow of my story?"[85] On the one hand, the "hollow of [the] story" recalls the hollow of the drum Yolanda plays in the last chapter (the place where she puts Schwarz after taking him from his mother) and the hollowness of John's aforementioned cavernous mouth. But the collapse of time that transpires here (referencing events that happen later in the narrative's chronological time, though earlier in the narrative's linear time) suggests that the story being told is not simply Yolanda's but also that of all the García girls. Even the juxtaposed images of a lurking, wailing cat, a violation, an opening mouth, and art intimate as much. After all, Yolanda is not the only García sister preoccupied with a cat. Sandi too is drawn to cats. This fascination is connected to Sandi's

CLAMPED MOUTHS AND MUTED CRIES / 193

artistic expression as a child, the violation she sees Don José commit, and the cries she releases in turn. Although neither Sofía nor Carla is explicitly linked to a cat, both characters, like Yolanda and Sandi, experience violations that are tied to their expression. For these reasons, the "thing" that Alvarez describes in the narrative's final sequence must be ambiguous. The wail that the "thing" releases because of a violation at art's center underscores the relation that the text draws between creative expression and violation. Alvarez illustrates the tremendous harm that undergirds such violation. Yet by emphasizing that the "I" *hears* the "thing" wailing at night, Alvarez concludes her story by presenting a cry that is not stifled but is audible. The "black furred thing" ultimately makes itself heard.

# Conclusion: Hope in the Interstices

*Wild tongues can't be tamed, they can only be cut out. . . . I will no
longer be made to feel ashamed of existing. I will have my voice. . . . I will
overcome the tradition of silence.*
—GLORIA ANZALDÚA, *BORDERLANDS/LA FRONTERA: THE NEW MESTIZA*

*Intersections of Harm* closes as it opens, returning to the image of stifled expression presented in its introductory epigraph about the patient at the dentist's office who is subjected to linguistic suppression. While emphasizing the violence undergirding any attempt to tame allegedly wild tongues, in the epigraph above, Anzaldúa reveals the impossibility of carrying out this feat. The "wild tongues'" resistance is simply too powerful. The only way to combat this resistance is to cut out the tongues altogether and impose a "tradition of silence."[1] This act, however, is preempted with both the affirmation of voice and subjecthood and also the determination to overcome this muzzling tradition. Despite depicting the harm imposed on borderlands subjects, Anzaldúa ultimately emphasizes these subjects' resistance, self-affirmation, and determination, effectively underscoring the hope that lies in the interstices of her narrative.

This same type of hope can be found in the texts I have analyzed. *The Ladies' Gallery, Impossible Motherhood, Geographies of Home, So Far from God, Dreaming in Cuban,* and *How the García Girls Lost Their Accents* all illustrate the intersections of psychological, physical, and geopolitical harm, but they also signal the hope that can be found therein. Although it might prove challenging to find tangible hope in Irene Vilar's first memoir that emphasizes the cyclicality and reproduction of gendered harm, Vilar's second memoir concludes with a hopeful direct address to her daughter: "You are becoming my origins."[2] This assertion reveals how the daughter allows for the possibility of the author's own rebirth and a chance at a new life in defiance of the doomed destiny she fears she has inherited. Despite the harm that befalls each of the protagonists in Loida Maritza Pérez's novel, the text ultimately underscores the importance of making the best out of trying circumstances, presenting a potentially hopeful message of perseverance in the face of seemingly insurmountable obstacles. Ana Castillo's call to action in the wake of so much deadly devastation, meanwhile, reveals how harm, hope, and activism can and should intertwine. Cristina García's ambiguous ending to her novel and invocation of *duende* in the final pages reconfigure the symbolism attached to the iconic image of the submerged archetypal "madwoman," arguably transforming this image from one of death to one of hopeful artistic attainment and freedom. And Julia Alvarez's frightful closing image of a haunting "black furred thing" that "wail[s] over a violation" at art's center nevertheless effectively and hopefully makes its voice heard.[3] In all of these ways, each writer demonstrates how harm does not preclude the possibility of hope.

This does not mean that hope is plentiful in these narratives. It can be agonizingly difficult to detect. Hope resides in the narratives' interstices, in the spaces (however narrow they might be) "between and among" the abundant representations of overwhelming harm. Hope exists in such spaces because the wounds, fissures, and ruptures therein allow for the possibility, and indicate the necessity, of change.[4] Hope neither manifests itself in readily recognizable ways nor presents itself in conventionally happy endings. As shown in the examples above, hope arises from ambiguity. The possibility of change, no matter how remote it may seem, springs from such ambiguity. Although all of the writers illustrate how harm begets harm, they also demonstrate that harm can foster hope. Indeed, it is paradoxically in the depictions of harm that the writers portray hope. By writing about such dire topics, and using their words "to penetrate the privatism of our lives," Vilar, Pérez, Castillo, García, and Alvarez enact what Cherríe Moraga labels "the ultimate optimis[m]."[5]

Although the bulk of *Intersections of Harm* focuses on representations of harm, it too contains hopeful messages and has the same optimistic spirit described by Moraga. These messages and spirit emanate from the narratives I analyze, are paralleled in my structure, and are inspired by those articulated by Moraga in her "Foreword to the Second Edition" of *This Bridge Called My Back*. Like Moraga, I believe that "people are capable of change" and envision my target audience as "the people of color we do reach and the people they touch . . . people for whom books have been as common to their lives as bread . . . [and] anyone who will listen with their ears open (even if only a crack) to the currents of change around them."[6] My focus on the intersections of harm done to body, mind, and place is not intended to elicit a sense of defeat or despair in the reader. Quite the opposite: it is intended to serve as an optimistic call to action that compels readers, at the very least, to question the types of conditions that foster such harm. Recognizing and questioning such conditions are critical steps toward effecting change.

I take Moraga's words about writing, remembering, and envisioning to heart by "remember[ing], not out of nostalgia but out of hope," by "remember[ing] in order to envision," by "look[ing] backward in order to look forward."[7] My emphasis on *historia* and examination of texts in a deliberately disrupted chronological sequence are ways of trying to envision a more hopeful future. My structure resembles the nonlinear one of the narratives themselves and to some degree mirrors the reverse chronological structure of *How the García Girls Lost Their Accents*. Although my (primarily) reverse chronological positioning of the texts admittedly does not traverse much historical time, certainly not in the way the narratives themselves span time, my chapter order nevertheless attempts to gesture toward the importance of what Homi Bhabha terms a "'projective' past," or looking back in order to move forward.[8] *Intersections of Harm* underscores how the past is scripted onto the present; how history shapes story and story shapes history; how a re-turn to and remembrance of the past allow for the possibility of creating social change in the present and for the future. Hope springs from the seemingly paradoxical progressive impulse generated by a remembrance of things past. Only in re-turning to the past can we undo the feeling of inevitability that may be associated with it and create paths that may deviate from its otherwise supposedly projected course. Hope lies in the crevices where this deviation becomes possible.

## From Shackles to Crossroads

Anzaldúa's *Borderlands* is a prime example of a text that grapples with *Intersections of Harm*'s main polemics. While blurring genres and dismantling the divide distinguishing literature from theory from history, *Borderlands* highlights connections between individual and collective; emphasizes the junction of body, mind, and place; signals the importance of *historia* telling; shows the relation between deviance and defiance; underscores the centrality of interstices, intersections, and ambiguity; and contains a message of hope in the face of devastating harm. As much as it shapes my theorization throughout this manuscript, *Borderlands* could be a primary text worthy of examination in its own right.

Although an in-depth analysis of *Borderlands* is beyond the scope of this book, let me call your attention to the last two sections of "Movimientos de rebeldía y las culturas que traicionan" in Anzaldúa's shapeshifting text. Here, Anzaldúa mentions the omnipresent dangers of life in the borderlands, dangers particularly potent for women of color. She labels this exposure to harm intimate terrorism and explains how such exposure instills a sense of constant fear and animalization, leading women of color to feel trapped in cells:

> Alienated from her mother culture, "alien" in the dominant culture, the woman of color does not feel safe within the inner life of her Self. Petrified, she can't respond, her face caught between *los intersticios*, the spaces between the different worlds she inhabits.
> The ability to respond is what is meant by responsibility, yet our cultures take away our ability to act—shackle us in the name of protection. Blocked, immobilized, we can't move forward, can't move backwards. That writhing serpent movement of life, swifter than lightning, frozen.[9]

In this description, Anzaldúa conjoins ideas of body, mind, and place and ties individual to collective. Her characterization of petrification unites body with mind. Petrification causes physical and psychic immobility, highlighting the corporeal and psychological effects of intimate terrorism. The description of the interstices where the woman/women of color is/are caught, meanwhile, elucidates how physical place and mental place cause this/these woman/women to feel frozen "between and among" spaces. Switching from the third-person singular female pronoun to the first-person plural one, and revealing the interchangeability of this pronoun use, Anzaldúa emphasizes how intimate terrorism is experienced at the individual and collective level at once. The veneer behind which intimate terrorism hides, as Anzaldúa puts it, is protection. Yet through Anzaldúa's imagery and word choice, she questions whether protection can really serve its function if it shackles and petrifies women of color.

Despite the immobilizing harm referenced here, Anzaldúa shows that such immobilization need not be permanent. "There in front of us is the crossroads and choice," she writes, "to feel a victim where someone else is to blame . . . or to feel strong, and, for the most part, in control."[10] The crossroads, an interstitial space where paths intersect and divide, are accompanied by the idea of choice, however constrained this choice might be. Rather than remain frozen in the fissures, it is important to muster inner strength and self-control in order to combat the oppressive obstacles that seek to stifle "the ability to respond." Although this assertion risks succumbing to the type of problematic victim-oppressor dualistic rhetoric that Anzaldúa troubles elsewhere in her narrative and risks overestimating the degree of choice really available to those who experience intimate terrorism, Anzaldúa concedes that the process of reasserting control is difficult at best. She is not advocating a neoliberal "pull yourself up by your bootstraps" model of accountability or responsibility in her discussion of choice that would ignore the all-too-powerful debilitating institutionalized structures of oppression that women of color regularly confront. She is proposing that resignation is not the answer to oppression.

With this suggestion, Anzaldúa highlights the hope that can be found in the crossroads. This hope consists of taking back at least some control from the forces that have sought to remove it altogether. In *This Bridge Called My Back* and *Borderlands* alike, Anzaldúa provides some suggestions about how to keep or regain at least part of this control. According to Anzaldúa, this maintenance or reclamation of control consists of nurturing and listening to one's voice, even when surrounding forces seek to suppress it or make it difficult for voice to be heard. To this end, in *This Bridge Called My Back*, she urges women of color to find the muse within and write no matter the location and no matter the would-be censors.[11] In *Borderlands*, she suggests that the petrified woman/women referenced above draw(s) individual strength from both a collective history of resistance and a fire that burns within no matter how small the flame, a fire that refuses to be extinguished. Anzaldúa's emphasis on an inner strength that is fueled by a collective one underscores her message of hopeful defiance. This individual hopeful defiance is tied to a collective "history of [women's] resistance" and "[female] rites of defiance" marked by mourning, wailing, protest, wounding, solitude, and rebelliousness.[12]

These same types of images of female resistance and defiance can also be found in the primary texts analyzed in *Intersections of Harm*, even though the *historias* specific to each are distinct. *The Ladies' Gallery* highlights a matrilineal heritage of suffering, solitude, and psychological devastation but is told from the perspective of the granddaughter who has somehow survived this woeful legacy and written it down as a way of "try[ing] other ways of being."[13] *Impossible Motherhood*, with its focus on Irene's repeated abortions, centers on the idea of circumscribed choice and highlights a pattern of self-inflicted and externally inflicted wounds paradoxically accompanied by perpetual mourning and perpetual hope for a life outside of the cycle of physical, psychological, and geopolitical harm. In her critical attention to her individual and collective struggles with seized freedoms, Vilar takes the responsibility for which Anzaldúa calls in the passage cited above by refusing to remain shackled; instead she writes and remembers, "opening the possibility to a less violent world."[14] *Geographies of Home* ends with an emphasis on resilience in the wake of devastating harm. *So Far from God* presents protagonists who are marked either by their defiance of gendered or (hetero)sexist norms or their wailing rites, and it underscores the vital interconnectedness among rebellion, protest, and survival. Revolution is foregrounded in *Dreaming in Cuban*, as each of the female protagonists rebels via creative expression to articulate her own resistance to gendered, racialized, and/or political ideologies. Likewise, *How the García Girls Lost Their Accents* portrays readily silenced expressions of defiance, as each of the characters struggles to make her cries heard. The similar imagery across these narratives reveals how the protagonists therein fight to undo the shackles that confine them and situate themselves in the type of crossroads signaled by Anzaldúa, one marked by female resistance and hope amid harm.

The crossroads are an interstitial and intersectional place where inner resistance battles outer resistance. The hope that exists in such a fraught place lies in the lack of complacency and refusal to remain immobilized therein. Mobility and fluidity, in terms of temporality and spatiality, are key ingredients for unraveling the shackles that confine. The deviation that can result from "looking backward in order to look forward" and from moving "between and among" space(s) allows for the possibility of change, one that is needed to break free from the shackles that petrify. Hope necessitates temporal, spatial, *and* political movement/revolution. And if the personal is political and the political is personal, then, as Moraga and Anzaldúa claim in their introduction to *This Bridge Called My Back*, "the revolution [must] begin at home."[15]

## A Home of One's Own

All of the primary texts examined in this book underscore the centrality of home in their narratives. For Vilar, home is a yearning for rootedness and belonging amid the perpetual turbulence and upheaval she has witnessed and experienced. Pérez concludes her novel by emphasizing the connections among home, memories, and self. Castillo introduces the concept of home in her critique of the Anglo takeover of lands that once belonged to the native inhabitants of Tome, and she links homelessness to militarized and racialized dispossession. Through her protagonist Pilar, García ties home to belonging, as she highlights the difficulties Pilar faces as a Cuban American who is trying to figure out where home is and what it means to her. Likewise, Alvarez questions what home means and where it exists for migrant subjects who carry their homeland with them while coming of age in an adopted country and who, upon returning to their homeland, realize that homeland and home are not necessarily synonymous. In all of these cases, home is by no means a fixed or readily identifiable site; it is ever mobile.

Similarly, like Henri Lefebvre and Doreen Massey, who insist on the fluidity and constructedness of space, and like bell hooks, who maintains that "[home] is locations," throughout *Borderlands*, Anzaldúa describes home as a "thin edge of / barbwire" and a nomadic site carried on one's back.[16] Anzaldúa thus locates home in an interstitial space, one that is neither here nor there but in the space in between. Anzaldúa elaborates: "If going home is denied me then I will have to stand and claim my space, making a new culture—*una cultura mestiza*—with my own lumber, my own bricks and mortar and my own feminist architecture."[17] Portraying home as located on one's back, depicting home as a potentially alienating place, describing home as a "thin edge of / barbwire," and characterizing home as a perpetually shifting, interstitial site that is reconstructed by oneself, Anzaldúa—like Vilar, Pérez, Castillo, García, and Alvarez— shows how home is a concept tied to body, mind, and place at once. Ending her section on resistance with this architectural metaphor, Anzaldúa underscores the importance of claiming and carving a space for oneself.

Unlike the space invoked by Virginia Woolf, this home more closely resembles the one depicted by Sandra Cisneros in *The House on Mango Street*. Cisneros describes her protagonist Esperanza's deep desire for a house of her own where she can feel like she belongs, even though Esperanza ultimately realizes that what she seeks isn't so much a physical house as a psychological home. This home recalls the one Anzaldúa references in her essay, "Speaking in Tongues: A Letter to Third World Women Writers," when she urges writers to "forget the room of one's own" and find a space, *any* space, in which to write.[18] *This* is the space in the crossroads: the one "between and among" spaces, the ambiguous one, the intersectional one, the embattled one, the one where belonging can be found even in the face of perpetual unbelonging, and the one where hope can be gleaned amid pervasive harm.

# NOTES

## Introduction

1. Anzaldúa uses this passage to introduce the concept of linguistic terrorism, or the idea that certain languages are "right" and others are "wrong." Immediately after presenting the dentist anecdote, she describes attacks on "accented" English in classroom settings and declares, "El Anglo con cara de inocente nos arrancó la lengua" (The Anglo, wearing an innocent expression, cut out our tongue[s]). The juxtaposition of these snapshots suggests that the dentist quite possibly is Anglo, or at least is allied with the Anglo whom Anzaldúa claims "cut out our tongue(s)." Anzaldúa, *Borderlands*, 54.

2. Ibid., 59.

3. Ibid., 53.

4. I use the term *Latina/o* to describe someone with roots in Latin America who has spent formative years in the United States. I view the label as a U.S. construct, in line with the ways Latina/o studies scholars Suzanne Oboler and Marta Caminero-Santangelo define the term. I primarily use *Latina/o* in lieu of the governmentally imposed label *Hispanic* because of the grassroots origins of the term *Latina/o* and because of its built-in recognition of the heterogeneous makeup of peoples who fall under its parameters.

5. Castillo uses the term *Xicana* in place of *Chicana* to sidestep the cultural nationalism associated with the latter label and the subjugation of women in the name of *Raza* politics. Although I wholeheartedly stand by the antisexist impulse behind Castillo's choice of terminology, I mostly use the term *Chicana/o* in this book since that is the term most often recognized and adopted as a grassroots alternative to the identity label *Mexican American*. I use *Mexican American* when referring to subjects who do not explicitly identify with the type of grassroots politics that *Chicana/o* and *Xicana* connote. Castillo, *Massacre of the Dreamers*, 226.

6. Anzaldúa, *Borderlands*, 46.

7. Sandoval, *Methodology of the Oppressed*, 58.

8. Becerra et al., "The Hispanic Patient," 1.

9. This awareness was linked to the widespread "disseminat[ion of the label *Hispanic*] by state agencies after 1970" and a shift in the 1970 census that for the first time asked, "'Is this person's origin or descent' . . . 'Mexican'; 'Central or South American'; 'Puerto Rican'; 'Cuban'; 'Other Spanish'; or 'No, none of these.'" Oboler, *Ethnic Labels, Latino Lives*, xiii; Caminero-Santangelo, *On Latinidad*, 221.

10. Caminero-Santangelo, *The Madwoman Can't Speak*, 5–6. During the same decade when Latina/o mental health concerns finally were being addressed in the United States, a number of important ideas about psychology were being widely disseminated throughout the world. Frantz Fanon was situating Freudian psychoanalytic theories in the contexts of racial subjugation and colonization (in the Caribbean and Africa), and he posited a connection among body, mind, and place. Michel Foucault was challenging the relationship between care and control while criticizing the criminalization of mental illness in eighteenth-century European asylums. Jacques Lacan was writing about the pivotal role of language in constructions of mental health and illness and emphasizing the idea of the lack in relation to subject formation. Meanwhile, the antipsychiatry movement and community psychology began to emerge in the United States. Led by scholars like R. D. Laing and Thomas Szasz, the former charged psychiatry with harming rather than helping its patients and claimed that mental illness was a questionable, socially constructed phenomenon. The latter grew from similar vexations; it developed out of a frustration with the ways dominant modes of therapy framed power as residing in therapists and institutions, and it repositioned power as something that sprang from the community. Uniting these strands of thought was a reconceptualization of dominant understandings of care, mental health, and mental illness. Such reconceptualizations of care inform my literary analysis. I draw from these schools of thought to question the ready ascriptions of deviance and the type of treatment afforded to Latinas as portrayed in recent Latina literary production and also to posit an integral relation among body, mind, and place.

11. In "The Hispanic Patient," Becerra et al. indicate as much: they note a disparity between the small number of Latinas/os utilizing services relative to those allegedly requiring such care, and they comment on the lack of appropriate health care given to Latinas/os when they do seek it. In their psychological research, Rogler et al. likewise observe that Latinas/os, unlike white Anglos, tend to seek care under duress. They also note that Latinas/os are liable to be diagnosed with severe mental disorders and are "more likely to be diagnosed as schizophrenic and then treated in a psychiatric emergency room than [are] non-minority patients" (*Hispanics and Mental Health*, 17).

12. Special Populations Sub-Task Panel on Mental Health of Hispanic Americans, *Report to the President's Commission on Mental Health*, 3.

13. Santiago-Irizarry, *Medicalizing Ethnicity*, 55, 147.

14. Special Populations Sub-Task Panel on Mental Health of Hispanic Americans, *Report to the President's Commission on Mental Health*, xv, 2, 40.

15. Santiago-Irizarry, *Medicalizing Ethnicity*, 46.

16. Ibid., 156.

17. Ibid., 38–39.

18. U.S. Department of Health and Human Services, *Mental Health*, 131.

19. Ibid., 133.

20. I say "Latino literature" instead of "Latina/o literature" because writing by Latinos began to be widely disseminated in the 1960s and 1970s, whereas writing by Latinas only began to be widely published in the 1980s and 1990s. McCracken, *New Latina Narrative*, 4.

21. Dalleo and Machado Sáez, *The Latino/a Canon and the Emergence of Post-Sixties Literature*, 3.

22. In *The Latino/a Canon and the Emergence of Post-Sixties Literature*, Machado Sáez and Dalleo note that many of the allegations that post-1960s Latina/o literature is apolitical come from Latino/a studies scholars whom they describe as anticolonialists. They explain that anticolonialists' nostalgia for the "ghetto"-resistant literary traditions of the 1960s affects their perception of literature produced thereafter. According to Machado Sáez and Dalleo, anticolonialists define resistance narrowly, based on its manifestation in the "ghetto" traditions. Because post-1960s literature looks different from that produced in the 1960s, it has been marked as apolitical by anticolonial scholars.

23. I say "Latino" rather than "Latina/o" not because women didn't form part of these movements but because women's concerns were cast aside in them.

24. Bost, *Encarnación*, 31.

25. Moraga and Anzaldúa, "Foreword to the Second Edition," in *This Bridge Called My Back*.

26. Ibid., xix.

27. Vilar, *Impossible Motherhood*, 35.

28. Vilar, *The Ladies' Gallery*, 7.

29. Vilar, *Impossible Motherhood*, 202.

30. Sections of this paragraph are drawn from my article "Still Hands."

31. García, *Dreaming in Cuban*, 240.

32. Anzaldúa, *Borderlands*, 58–59.

33. Vilar, *Impossible Motherhood*, 34.

34. Caminero-Santangelo, *On Latinidad*, 219.

35. Bhabha, *The Location of Culture*, 27.

36. Anzaldúa, *Borderlands*, 79.

## 1 / Rape's Shadow

1. *The Ladies' Gallery* originally was published under the title *A Message from God in the Atomic Age: A Memoir*. I use the present tense to describe the past events that transpire within both memoirs per literary convention. I refer to Vilar by her surname when referring to her as writer of the memoirs and by her given name, Irene, when describing her position within the books.

2. Vilar, *The Ladies' Gallery*, 170.

3. *La Operación*.

4. Between 1945 and 1964, more than one third of Puerto Ricans migrated to the U.S. mainland. Oboler, *Ethnic Labels, Latino Lives*, 39; *La Operación*.

5. Briggs, *Reproducing Empire*, 199.

6. Ibid., 46, 51.

7. Ibid., 108.

8. Admittedly the use of the birth control pill—and a birth control movement—existed on the island prior to the mainland's involvement there. There is a difference,

though, between a self-propelled movement that advocates birth control for the sake of reproductive liberty and one imposed from without that encourages birth control under the guise of addressing widespread poverty or, worse, under what could be considered coercive circumstances. Briggs, *Reproducing Empire*, 90.

9. Ibid., 122.

10. *La Operación*.

11. Vilar, *Impossible Motherhood*, 204.

12. *La Operación*; Briggs, *Reproducing Empire*, 107. Briggs is quick to warn that there is not much support for the Puerto Rican Nationalist Party's or the mainland reproductive rights movement's allegations that eugenics was to be held (primarily) responsible for the rise in Puerto Rican women's sterilizations thereafter, as the Eugenics Board did not order the majority of surgical sterilizations performed between 1940 and 1970. Unlike the filmmaker Ana María García, who suggests that the sterilization of Puerto Rican women was based on a sinister agenda, as documented in her interviews with Puerto Rican women who painfully recount having undergone *la operación* without having fully understood what that procedure entailed, Briggs disputes claims that the vast majority of Puerto Rican women who had been sterilized did so involuntarily. Briggs instead points out that there is no record indicating as much in survey data, and she observes that such data "consistently found that women were overwhelmingly pleased with having obtained sterilization" (149, 153).

13. Although Vilar's father's and brothers' substance abuse plays an important role in her subject formation and relates to larger issues of addiction that she depicts, an exploration of her male relatives is beyond the scope of *Intersections of Harm*, even though I recognize that this subject merits further consideration. I do not delve into it largely because I am primarily interested in exploring the female legacy at the heart of Vilar's narratives, but also because Vilar herself privileges a matrilineal analysis.

14. Edward Said writes, "If there is anything that radically distinguishes the imagination of anti-imperialism, it is the primacy of the geographical in it. Imperialism after all is an act of geographical violence. . . . For the native, the history of his/her colonial servitude is inaugurated by the loss to an outsider of the local place, whose concrete geographical identity must thereafter be searched for and somehow restored" (quoted in Brady, *Extinct Lands, Temporal Geographies*, 145).

15. Vilar, *The Ladies' Gallery*, 21, 73, 72.

16. Although much has been written about Lolita Lebrón, I focus on her portrayal in Vilar's memoirs. My reading of her is therefore mediated by Vilar's representation of her.

17. Vilar, *The Ladies' Gallery*, 262.

18. Morgan writes, "Our history, values, voices, and (cross-cultural) culture have been taken from us—manifest in patriarchal seizure of our basic 'land.' Our own *bodies* have been taken from us, mined for their natural resources (sex, children, and labor), and alienated/mystified, whether as stereotypical virgin, whore, or mother. It follows that as women, to reclaim our lives we must reclaim our flesh" (in Vilar, *Impossible Motherhood*, xvi).

19. Morgan in Vilar, *Impossible Motherhood*, xvi, ix.

20. Moraga, *The Last Generation*, 149, 150, 172. Moraga, however, situates this analogy in the context of struggles faced by Chicanas, women of color, lesbians,

and gay men, and she emphasizes the importance of historical, cultural, and sexual specificity in any decolonial undertaking. She also expressly advances a U.S. Third World feminist praxis.

21. Ibid., 173.

22. According to Mohanty, Third World feminist writings comprise "(1) the idea of the simultaneity of oppressions as fundamental to the experience of social and political marginality and the grounding of feminist politics in the histories of racism and imperialism; (2) the crucial role of a hegemonic state in circumscribing their/our daily lives and survival struggles; (3) the significance of memory and writing in the creation of oppositional agency; and (4) the differences, conflicts, and contradictions internal to third world women's organizations and communities. In addition, they have insisted on the complex interrelationships between feminist, antiracist, and nationalist struggles" ("Introduction," 10).

23. Vilar, *The Ladies' Gallery*, 22.

24. Vilar's self-characterization as countryless could be considered an invocation of Virginia Woolf's declaration, quoted by Adrienne Rich: "As a woman I have no country. As a woman I want no country. As a woman my country is the whole world" ("Notes toward a Politics of Location," 211). Given Vilar's professed interest in Woolf's writings, it is possible to read Vilar's depiction of herself as countryless in this light and to read her countrylessness as an articulation of global citizenship in turn. However, considering that she describes herself as a type of colonized subject by virtue of Puerto Rico's de facto status as a U.S. colony, it also makes sense to read this self-description in relation to the Xicana writer Ana Castillo's denial of global citizenship. Similarly defining herself as "a countryless woman," Castillo states, "I CANNOT SAY I AM A CITIZEN OF THE WORLD as Virginia Woolf . . . ; nor can I make the same claim to U.S. citizenship as Adrienne Rich. . . . I am treated at best, as a second class citizen, at worst, as a non-entity. I am commonly perceived as a foreigner everywhere I go. . . . This international perception is based on my color and features. I am neither black nor white" (*Massacre of the Dreamers*, 21).

25. Massey, *Space, Place and Gender*, 171.

26. Moraga, *The Last Generation*, 190.

27. Vilar, *Impossible Motherhood*, 10.

28. Vilar, *The Ladies' Gallery*, 48.

29. Ibid., 3, 94. Similarly, in a 1954 issue, "*Newsweek* portrays the nationalists as 'fanatics' on an 'insane' mission" (Oboler, *Ethnic Labels, Latino Lives*, 191).

30. Vilar, *The Ladies' Gallery*, 260, 262.

31. Ibid., 263, 264, 266.

32. Vilar's description of Lolita thus resonates with the antipsychiatry movement's claims that the psychiatric system inflicts more harm than good.

33. Vilar, *The Ladies' Gallery*, 270.

34. The connection Vilar draws between incarceration and institutionalization evokes images from Foucault's *Madness and Civilization* and his analyses of eighteenth century European asylums that functioned as prisons and Szasz's *The Manufacture of Madness*, which illustrates how European asylums were founded not as "medical or therapeutic facilities" but "as prisonlike structures for the confinement of socially undesirable persons" (126–27).

35. Fanon, *The Wretched of the Earth*, 20.

36. Again, an analogy could be drawn to the colonized Algerians described in *The Wretched of the Earth* who act hysterical to endure the hardships suffered under colonization.

37. Estroff, *Making It Crazy*, 109–10.

38. Vilar, *The Ladies' Gallery*, 263.

39. Ibid., 265.

40. Ibid., 4. The indirect reference to Woolf merits attention not only because of Woolf's emphasis on women's writing but also because of her mental breakdowns and suicide by drowning. Considering the legacies of mental illness and (attempted) suicide in Vilar's family, the reference to a room of one's own evokes the ideas of female self-expression *and* female harm.

41. Ibid. Lolita's writing while incarcerated also elucidates the centrality of writing for U.S. Third World feminists. Writing, regardless of the place where it can be carried out, is vital to making audible the voices of women of color that readily are silenced.

42. Vilar, *Impossible Motherhood*, 11.

43. Bhabha, *The Location of Culture*, 163; Vilar, *Impossible Motherhood*, 11.

44. Vilar, *Impossible Motherhood*, 12.

45. Ibid., 205.

46. Ibid.

47. Vilar's portrayal here resonates with that found in *The Wretched of the Earth* that similarly emphasizes how a pathological environment can perpetuate individual pathology.

48. Vilar, *Impossible Motherhood*, 204.

49. Vilar, *The Ladies' Gallery*, 140.

50. Showalter, *The Female Malady*, 84–86.

51. Vilar, *The Ladies' Gallery*, 128.

52. Writing about a specifically colonized subjectivity, Ngugi bestows internalized oppression with the name of colonial alienation and defines this as "the domination of the mental universe of the colonized," which "resulted in the disassociation of the sensibility of that child from his natural and social environment" (*Decolonising the Mind*, 16–17). Similarly, in her discussion of the *Coatlicue* state, a state that builds on Carl Jung's shadow concept and encompasses the "underground" aspects of the self, Anzaldúa details the effects of colonialism and sexism, as she writes about feeling deformed, alien, abnormal, and ashamed, and as she describes her bodily betrayal (*Borderlands*, 42–43).

53. Vilar, *The Ladies' Gallery*, 128.

54. Ibid., 121, 122, 126.

55. Ibid., 249, 243–44.

56. Fanon, *Black Skin, White Masks*, 111.

57. Commenting on the memoir's structure, Laura Kanost asserts, "The illness-narrative portion of Vilar's memoir is visually marked as separate through the use of italics, and yet through its persistent recurrence it structures the entire work, thus signaling the interconnected relationship between the illness experience and all the other strands of the memoir." She adds, "By contextualizing her hospitalization within her own life story as well as the stories of her mother and grandmother, Vilar represents mental illness as one pivotal life experience among many" ("Re-Placing the Madwoman," 108).

58. Vilar, *The Ladies' Gallery*, 260, 200, 321.

59. Ibid., 309, 310, 311–12.

60. Ibid., 306.

61. Kanost, "Re-Placing the Madwoman," 111–12.

62. Fanon, *Black Skin, White Masks*, 126–27.

63. Vilar, *The Ladies' Gallery*, 99, 60–61.

64. Ibid., 15, 154, 61–62, 175, 214.

65. Vilar, *Impossible Motherhood*, 99–100.

66. Vilar, *The Ladies' Gallery*, 175.

67. The only revealing information Vilar provides about her "master," lover, and first husband is that he is a Jewish, Argentinean professor of Latin American literature at Syracuse University. During a class discussion, one of my students likened Irene's first husband to *Harry Potter*'s Voldemort, noting that the husband's namelessness in the memoir renders him virtually omnipotent as he who *need not* be named.

68. Vilar, *Impossible Motherhood*, 54.

69. Ibid., 83.

70. Bhabha, *The Location of Culture*, 13, 15.

71. Vilar, *Impossible Motherhood*, 76.

72. Ibid., 76, 93.

73. Ibid., 51.

74. Ibid., 86.

75. Ibid., 83, 202.

76. I use the term *antichoice* rather than *pro-life* because the latter incorrectly implies that those who believe in a woman's right to choose are antilife.

77. Foucault, *The History of Sexuality*, 93.

78. Vilar, *Impossible Motherhood*, 2, 204.

79. Briggs, *Reproducing Empire*, 161.

80. Vilar, *Impossible Motherhood*, 202–3.

81. Ibid., 52, 85, 90, 91, 154, 193.

82. Vilar, *The Ladies' Gallery*, 176, 318.

83. Ibid., 318.

84. This essentialized construction is akin to that which Vilma Santiago-Irizarry criticizes in *Medicalizing Ethnicity*, an ethnographic study that examines how mental health care practitioners medicalized Latina/o patients by virtue of their *latinidad*.

85. Vilar, *Impossible Motherhood*, 204.

86. Vilar, *The Ladies' Gallery*, 7.

87. Ibid.

88. Kanost, "Re-Placing the Madwoman," 108.

89. On the back cover of *Impossible Motherhood*, Junot Díaz describes the memoir as depicting "a harrowing underworld."

90. Vilar, *Impossible Motherhood*, 101, 137.

91. Kanost, "Re-Placing the Madwoman," 107.

92. Trigo, "Memoirs for the Abject," 132.

93. Vilar, *Impossible Motherhood*, 219–20.

94. Ibid., 222.

## 2 / Violated Bodies and Assaulting Landscapes in Loida Maritza Pérez's *Geographies of Home*

1. hooks, *Yearning*, 148.
2. Pérez, *Geographies of Home*, 23–24.
3. Massey, *Space, Place and Gender*, 171.
4. Wilson, *The Sphinx in the City*, 7.
5. Ibid., 135–36.
6. Ngugi, *Decolonising the Mind*, 16–17.
7. Pérez, *Geographies of Home*, 24.
8. Anzaldúa, *Borderlands*, 20.
9. Throughout *Geographies of Home*, Pérez, like Villa, highlights the fear imparted by the urban setting, and she paints the building where the bulk of the family members reside as "dilapidated," "condemned," and situated in a decaying neighborhood. In his analysis of "Neighbors," Villa also reads the short story's protagonist Aura "as a metonymic figure for the disintegration of her neighborhood, in which the dysfunctions of the larger barrio community are reflected on her mind and body." He emphasizes the roles that temporality, entrapment, uprooting, and alienation play in the geographic transformations/deformations of the *barrio*, just as Pérez underscores the centrality of time, claustrophobia, uprootedness, and isolation in her depiction of Aurelia and her family in a less than neighborly New York City neighborhood. Pérez, *Geographies of Home*, 21; Villa, *Barrio-Logos*, 117–18.
10. Villa, *Barrio-Logos*, 117.
11. Pérez, *Geographies of Home*, 133.
12. Ibid., 255.
13. Ibid., 295.
14. Bhabha, *The Location of Culture*, 361.
15. Pérez, *Geographies of Home*, 146, 109.
16. Ibid., 148.
17. Ibid., 108–9. The description of Marina's manic episode echoes Fanon's characterization of the colonized Algerians in *The Wretched of the Earth*. Just as Marina is dismissed as "possessed" for her "spasmodic" convulsions in church, the colonized depicted by Fanon are classified as "hysterical" for their spasmodic affectivity.
18. Fanon, *The Wretched of the Earth*, 20.
19. Ibid., 19.
20. Pérez, *Geographies of Home*, 148.
21. Ibid., 151, 152–53.
22. Ibid., 156.
23. Poe, "Annabel Lee," 477–79. Pérez admits that Poe is one of the writers who has "had the greatest impact on [her]" (*Geographies of Home*, 8).
24. DeGuzmán, *Spain's Long Shadow*, 26, 46. Toni Morrison defines "American Africanism" as "an investigation into the ways in which a nonwhite, Africanlike (or Africanist) presence or persona was constructed in the United States, and the imaginative uses this fabricated presence served." She relays her "alarmed distrust" of a scholar who claims that "Poe has little to say about the darky," explaining that literary representations of race do not exist solely in the works of those who are recipients of racism but also in the works of "those who perpetuate it" (*Playing in the Dark*, 6, 10–11).

25. Eng, *Racial Castration*, 14–15.

26. Pérez, *Geographies of Home*, 156–57.

27. I place the term *endings* in scare quotes since some of these characters' "endings" are more ambiguous than others and do not necessarily signify the characters' deaths. I use the phrase *foreshadowed "endings"* since Celia steps into the ocean more than once in *Dreaming in Cuban*. Like Ophelia and Celia, Anabelle is distinguished by her long, tangled, or disheveled hair. Like Ophelia, who suffers a "muddy death," in Anabelle's final moments, she is clothed in a "mud-smeared dress." The description of the dress worn by Anabelle as she steps into the eye of the hurricane resembles that of Ophelia, the Lady of Shalott, and Celia when they are underwater. Ophelia's "clothes spread wide," and her "garments, heavy with their drink, / Pull'd the poor wretch"; a stormy wind carries the Lady of Shalott downstream "Lying, robed in snowy white / That loosely flew to left and right"; Celia "wades into the ocean [that] pulls on her housedress like weights on her hem"; and a strip of fabric belonging to Anabelle's dress "fluttered behind her" with her "remaining appendage too water-logged to propel her off the ground." The birdlike imagery Pérez invokes—as she likens Anabelle to "one who had lost a wing"—recalls that found at the end of *The Awakening* when Chopin draws attention to a "bird with a broken wing [that] was beating the air above, reeling, fluttering, circling disabled down, down to the water" immediately before describing Edna's final walk out to sea. Just as Anabelle is "impervious to whatever affected the body she inhabited like a shell," Ophelia is characterized as "incapable of her own distress." Not only does Anabelle not make any "effort to protect herself," but she "offer[s] herself to the wind" and "plac[es] herself directly in harm's way," much as the Lady of Shalott knowingly sails toward her impending death and as Edna and Celia purposefully walk out to sea in their moments of awakening/arguable suicides. Shakespeare, *The Tragedy of Hamlet*, 1177; Pérez, *Geographies of Home*, 156–57; Tennyson, "The Lady of Shalott," 81–87; García, *Dreaming in Cuban*, 7; Chopin, *The Awakening*, 108.

28. Gilbert and Gubar, *The Madwoman in the Attic*, 614–18, 620.

29. Pérez, *Geographies of Home*, 158.

30. Ibid.

31. Ibid., 151.

32. Ibid., 158. Here I am thinking of Gayatri Spivak's question about whether the subaltern can speak and Marta Caminero-Santangelo's contention that the madwoman ultimately is trapped in silence.

33. Pérez, *Geographies of Home*, 159.

34. Bost, *Encarnación*, 31, 34.

35. Anzaldúa defines the *Coatlicue* state as one that entails "duality in life, a synthesis of duality, and a third perspective—something more than mere duality or a synthesis of duality." Drawing from mythology and Jungian psychology and likening *Coatlicue* to Medusa, Anzaldúa further describes the *Coatlicue* state as a furtive "underground" that is associated with abnormality, monstrosity, evil, darkness, negativity, and beastliness and that instills a sense of shame (*Borderlands*, 42–47).

36. Ibid., 16.

37. For a detailed analysis of Jung's influence on Anzaldúa's Shadow-Beast, see DeGuzmán, *Buenas Noches, American Culture*, 31–33.

38. Storr, *The Essential Jung*, 87.

39. Pérez, *Geographies of Home*, 212.

40. As in Morrison's *The Bluest Eye*, which portrays the Breedlove abode as anything but loving and as standing in stark contrast to the happy home of the iconic Dick and Jane books, Pasión and Rebecca's house in *Geographies of Home* is depicted as far less than ideal. Indeed, a number of parallels could be drawn between *Geographies of Home* and *The Bluest Eye*. Pérez's portrayal of the inhospitable New York City setting resembles Morrison's depiction of the "unyielding earth" and environment hostile to the growth of marigolds. Likewise, the places where the characters reside in both novels are characterized by negativity: deprivation, poverty, and smell are but a few key terms used to depict such spaces. Both writers also deploy images of dirt in relation to female characters, with dirt representing Pecola and Rebecca in Morrison and Pérez's respective texts. Morrison, *The Bluest Eye*, 6.

41. Pérez, *Geographies of Home*, 55–56, 59, 171, 62, 192–94.

42. Lefebvre, *The Production of Space*, 99.

43. Pérez, *Geographies of Home*, 55–56.

44. Ibid., 170.

45. Anzaldúa, *Borderlands*, 23.

46. Genesis 28.

47. There are too many examples of U.S. governmental interference in the lives of women of color to name. A couple of examples include the quarantining of Mexicans in the U.S.-Mexico borderlands in the early twentieth century and the testing of the bodies of black and Puerto Rican women in the latter half of the twentieth century under the guise of advancement of reproductive technologies.

48. The feminist critic Carisa Showden argues that it is important to recognize that agency and "victimization" are not mutually distinct categories and to reframe how we view intimate partner violence so that the onus for abuse is not placed entirely on survivors. Showden claims that we need to move away from asking, "Why doesn't she leave?" to asking, "Why does he hit her?" In the context of *Geographies of Home*, though, Rebecca's family members treat her as if she refuses to assert any agency because she stays with Pasión; they focus on her individual actions as if they existed in a geopolitical vacuum; and they place full responsibility on Rebecca for remaining with Pasión rather than examining the "coercive control" he wields over her. Showden, *Choices Women Make*, 38, 40, 47, 49.

49. As Emi Koyama, a harm-reduction advocate, explained at Chicago's Color of Violence II: Building a Movement Conference in March 2002, it is of the utmost importance to respect how people see fit to survive their situations, particularly given evidence that it sometimes is considered more dangerous for survivors to leave their batterers than to remain with them. Like Iris López, who refers to the mass sterilization of Puerto Rican women as a form of "constrained choice" (examined in chapter 1), and like Carisa Showden, who explores the relation among coercion, control, and intimate partner violence, Dorothy Roberts suggests that the word *choice* does not recognize the extent to which survivors of violence who also are women of color experience coercion daily. For these reasons, women of color might well be reticent to get out of their abusive situations and turn to receive aid. Indeed, "many women of color [who are survivors of domestic violence] are already suspicious of mental health practitioners, expect to be inadequately served, may underestimate the extent and kind of assistance they require, and as a result may never consider

seeking mental health care at all"; "perhaps because of the distrust of public agencies, women of color are [also] less likely to report rape than nonminority women." Given the rampant cultural insensitivity of mental health services in this country, it comes as no surprise that women of color who have been subject to extreme violence would be wary of seeking mental health care treatment. Kanuha, "Women of Color in Battering Relationships," 440; Vasquez, "Latinas," 126.

50. Falicov, *Latino Families in Therapy*, 151.

51. Pérez, *Geographies of Home*, 300.

52. Hurtado, *The Color of Privilege*, 45.

53. I thank Paula Straile for asking whether Rebecca was a reference to Pocahontas during the 2002 American Comparative Literature Association Conference.

54. Sandín, *Killing Spanish*, 68.

55. Pérez, *Geographies of Home*, 38.

56. Duany, "Reconstructing Racial Identity," 148.

57. Ibid., 152.

58. Fanon, *Black Skin, White Masks*, 191.

59. Pérez, *Geographies of Home*, 16.

60. Bhabha, *The Location of Culture*, 284, 296, 14–15.

61. Sandín, *Killing Spanish*, 73.

62. Pérez, *Geographies of Home*, 16. According to the Mayo Clinic website, symptoms of posttraumatic stress disorder (PTSD) include flashbacks and "upsetting dreams," and rape survivors are among those especially susceptible to developing PTSD.

63. Pérez, *Geographies of Home*, 16–17.

64. Ibid., 17–18.

65. Ibid., 17, 16.

66. Lefebvre, *The Production of Space*, 185–86.

67. Pérez, *Geographies of Home*, 18.

68. Brady, *Extinct Lands, Temporal Geographies*, 53; Pérez, *Geographies of Home*, 18.

69. Pérez, *Geographies of Home*, 18.

70. I say that the neighborhood presumably previously consisted of white families based on Pérez's phrasing. Pérez positions the prior middle-class residents in contrast to the current "black and Hispanic" ones. The three main groups presented in the novel are Latinas/os, blacks, and whites, even while the narrative recognizes that these categories need not be mutually exclusive. Since Pérez describes blacks and Latinas/os as other than middle class in this passage, the reader can infer that the former residents were white (ibid., 84).

71. Ibid., 85.

72. Ibid.

73. Ibid.

74. Eng, *Racial Castration*, 7–9, 15.

75. Pérez, *Geographies of Home*, 85.

76. Ibid., 32.

77. Anzaldúa, *Borderlands*, 43; Pérez, *Geographies of Home*, 112.

78. Pérez, *Geographies of Home*, 113.

79. I thank Pablo Ramirez for pointing out to me that the Ku Klux Klan has constructed Cain in this way.

80. Considering Sue Estroff's observations that medication perpetuates the stigma of pathologization, Marina's decision not to take her pills can be interpreted as a rejection of her "madness" and a means of inserting herself in the nonmedicated, "sane" world.

81. In this respect, Marina's parents' attitudes mirror that found in the psychological research done by Valli Kanuha, who notes "the paradoxical belief held by many women of color that they must care for their families first—and by extension their 'race' first—by persevering under dire circumstances or seeking help for themselves" ("Women of Color in Battering Relationships," 440).

82. Pérez, *Geographies of Home*, 290.

83. Ibid., 280–81, 283.

84. Anzaldúa, *Borderlands*, 36–38.

85. Pérez, *Geographies of Home*, 286–87.

86. Ibid., 288, 290.

87. Bhabha, *The Location of Culture*, 195.

88. Pérez, *Geographies of Home*, 17, 284–85, 290, 311.

89. Ibid., 1, 71.

90. Ibid., 282.

91. Rich, "Notes," 212.

92. Villa, *Barrio-Logos*, 209.

93. Sandín, *Killing Spanish*, 65.

94. Pérez, *Geographies of Home*, 289.

95. Fanon, *Black Skin, White Masks*, 110–16.

96. Pérez, *Geographies of Home*, 300.

97. Villa, *Barrio-Logos*, 165.

98. Pérez, *Geographies of Home*, 320–21.

99. Ibid., 321.

100. Ibid., 2, 321.

101. Ibid., 291; Villa, *Barrio-Logos*, 5; Massey, *Space, Place and Gender*, 11.

102. Cisneros, *The House on Mango Street*, 105.

## 3 / Madness's Material Consequences in Ana Castillo's *So Far from God*

1. Laura Pulido defines *subaltern* as having a "lack of voice . . . , or at best, a voice that is barely audible" (*Environmentalism and Economic Justice*, 128). Although the Tome community members of *So Far from God* are not silent, they lack the power associated with the ability to have a voice that is readily *heard*.

2. Although Domingo is not exempt from the harm his family experiences, I do not focus on him since he is absent for much of the narrative and since Castillo puts women at the center of her tale.

3. Castillo, *So Far from God*, 157.

4. Elisabeth Mermann-Jozwiak, Sandra Cisneros, and Susan Thananopavarn comment on the *telenovela*-like and comedic style of the text; Ralph Rodriguez describes the book as a romance; Silvio Sirias and Richard McGarry read the novel as a religious allegory; and Michael Porsche, Roland Walter, B. J. Manríquez, and Frederick Luis Aldama characterize the text as magical realism. Caminero-Santangelo, *On Latinidad*, 247.

5. Alaimo, "Trans-corporeal Feminisms and the Ethical Space of Nature," 238, 250.

6. The title of this section is partly a response to what I interpret to be the Mexican writer Octavio Paz's misogynist representation of La Malinche and her legacy in "Los hijos de la Malinche," in *The Labyrinth of Solitude*. His chapter title is translated as "The Sons of La Malinche" in the English version of the book, although the word *hijos* can refer to sons or children. Appropriating this title, with a twist, I seek to highlight the legacy left to the "daughters" of La Malinche.

7. Castillo, *So Far from God*, 77, 37.

8. According to Wendy Faris, a magical realist text "contains an 'irreducible element' of magic, something we cannot explain according to the laws of the universe as we know them. In the terms of the text, magical things 'really' do happen" and are presented in "a matter-of-fact way . . . without undue questioning or reflection" (quoted in Caminero-Santangelo, *On Latinidad*, 144).

9. Caminero-Santangelo, *On Latinidad*, 143–45.

10. Ralph Rodriguez focuses on the religious symbolism of the protagonists' names, citing Alban Butler's description of these mythical figures: "The Roman widow St. Wisdom and her three daughters suffered for the faith under the emperor Hadrian. According to a spurious legend St. Faith, aged twelve, was scourged, thrown into a boiling pitch, taken out alive, and beheaded; St. Hope, aged ten, and St. Charity, aged nine, being unhurt in a furnace, were also beheaded; and their mother suffered while praying over the bodies of her children. Some have maintained that the whole story is a myth, but the universality of their *cultus* both in the East and the West suggests that there may have been early martyrs of these names" ("Chicana/o Fiction from Resistance to Contestation," 79–80).

11. Quoting Stafford Poole, Theresa Delgadillo writes, "Historically, Our Lady of Guadalupe has been deployed in the service of both accommodation, that is, to win Indian converts to the Church, and rebellion, to symbolize Mexican nationalism against Spanish domination . . . and to figure native claims to land and other rights" ("Forms of Chicana Feminist Resistance," 898).

12. Castillo, *So Far from God*, 88.

13. While an analysis of Francisco merits further consideration, it is beyond the scope of this book, primarily because I focus on how *women* protagonists deal with harm, even though I realize that the way male protagonists experience harm affects how the women experience it. Worth mentioning is that Francisco is a Vietnam War veteran. It is thus possible to view his obsessive fervor as stemming from more than religious fanaticism, staunch patriarchy, homophobia, or even possessive "love"; it could follow from militarized violence and correspond with the type of posttraumatic stress disorder not uncommon among veterans. For a more in-depth engagement with Castillo's portrayal of Francisco, refer to Sirias and McGarry, "Rebellion and Tradition in Ana Castillo's *So Far from God* and Sylvia López-Medina's *Cantora*"; Delgadillo, "Forms of Chicana Feminist Resistance."

14. Castillo, *So Far from God*, 211.

15. When I use the term *tragedy*, I am not deploying it as a genre opposed to comedy or one related to Greek theater that follows from an individual character's flaw. I use the term as it is commonly understood, as a marker of deep sadness. The way Castillo deploys the tragic corresponds with her use of the comic.

16. Castillo, *So Far from God*, 211.

17. The imagery Castillo uses here resonates with that in Alice Walker's *In Search of Our Mothers' Gardens*. In her title essay, Walker describes the deaths of black southern

women, treated like mules during their lifetimes and unmourned in their deaths: "[These women] forced their minds to desert their bodies and their striving spirits sought to rise, like frail whirlwinds from the hard red clay. And when those frail whirlwinds fell, in scattered particles, upon the ground, no one mourned. Instead, men lit candles to celebrate the emptiness that remained, as people do who enter a beautiful but vacant space to resurrect a God" (232). Striking here is the juxtaposition of body, mind, and place. The women seek to separate their minds from their bodies and the unyielding earth, while the men treat the emptiness the women leave in their wake as a religious space of worship. While Walker's passage highlights the women's desire to soar above "the hard red clay," Castillo's depiction invokes a downward movement into a soft and yielding earth. Yet Castillo's emphasis on the nothing that remains of Caridad's and Esmeralda's bodies—juxtaposed against a description of the natural environment—underscores the extremity of the harm to which her characters, like the women Walker describes, have been subjected and troubles the romanticized idea that the deaths represent eternal life.

18. Thank you to one of my anonymous reviewers for pointing out the link between Loca and Christina the Astonishing.

19. The term *loca* translates as "mad (one)," while *santa* translates as "saintly" or "saint."

20. *Locura* is linked to sexual and social deviance. The phrase *la vida loca*— despite its popularization in 1999 by pop singer Ricky Martin as representing a life of danger, lust, and sexual intrigue— is often used to describe gang life, as illustrated in Luis Rodríguez's memoir *Always Running: La Vida Loca: Gang Days in L.A.* and Yxta Maya Murray's novel *Locas*. The term *loca* thus refers to clinical and nonclinical understandings of deviance.

21. Torres, introduction to *Tortilleras*, 6.

22. Tim Dean elaborates on this subject in his analysis of barebacking subculture in *Unlimited Intimacy*. Just as he argues that it is important to move beyond pathologizing criticism or defense of barebacking subculture in the wake of AIDS awareness and instead examine the complexities within this subculture—including its defiance, affirmation, and desire for "unlimited intimacy"—I maintain that Loca's diagnosis as HIV positive in *So Far from God* is necessarily complex and needs to be read as such. Neither to be taken at face value nor dismissed outright, Loca's medical diagnosis further marks her aberration from her community, even while her death marks her veneration by this same community.

23. Walker, *In Search of Our Mothers' Gardens*, 232.

24. Pérez, "Caminando con La Llorona," 105.

25. Sharpe, "Learning to Live without Black Familia," 247.

26. DeGuzmán, *Buenas Noches, American Culture*, 36.

27. Moraga, *Loving in the War Years*, 37.

28. Anzaldúa, *Borderlands*, 36–37.

29. Castillo, *So Far from God*, 226.

30. Delgadillo analyzes *So Far from God* through the lens of a hybrid spirituality, pointing out that hybridity and syncretism are distinct concepts. "Unlike the concept of syncretism, which emphasizes the reconciliation of diverse beliefs, systems, or practices in a new form, the conceptions of cultural hybridity," Delgadillo explains, "allow us to recognize the heterogeneity and ongoing negotiations that constitute

culture in general, and the unique way this is performed in Castillo's text" ("Forms of Chicana Feminist Resistance," 893).

31. Castillo, *So Far from God*, 223–24.

32. Ibid., 225, 224.

33. Ibid., 226, 227.

34. Ibid., 229.

35. This is the first time in the narrative that the acronym AIDS is used. Prior to Loca's surgery, she is said to have HIV.

36. Castillo, *So Far from God*, 228.

37. Falicov, *Latino Families in Therapy*, 142.

38. Castillo, *So Far from God*, 235.

39. Ibid., 138, 39, 48, 47.

40. Even the setting of the narrative illustrates the interstitial politics within the text. Lying between the United States and Mexico, formerly part of Mexico and now part of the United States, and subject to Spanish and U.S. colonization alike, the narrative's borderlands setting parallels the protagonists' bordered subjectivities, revealing a link between physical place and psychological space. In her portrayal of Esperanza and Fe, Castillo also speaks to the actual militarization of New Mexico and the racialization that accompanies such militarization.

41. Castillo, *So Far from God*, 134, 159, 160, 84.

42. Ibid., 159, 160.

43. Ibid., 32.

44. Ibid., 85, 158.

45. Ibid., 171, 178, 181.

46. Ibid., 178, 179, 181, 183, 185, 186–87.

47. Castillo's portrayal of the health care system with which Fe interacts recalls that presented by the antipsychiatry movement: both elucidate the harm exacted by medical systems.

48. Castillo, *So Far from God*, 186.

49. Ibid., 178.

50. Ibid., 187.

51. Ibid.

52. Ibid., 188–89.

53. Platt, "Ecocritical Chicana Literature," 152.

54. Castillo, *So Far from God*, 181.

55. Ibid., 188.

56. Hernández, *Sun Mad*.

57. Benjamin F. Chavis Jr. defines environmental racism as "racial discrimination in environmental policy making. It is racial discrimination in the enforcement of regulations and laws. It is racial discrimination in the deliberate targeting of communities of color for toxic waste disposal and the siting of polluting industries. It is racial discrimination in the official sanctioning of the life-threatening presence of poisons and pollutants in communities of color. And it is racial discrimination in the history of excluding people of color from the mainstream environmental groups, decision making boards, commissions, and regulatory bodies" (quoted in Platt, "Ecocritical Chicana Literature," 140).

58. Pulido, *Environmentalism and Economic Justice*, 26.

59. Castillo, *So Far from God*, 139.

60. Ibid., 242–43.

61. Castillo, *Massacre of the Dreamers*, 61, 170.

62. Castillo, *So Far from God*, 146.

63. Pulido, *Environmentalism and Economic Justice*, xix.

64. Castillo, *So Far from God*, 147–48.

65. Ibid., 144, 142.

66. Pulido, *Environmentalism and Economic Justice*, 131.

67. Caminero-Santangelo maintains "that by lampooning M.O.M.A.S...., Castillo is precisely rejecting a preexisting and essentialized panethnic Latino identity as somehow inherently resistant" (*On Latinidad*, 158).

68. Xicanisma refers to a Chicana feminist politics that reclaims *indigenismo* and "the forsaken feminine" and rejects colonization. Castillo, *Massacre of the Dreamers*, 12.

69. Moraga, *The Last Generation*, 190.

70. Castillo, *So Far from God*, 155.

## 4 / Artistic Aberrance and Liminal Geographies in Cristina García's *Dreaming in Cuban*

1. García, *Dreaming in Cuban*, 235. Sections of this chapter are drawn from my article "Still Hands."

2. López, "Women on the Verge of a Revolution," 36.

3. García, *Dreaming in Cuban*, 159.

4. López, "Women on the Verge of a Revolution," 38–39.

5. García, *Dreaming in Cuban*, 44, 41.

6. Sandín, *Killing Spanish*, 68.

7. García, *Dreaming in Cuban*, 195.

8. Ibid., 36.

9. Ibid., 51.

10. The incompatible association Celia's doctors draw speaks to Foucault's observations about the connection between medical care and control, Showalter's research on the feminization of "madness," and Thomas Szasz's contention that the psychiatric system is designed to hurt its patients.

11. Estroff explains that patients perform "craziness" since they cannot escape being labeled such (*Making It Crazy*, 109–10).

12. García, *Dreaming in Cuban*, 50–51.

13. Ibid., 37, 157.

14. The comparison of this disease to tuberculosis is striking because Berta later dies of tuberculosis and because García arguably is invoking both the subject of Edgar Allen Poe's "Annabel Lee" and Poe's deceased wife, on whom Annabel is based and who died of tuberculosis. In the poem, Annabel's illness is never named. Instead, she is described as being killed by "a chilling wind." Considering the similar setting and water imagery in Poe's poem and García's novel, García's reference to a "disease" like tuberculosis invites comparisons between both pieces. Poe, "Annabel Lee," 477–78.

15. García, *Dreaming in Cuban*, 118.

16. Ibid., 159.

17. Ibid., 195.

18. The literary critics Andrea O'Reilly Herrera and Katherine Payant maintain that Gustavo functions as a symbolic, "nostalgic," and "romantic" Spanish colonizer who "exploited the beauty and riches of Cuba and then left." Herrera, "Women and the Revolution in Cristina García's 'Dreaming in Cuban,'" 87; Payant, "From Alienation to Reconciliation in the Novels of Cristina García," 166.

19. García Lorca, "The Duende," 155.

20. García, *Dreaming in Cuban*, 95.

21. García Lorca, "The Duende," 162.

22. García, *Dreaming in Cuban*, 112.

23. López, "Women on the Verge of a Revolution," 108.

24. García, *Dreaming in Cuban*, 243.

25. Ibid.

26. Gilbert and Gubar, *The Madwoman in the Attic*, 617–18.

27. Ferré, "On Destiny, Language, and Translation, or, Ophelia Adrift in the C & O Canal," 33.

28. García, *Dreaming in Cuban*, 243.

29. Ibid., 244.

30. Ibid., 243.

31. Ibid., 3. Although *gusano* means "worm" in Spanish, the term connotes betrayal and has been used to refer to Cubans who fled Cuba because of the Revolution.

32. Herrera, "Women and the Revolution in Cristina García's 'Dreaming in Cuban,'" 86, 72.

33. García, *Dreaming in Cuban*, 245.

34. Felicia's view of *santería* as a type of poetry speaks to Alice Walker's description of black women, perceived as crazy saints by those around them, as artists. The relation Walker draws among black femininity, misconstrued sainthood, madness, and artistry resonates with García's portrayal of Felicia, who is affiliated with blackness, *santería*, madness, and artistry (in her understanding of *santería*). Walker, *In Search of Our Mothers' Gardens*, 233.

35. García, *Dreaming in Cuban*, 186, 110, 88, 86, 121, 90, 91.

36. Ibid., 47.

37. Ibid., 78–79.

38. Collins, *Black Feminist Thought*, 129; Fanon, *Black Skin, White Masks*, 98.

39. Collins, *Black Feminist Thought*, 129; Briggs, *Reproducing Empire*, 40.

40. Carby, *Reconstructing Womanhood*, 32, 38.

41. Briggs, *Reproducing Empire*, 64, 60.

42. García, *Dreaming in Cuban*, 82.

43. To avoid confusion, I refer to Felicia by her given name, and I refer to Felicia Gutierrez by her full name or as Felicia's namesake.

44. García, *Dreaming in Cuban*, 82; Brontë, *Jane Eyre*, 130, 258, 131, 377.

45. It is difficult to view anyone who keeps his secret wife confined as anything other than abusive.

46. García, *Dreaming in Cuban*, 151.

47. Ibid., 155.

48. Ibid., 85–89, 107, 154, 91.

49. Szasz, *The Manufacture of Madness*, 126–27; García, *Dreaming in Cuban*, 106.

50. Foucault, *Madness and Civilization*, 46.

51. García, *Dreaming in Cuban*, 107, 109.

52. Anzaldúa, *Borderlands*, 65; DeGuzmán, *Buenas Noches, American Culture*, 1.

53. García, *Dreaming in Cuban*, 184, 189.

54. Ibid., 214.

55. Ibid., 45.

56. Gilman, "The Yellow Wallpaper," 35.

57. García, *Dreaming in Cuban*, 45.

58. Frantz Fanon discusses pervasive racist ideologies tying blackness to filth and depicting blacks as "disgusting," "walking dung-heap[s]" (*Black Skin, White Masks*, 98).

59. García's attention to Felicia's sleeplessness and psychic restlessness corresponds with Shakespeare's, Fanon's, and Anzaldúa's writings linking insomnia with mental illness. Shakespeare highlights how Macbeth's insanity is marked by sleeplessness; Fanon mentions that insomnia is a common symptom among his patients who struggle with mental disorders; and Anzaldúa ties her insomnia to feelings of craziness.

60. García, *Dreaming in Cuban*, 83.

61. Ibid., 46.

62. Ibid., 45.

63. Ibid., 95.

64. Ibid., 82, 184.

65. López, "Women on the Verge of a Revolution," 35.

66. Ibid., 33–35, 42.

67. García, *Dreaming in Cuban*, 167, 172.

68. Bordo, "The Body and the Reproduction of Femininity," 511.

69. García, *Dreaming in Cuban*, 21.

70. Ibid., 70.

71. Ibid., 70–71.

72. Ibid., 72. This scene arguably heralds the one in *Geographies of Home* where Marina enters the bathroom upon reliving her rape. Both scenes use similar scrubbing imagery.

73. García, *Dreaming in Cuban*, 129, 175, 133.

74. Ibid., 174.

75. Ibid.

76. Ibid., 196, 197. The turn to song links Lourdes to Celia, who is prompted to sing at the novel's close. García thus depicts both characters as potentially coming to voice by the book's end.

77. García, *Dreaming in Cuban*, 197.

78. Ibid., 227. The animal imagery and ecocritique here heralds that found in García's second novel, *The Agüero Sisters*.

79. García, *Dreaming in Cuban*, 222.

80. Ibid., 227.

81. Ibid.

82. Ibid., 236.

83. Ibid., 29.

84. Ibid., 138, 141.

85. Ibid., 141.

86. Ibid., 141, 177, 132.

87. Ibid., 171. Given the novel's repeated mention of cancer, Jorge's comparison of censored expression to cancer is charged. Jorge and his son, Javier, both battle cancer. García implies that Celia too contracts it: she undergoes a mastectomy and has a scar resembling that of her son. Since this scene with Celia is mentioned in passing, and since the cancer primarily affects the male characters in the text, further elaboration on this topic is beyond the scope of my analysis.

88. Ibid., 235.

89. Ibid., 59.

90. Bost, *Encarnación*, 78–79, 90; Anzaldúa, *Borderlands*, 75, 73.

91. García, *Dreaming in Cuban*, 139–40.

92. Ibid., 28, 220.

93. Ibid., 135.

94. Ibid., 202.

95. Ibid., 202, 201, 244.

96. Ibid., 72, 201.

97. Bost emphasizes this idea throughout her book, introducing it in her opening page, as she writes, "Bodies are never static" (*Encarnación*, 1).

98. López, "Women on the Verge of a Revolution," 103.

99. Anzaldúa, *Borderlands*, 79.

100. García, *Dreaming in Cuban*, 138, 28.

101. Caminero-Santangelo, *On Latinidad*, 104.

5 / Clamped Mouths and Muted Cries

1. Ellen McCracken persuasively argues that reviews of Alvarez's novel, like "How Assimilation Rips at Cultural Roots of Four Girls," *San Diego Tribune*, May 17, 1991, and "Garcia Girls Transcends Tale of Family's Assimilation," *San Antonio Express-News*, August 18, 1991, fail to understand how Alvarez's book "belies the smooth integration of the Latina immigrant into the U.S. mainstream." McCracken, *New Latina Narrative*, 28.

2. Caminero-Santangelo, "'The Territory of the Storyteller,'" 17.

3. Ruiz, "The Empowerment of Language-Minority Students," 320, 321.

4. Anzaldúa, *Borderlands*, 58.

5. Ibid., 53.

6. Alvarez, *How the García Girls Lost Their Accents*, 28.

7. Ibid.

8. Ibid., 28–30.

9. Ibid., 39.

10. Ibid., 113, 117, 118.

11. Ibid., 119–20.

12. Ibid., 160.

13. Lefebvre, *The Production of Space*, 27.

14. Alvarez, *How the García Girls Lost Their Accents*, 151.

15. hooks, *Yearning*, 148.

16. Alvarez, *How the García Girls Lost Their Accents*, 151.

17. Ibid., 153.

18. I insert the term *accented* in scare quotes because, as Frances Aparicio maintains, *everyone* speaks with an accent. Although some accents are more normativized

than others, the idea of an accentless English is a myth. The title of Alvarez's novel highlights the pervasiveness of this myth.

19. Alvarez, *How the García Girls Lost Their Accents*, 164.

20. Rich, "Notes," 212.

21. Alvarez, *How the García Girls Lost Their Accents*, 157.

22. Ibid., 160.

23. Ibid., 161–62.

24. Anzaldúa, *Borderlands*, 59.

25. Alvarez, *How the García Girls Lost Their Accents*, 162.

26. "Interview with Author Julia Alvarez." Alvarez discusses this scene in relation to the removal of *How the García Girls Lost Their Accents* from schools in Johnston County, North Carolina, in 2007. She describes a double silencing, the one that comes from banning the novel and the one that transpires within the text; she emphasizes the weight words carry; and she stresses the importance of educating "students about the power of words and stories to convey to others those awful moments when we are bereft, helpless, and need to share our story in order to feel human again."

27. Ruiz, "The Empowerment of Language-Minority Students," 321.

28. Anzaldúa, *Borderlands*, 69–70.

29. Alvarez, *How the García Girls Lost Their Accents*, 247.

30. Ibid., 243. The description of Don José as a mad artist draws on ready associations between creativity and madness, an affiliation that the psychiatrist Albert Rothenberg contests but one upon which Alvarez draws throughout her narrative. At the same time, the characterization of Don José troubles the ready gendering of madness as a female disease. Rothenberg destabilizes the relationship between creativity and "madness" throughout *Creativity and Madness*, first challenging the link between the two phenomena in his opening chapter (11–13).

31. Alvarez, *How the García Girls Lost Their Accents*, 157, 251.

32. Ibid., 251, 254, 253.

33. Ibid., 254, 255.

34. Barak, "'Turning and Turning in the Widening Gyre,'" 172; McCracken, *New Latina Narrative*, 108.

35. Alvarez, *How the García Girls Lost Their Accents*, 170–171.

36. Ibid., 179.

37. Duany, "Reconstructing Racial Identity," 165.

38. Alvarez, *How the García Girls Lost Their Accents*, 180, 182.

39. Ibid., 181.

40. Fanon, *Black Skin, White Masks*, 98.

41. Alvarez, *How the García Girls Lost Their Accents*, 182.

42. Ibid., 51.

43. Ibid., 51–52.

44. Bordo, "The Body and the Reproduction of Femininity," 511, 509.

45. Alvarez, *How the García Girls Lost Their Accents*, 55.

46. Ibid., 56.

47. Thanks to Joy Kasson for asking if a parallel could be drawn between the book's structure and content and if this parallelism meant that the text could be read through a psychodynamic lens.

48. Alvarez, *How the García Girls Lost Their Accents*, 131.

49. Ibid., 54.

50. Fanon, *Black Skin, White Masks*, 98.

51. This depiction is also potentially problematic since it risks usurping an iconic black trickster figure and reinscribing this figure as brown or at least nonblack.

52. Gates, *The Signifying Monkey*, 52, 77.

53. Alvarez, *How the García Girls Lost Their Accents*, 68.

54. Ibid., 78, 79.

55. Ibid., 74.

56. Ibid.

57. Ibid., 72, 76.

58. Ibid., 72.

59. Illustrating how a hostile environment can foster pathology, Alvarez presents madness in a manner similar to Fanon and Alice Walker. Like Alvarez, Walker emphasizes how stifled expression in a repressive environment can help explain why women of color, particularly those who are gifted poets, might go mad (*In Search of Our Mothers' Gardens*, 234–35).

60. Alvarez, *How the García Girls Lost Their Accents* 73; Anzaldúa, *Borderlands*, 37.

61. Alvarez, *How the García Girls Lost Their Accents*, 75.

62. Ibid.

63. Ibid.; Anzaldúa, *Borderlands*, 53.

64. Anzaldúa, *Borderlands*, 53.

65. Estroff, *Making It Crazy*, 109–10.

66. Audre Lorde, "The Master's Tools Will Never Dismantle the Master's House," in Moraga and Anzaldúa, *This Bridge Called My Back*, 98–101.

67. Alvarez, *How the García Girls Lost Their Accents*, 78.

68. Mimicry is "almost the same but not quite." It is subversive because of its ambivalence, one that adopts the colonial discourse to question it. It is threatening because it undermines notions of difference that are central to systems of colonization by instead relying on a discourse of similarity, even if it is a feigned one. Bhabha, *The Location of Culture*, 122.

69. This encounter between Yolanda and John is reminiscent of the story of the Tower of Babel in its focus on the chaos that ensues from the multiplication of languages. The degree of misunderstanding between Yolanda and John resembles the colossal confusion that transpires in the biblical narrative when "the LORD did . . . confound the language of all the earth" (*Twenty-six Translations of the Bible*, 24–25).

70. Alvarez, *How the García Girls Lost Their Accents*, 81.

71. Dalleo and Machado Sáez, *The Latino/a Canon and the Emergence of Post-Sixties Literature*, 140.

72. Christian, *Show and Tell*, 103.

73. Alvarez, *How the García Girls Lost Their Accents*, 79.

74. Anzaldúa, *Borderlands*, 54.

75. Walker, *In Search of Our Mothers' Gardens*, 240–41.

76. Alvarez, *How the García Girls Lost Their Accents*, 79, 80.

77. Anzaldúa, *Borderlands*, 20–21.

78. Alvarez, *How the García Girls Lost Their Accents*, 226–27.

79. Walker, *In Search of Our Mothers' Gardens*, 249–50.

80. Alvarez, *How the García Girls Lost Their Accents*, 141, 143, 89.

81. Ibid., 19–20.

82. Ibid., 14–15, 23.

83. Ibid., 290, 289.

84. In their analysis of *How the García Girls Lost Their Accents*, Machado Sáez and Dalleo situate Yolanda as Alvarez's double because she is a poet and storyteller (*The Latino/a Canon and the Emergence of Post-Sixties Literature*, 139).

85. Alvarez, *How the García Girls Lost Their Accents*, 289.

Conclusion

1. Anzaldúa, *Borderlands*, 54.

2. Vilar, *Impossible Motherhood*, 222.

3. Alvarez, *How the García Girls Lost Their Accents*, 290.

4. Sandoval, *Methodology of the Oppressed*, 58.

5. Moraga and Anzaldúa, *This Bridge Called My Back*, "Foreword to the Second Edition."

6. Ibid.

7. Moraga, *The Last Generation*, 190.

8. Bhabha, *The Location of Culture*, 361. I position these texts in a primarily reverse chronological order since *The Ladies' Gallery* disrupts my otherwise reverse sequence, as it was published in the middle of the time period this book spans. Yet I place my discussion of *The Ladies' Gallery* in my opening chapter because I pair it with Vilar's second memoir that was published after the other primary texts I analyze.

9. Anzaldúa, *Borderlands*, 20–21.

10. Ibid., 21.

11. Moraga and Anzaldúa, *This Bridge Called My Back*, 170, 173.

12. Anzaldúa, *Borderlands*, 21, 23.

13. Vilar, *The Ladies' Gallery*, 322.

14. Trigo, "Memoirs for the Abject," 132.

15. Moraga and Anzaldúa, *This Bridge Called My Back*, xxvi.

16. hooks, *Yearning*, 148; Anzaldúa, *Borderlands*, 3, 21.

17. Anzaldúa, *Borderlands*, 22.

18. Moraga and Anzaldúa, *This Bridge Called My Back*, 170.

# Works Cited

*Achieving the Promise: Transforming Mental Health Care in America: Final Report.* President's New Freedom Commission on Mental Health. Accessed December 18, 2014. store.samhsa.gov/shin/content//SMA03-3831/ SMA03-3831.pdf. July 22, 2003.

Alaimo, Stacy. "Trans-corporeal Feminisms and the Ethical Space of Nature." In *Material Feminisms*, edited by Stacy Alaimo and Susan Hekman, 237–64. Bloomington: Indiana University Press, 2008.

Alarcón, Norma. "*Traddutora, Traditora:* A Paradigmatic Figure of Chicana Feminism." In *Dangerous Liaisons: Gender, Nation, and Postcolonial Perspectives*, edited by Anne McClintock, Aamir Mufti, and Ella Shohat, 278–97. Minneapolis: University of Minnesota Press, 1997.

Alvarez, Julia. *How the García Girls Lost Their Accents.* New York: Plume, 1992.

Anzaldúa, Gloria. *Borderlands/La Frontera: The New Mestiza.* San Francisco: Aunt Lute Books, 1987.

Barak, Julie. "'Turning and Turning in the Widening Gyre': A Second Coming into Language in Julia Alvarez's *How the García Girls Lost Their Accents.*" *MELUS* 23, no. 1 (1998): 159–76.

Becerra, Rosina M., Marvin Karno, and Javier I. Escobar. "The Hispanic Patient: Mental Health Issues and Strategies." In *Mental Health and Hispanic Americans: Clinical Perspectives*, edited by Rosina M. Becerra, Marvin Karno, and Javier I. Escobar, 1–13. New York: Grune & Stratton, 1982.

Bhabha, Homi. *The Location of Culture.* 1994. London: Routledge, 2004.

Bordo, Susan. "The Body and the Reproduction of Femininity." 1993. In *The Gendered Society Reader*, 4th ed., edited by Michael Kimmel and Amy Aronson, 503–17. New York: Oxford University Press, 2011.

Bost, Suzanne. *Encarnación: Illness and Body Politics in Chicana Feminist Literature.* New York: Fordham University Press, 2010.

Brady, Mary Pat. *Extinct Lands, Temporal Geographies: Chicana Literature and the Urgency of Space.* Durham, NC: Duke University Press, 2002.

Briggs, Laura. *Reproducing Empire: Race, Sex, Science, and U.S. Imperialism in Puerto Rico.* Berkeley: University of California Press, 2002.

Brontë, Charlotte. *Jane Eyre.* Edited by Richard J. Dunn. New York: Norton, 1987.

Caminero-Santangelo, Marta. *The Madwoman Can't Speak: Or Why Insanity Is Not Subversive.* Ithaca, NY: Cornell University Press, 1998.

———. *On Latinidad: U.S. Latino Literature and the Construction of Ethnicity.* Gainesville: University Press of Florida, 2007.

———. "'The Territory of the Storyteller': An Interview with Julia Alvarez." Edited by Marta Caminero-Santangelo and Roy C. Boland. *Antipodas: Journal of Hispanic and Galician Studies* 10 (1998): 15–24.

Carby, Hazel V. *Reconstructing Womanhood: The Emergence of the Afro-American Woman Novelist.* New York: Oxford University Press, 1987.

Castillo, Ana. *Massacre of the Dreamers.* New York: Plume, 1994.

———. *So Far from God.* New York: Plume, 1993.

Cheng, Anne Anlin. *The Melancholy of Race: Psychoanalysis, Assimilation, and Hidden Grief.* New York: Oxford University Press, 2001.

Chopin, Kate. *The Awakening.* Edited by Margo Culley. New York: Norton, 1994.

Christian, Karen. *Show and Tell: Identity as Performance in U.S. Latina/o Fiction.* Albuquerque: University of New Mexico Press, 1997.

Cisneros, Sandra. *The House on Mango Street.* New York: Vintage Contemporaries, 1991.

Collins, Patricia Hill. *Black Feminist Thought: Knowledge, Consciousness, and the Politics of Empowerment.* 2nd ed. Edited by Judith L. Raiskin. New York: Routledge, 2000.

Dalleo, Raphael, and Elena Machado Sáez. *The Latino/a Canon and the Emergence of Post-Sixties Literature.* New York: Palgrave Macmillan, 2007.

Dean, Tim. *Unlimited Intimacy: Reflections on the Subculture of Barebacking.* Chicago: University of Chicago Press, 2009.

DeGuzmán, María. *Buenas Noches, American Culture: Latina/o Aesthetics of Night.* Bloomington: Indiana University Press, 2012.

———. *Spain's Long Shadow: The Black Legend, Off-Whiteness, and Anglo-American Empire.* Minneapolis: University of Minnesota Press, 2005.

Delgadillo, Theresa. "Forms of Chicana Feminist Resistance: Hybrid Spirituality in Ana Castillo's *So Far from God.*" *Modern Fiction Studies.* 44, no. 4 (1998): 888–916.

Duany, Jorge. "Reconstructing Racial Identity: Ethnicity, Color, and Class among Dominicans in the United States and Puerto Rico." "Race and

National Identity in the Americas." Special issue of *Latin American Perspectives* 25, no. 3 (1998): 147–72.

Eng, David L. *Racial Castration: Managing Masculinity in Asian America.* Durham, NC: Duke University Press, 2001.

Eng, David L., and David Kazanjian, eds. *Loss: The Politics of Mourning.* Berkeley: University of California Press, 2003.

Estroff, Sue E. *Making It Crazy: An Ethnography of Psychiatric Clients in an American Community.* Berkeley: University of California Press, 1981.

Falicov, Celia Jaes. *Latino Families in Therapy: A Guide to Multicultural Practice.* New York: Guilford Press, 1998.

Fanon, Frantz. *Black Skin, White Masks.* Translated by Charles Lam Markmann. 1952. New York: Grove Press, 1967.

———. *The Wretched of the Earth.* Translated by Richard Philcox. 1961. New York: Grove Press, 2004.

Ferré, Rosario. "On Destiny, Language, and Translation, or, Ophelia Adrift in the C & O Canal." In *Voice-Overs: Translation and Latin American Literature,* edited by Daniel Balderstrom and Marcy Schwartz, 32–41. Albany: University of New York Press, 2002.

Foucault, Michel. *The History of Sexuality,* Vol. 1: *An Introduction.* Translated by Robert Hurley. 1976. New York: Vintage Books, 1990.

———. *Madness and Civilization: A History of Insanity in the Age of Reason.* Translated by Richard Howard. 1965. New York: Vintage Books, 1988.

Freud, Sigmund. *Dora: An Analysis of a Case of Hysteria.* Edited by Philip Rieff. New York: Touchstone, 1997.

———. "Mourning and Melancholia." Translated by Joan Riviere. In *A General Selection from the Works of Sigmund Freud,* edited by John Rickman, 124–40. New York: Liveright, 1957.

García, Alma. "The Development of Chicana Feminist Discourse, 1970–1980." In *Unequal Sisters: A Multicultural Reader in U.S. Women's History,* 2nd ed., edited by Vicki Ruiz and Ellen Carol DuBois, 531–44. New York: Routledge, 1994.

García, Cristina. *The Agüero Sisters.* New York: Knopf, 1997.

———. *Dreaming in Cuban.* New York: Ballantine Books, 1992.

García Lorca, Federico. "The Duende: Theory and Divertissement." In *Poet in New York,* translated by Ben Belitt, 154–66. New York: Grove Press, 1955.

Gates, Henry Louis, Jr. *The Signifying Monkey.* New York: Oxford University Press, 1988.

"Genesis." In *The Holy Bible, English Standard Version,* The New Classic Reference Edition, 1–53. Wheaton, IL: Crossway, 2001.

Gilbert, Sandra M., and Susan Gubar. *The Madwoman in the Attic: The Woman Writer and the Nineteenth Century Literary Imagination.* 1979. New Haven, CT: Yale University Press, 2000.

Gilman, Charlotte Perkins Stetson. "The Yellow Wallpaper." 1892. In *Out of Her*

*Mind: Women Writing on Madness*, edited by Rebecca Shannonhouse, 32–49. New York: Modern Library, 2000.

Green, Rayna. "The Pocahontas Perplex: The Image of Indian Women in American Culture." *Massachusetts Review* 16, no. 4 (1975): 698–714.

Halperin, Laura. "Still Hands: Celia's Transgression in Cristina García's *Dreaming in Cuban*." *Latino Studies* 6, no. 4 (2008): 418–35.

Hernández, Ester. *Sun Mad*. 1982. Screenprint on paper. Smithsonian American Art Museum, Washington, DC.

Herrera, Andrea O'Reilly. "Women and the Revolution in Cristina García's 'Dreaming in Cuban.'" *Modern Language Studies* 27, no. 3/4 (1997): 69–91.

hooks, bell. *Yearning: Race, Gender, and Cultural Politics*. Boston: South End Press, 1990.

Hurtado, Aída. *The Color of Privilege: Three Blasphemies on Race and Feminism*. Ann Arbor: University of Michigan Press, 1996.

"Interview with Author Julia Alvarez." National Coalition Against Censorship. Accessed December 18, 2014. ncac.org/update/interview-with-julia-alvarez/. January 29, 2008.

Kanost, Laura. "Re-placing the Madwoman: Irene Vilar's *The Ladies' Gallery*." *Frontiers: A Journal of Women Studies* 31, no. 3 (2010): 103–15.

Kanuha, Valli. "Women of Color in Battering Relationships." In *Women of Color: Integrating Ethnic and Gender Identities in Psychotherapy*, edited by Lillian Comas-Díaz and Beverly Greene, 428–54. New York: Guilford Press, 1994.

Khanna, Ranjana. *Dark Continents: Psychoanalysis and Colonialism*. Durham, NC: Duke University Press, 2003.

Lacan, Jacques. "The Mirror Stage as Formative of the Function of the I as Revealed in Psychoanalytic Experience." In *Écrits: A Selection*, translated by Alan Sheridan, 1–7. New York: Norton, 1977.

Lefebvre, Henri. *The Production of Space*. Translated by Donald Nicholson-Smith. Oxford: Blackwell, 1994.

López, Kimberle S. "Women on the Verge of a Revolution: Madness and Resistance in Cristina Garcia's *Dreaming in Cuban*." *Letras Femeninas* 22, nos. 1–2 (1996): 33–49.

Massey, Doreen. *Space, Place, and Gender*. Cambridge, UK: Polity Press, 1994.

McCracken, Ellen. *New Latina Narrative: The Feminine Space of Postmodern Ethnicity*. Tucson: University of Arizona Press, 1999.

Mermann-Jozwiak, Elisabeth. "*Gritos desde la Frontera*: Ana Castillo, Sandra Cisneros, and Postmodernism." *MELUS* 25, no. 2 (2000): 101–18.

Mohanty, Chandra Talpade. "Introduction: Cartographies of Struggle: Third World Women and the Politics of Feminism." In *Third World Women and the Politics of Feminism*, edited by Chandra Talpade Mohanty, Ann Russo, and Lourdes Torres, 1–47. Bloomington: Indiana University Press, 1991.

Moraga, Cherríe. *Heroes and Saints and Other Plays*. Albuquerque, NM: West End Press, 1994.

———. *The Last Generation: Prose and Poetry*. Boston: South End Press, 1993.

———. *Loving in the War Years: Lo que nunca pasó por sus labios*. Boston: South End Press, 1983.

Moraga, Cherríe, and Gloria Anzaldúa. *This Bridge Called My Back: Writings by Radical Women of Color*. Watertown, MA: Persephone Press, 1983.

Morrison, Toni. *The Bluest Eye*. 1970. New York: Vintage International, 2007.

———. *Playing in the Dark: Whiteness and the Literary Imagination*. Cambridge, MA: Harvard University Press, 1992.

Muñoz, José Esteban. *Disidentifications: Queers of Color and the Performance of Politics*. Minneapolis: University of Minnesota Press, 1999.

Ngugi wa Thiong'o. *Decolonising the Mind: The Politics of Language in African Literature*. London: Heinemann, 1981.

Oboler, Suzanne. *Ethnic Labels, Latino Lives: Identity and the Politics of (Re) Presentation in the United States*. Minneapolis: University of Minnesota Press, 1995.

*La Operación*. Directed by Ana María García. Latin American Film Project and Skylight Pictures, 1985.

Payant, Katherine B. "From Alienation to Reconciliation in the Novels of Cristina García." *MELUS* 26, no. 3 (2001): 163–82.

Pérez, Domino Renee. "Caminando con La Llorona: Traditional and Contemporary Narratives." In *Chicana Traditions: Continuity and Change*, edited by Norma E. Cantú and Olga Nájera-Ramírez, 100–113. Urbana: University of Illinois Press, 2002.

Pérez, Loida Maritza. *Geographies of Home*. New York: Penguin Books, 1999.

Platt, Kamala. "Ecocritical Chicana Literature: Ana Castillo's 'Virtual Realism.'" In *Ecofeminist Literary Criticism: Theory, Interpretation, Pedagogy*, edited by Greta Gaard and Patrick D. Murphy, 139–57. Urbana: University of Illinois Press, 1998.

Poe, Edgar Allan. "Annabel Lee." In *Selected Prose and Poetry*, 477–79. New York: Holt, Rinehart and Winston, 1963.

"Post-Traumatic Stress Disorder (PTSD)." Mayo Clinic. Accessed March 21, 2013. http://www.mayoclinic.com/health/post-traumatic-stress-disorder/ DS00246. April 8, 2011.

Pulido, Laura. *Environmentalism and Economic Justice: Two Chicano Struggles in the Southwest*. Tucson: University of Arizona Press, 1996.

Rappaport, Julian. *Community Psychology: Values, Research, and Action*. New York: Holt, Rinehart and Winston, 1977.

Rhys, Jean. *Wide Sargasso Sea*. 1966. New York: Norton, 1999.

Rich, Adrienne. "Notes toward a Politics of Location (1984)." In *Blood, Bread, and Poetry: Selected Prose 1979–1985*, 210–31. New York: Norton, 1986.

Roberts, Dorothy. *Killing the Black Body: Race, Reproduction, and the Meaning of Liberty.* New York: Vintage Books, 1997.

Rodriguez, Ralph E. "Chicana/o Fiction from Resistance to Contestation: The Role of Creation in Ana Castillo's *So Far from God.*" *MELUS* 25, no. 2 (2000): 63–82.

Rogler, Lloyd H., Robert G. Malgady, and Orlando Rodriguez. *Hispanics and Mental Health: A Framework for Research.* Malabar, FL: Robert E. Krieger, 1989.

Rothenberg, Albert. *Creativity and Madness: New Findings and Old Stereotypes.* Baltimore: Johns Hopkins University Press, 1990.

Ruiz, Richard. "The Empowerment of Language-Minority Students." In *Latinos and Education: A Critical Reader,* edited by Antonia Darder, Rodolfo D. Torres, and Henry Gutiérrez, 319–28. New York: Routledge, 1997.

Sandín, Lyn Di Iorio. *Killing Spanish: Literary Essays on Ambivalent U.S. Latino/a Identity.* New York: Palgrave Macmillan, 2004.

Sandoval, Chela. *Methodology of the Oppressed.* Minneapolis: University of Minnesota Press, 2000.

Santiago-Irizarry, Vilma. *Medicalizing Ethnicity: The Construction of Latino Identity in a Psychiatric Setting.* Ithaca, NY: Cornell University Press, 2001.

Scarry, Elaine. *The Body in Pain: The Making and Unmaking of the World.* New York: Oxford University Press, 1985.

Shakespeare, William. *The Tragedy of Hamlet, Prince of Denmark.* In *The Riverside Shakespeare.* Boston: Houghton Mifflin, 1974.

Sharpe, Christina. "Learning to Live without Black Familia: Cherríe Moraga's Nationalist Articulations." In *Tortilleras: Hispanic and U.S. Latina Lesbian Expression,* edited by Lourdes Torres and Inmaculada Pertusa, 240–57. Philadelphia: Temple University Press, 2003.

Showalter, Elaine. *The Female Malady: Women, Madness, and Culture in England, 1830–1980.* New York: Pantheon Books, 1985.

Showden, Carisa R. *Choices Women Make: Agency in Domestic Violence, Assisted Reproduction, and Sex Work.* Minneapolis: University of Minnesota Press, 2011.

Sirias, Silvio, and Richard McGarry. "Rebellion and Tradition in Ana Castillo's *So Far from God* and Sylvia López-Medina's *Cantora.*" *MELUS* 25, no. 2 (2000): 85–100.

Special Populations Sub-Task Panel on Mental Health of Hispanic Americans. *Report to the President's Commission on Mental Health.* Los Angeles: University of California, Spanish Speaking Mental Health Research Center, May 1978.

Spivak, Gayatri. "Can the Subaltern Speak?" In *Marxism and the Interpretation of Culture,* edited by Cary Nelson and Lawrence Grossberg, 271–313. London: Macmillan, 1988.

Storr, Anthony. *The Essential Jung.* 1961. Princeton, NJ: Princeton University Press, 1983.

Szasz, Thomas. *The Manufacture of Madness: A Comparative Study of the Inquisition and the Mental Health Movement.* New York: Harper & Row, 1970.

Tennyson, Alfred Lord. "The Lady of Shalott." 1842. In *Tennyson: Poems,* 81–87. New York: Everyman's Library, 2004.

Thananopavarn, Susan. "Conscientización of the Oppressed: Language and the Politics of Humor in Ana Castillo's *So Far from God.*" *Aztlán: A Journal of Chicano Studies* 37, no. 1 (2012): 65–86.

Thomas, Piri. *Down These Mean Streets.* 1967. New York: Vintage Books, 1997.

Torres, Lourdes. Introduction to *Tortilleras: Hispanic and U.S. Latina Lesbian Expression,* edited by Lourdes Torres and Inmaculada Pertusa, 1–15. Philadelphia: Temple University Press, 2003.

Trigo, Benigno. "Memoirs for the Abject: Irene Vilar's *Memoria.*" In *Remembering Maternal Bodies: Melancholy in Latina and Latin American Women's Writing,* 111–32. New York: Palgrave Macmillan, 2006.

*Twenty-six Translations of the Bible.* Edited by Curtis Vaughan, 24–25. Atlanta, GA: Mathis, 1985.

U.S. Department of Health and Human Services. *Mental Health: Culture, Race, and Ethnicity—A Supplement to Mental Health: A Report of the Surgeon General.* Rockville, MD: U.S. Department of Health and Human Services, 2001.

Vasquez, Melba J. T. "Latinas." In *Women of Color: Integrating Ethnic and Gender Identities in Psychotherapy,* edited by Lillian Comas-Díaz and Beverly Greene, 114–38. New York: Guilford Press, 1994.

Viego, Antonio. *Dead Subjects: Toward a Politics of Loss in Latino Studies.* Durham, NC: Duke University Press, 2007.

Vilar, Irene. *Impossible Motherhood: Testimony of an Abortion Addict.* New York: Other Press, 2009.

———. *The Ladies' Gallery: A Memoir of Family Secrets.* Translated by Gregory Rabassa. New York: Vintage Books, 1998.

Villa, Raúl Homero. *Barrio-Logos: Space and Place in Urban Chicano Literature.* Austin: University of Texas Press, 2000.

Walker, Alice. *In Search of Our Mothers' Gardens.* 1967. San Diego: Harcourt Brace Jovanovich, 1983.

Wilson, Elizabeth. *The Sphinx in the City: Urban Life, the Control of Disorder, and Women.* Berkeley: University of California Press, 1992.

# INDEX

# About the Author

Laura Halperin is an assistant professor in the Department of English and Comparative Literature and the Program in Latina/o Studies at the University of North Carolina, Chapel Hill. She is affiliated with UNC's Department of American Studies and Curriculum in Global Studies, and she is a member of the MLA Executive Committee of the Division of Chicana and Chicano Literature. Her work has appeared in *Latino Studies* and *The Routledge Companion to Latino/a Literature.*

CPSIA information can be obtained at www.ICGtesting.com
Printed in the USA
LVOW06s1931051115

461259LV00005B/313/P

9 780813 570365